Themes in Latin
American Cinema

Themes in Latin American Cinema

A Critical Survey

KEITH JOHN RICHARDS

Foreword by Alfonso Gumucio-Dagron

McFarland & Company, Inc., Publishers
Jefferson, North Carolina, and London

LIBRARY OF CONGRESS CATALOGUING-IN-PUBLICATION DATA

Richards, Keith John, 1953–
Themes in Latin American cinema :
a critical survey / Keith John Richards ;
foreword by Alfonso Gumucio-Dagron.
p.   cm.
Includes bibliographical references and index.

ISBN 978-0-7864-3538-8
softcover : 50# alkaline paper ∞

1. Motion pictures — Latin America — Plots, themes, etc.   I. Title.
PN1993.5.L3R53   2011   791.43098 — dc23   2011017863

BRITISH LIBRARY CATALOGUING DATA ARE AVAILABLE

Front cover image: Esteban looking back from the
clifftop in *Iluminados por el fuego* (still photography by
Gabriel Costa and Alfredo Rodríguez)

Manufactured in the United States of America

McFarland & Company, Inc., Publishers
Box 611, Jefferson, North Carolina 28640
www.mcfarlandpub.com

To all those who work
towards a truly independent
Latin America

Table of Contents

Acknowledgments

Thanks are due first and foremost to all of the nineteen filmmakers who collaborated with me on this project. Their single most important contribution was to concede interviews, but they also provided useful and interesting data — and, in many cases, invaluable encouragement.

I am also particularly grateful to the following people. Elizabeth Carrasco at the Cinemateca Boliviana in La Paz has been a boundless source of knowledge and support. The researcher, instructor, translator, and filmmaker Penny Simpson (with Joanne Hershfield, co-director and co-producer of the documentary *Nuestra Comunidad — Latinos in North Carolina*) was enormously helpful with contacts in Mexico, where she worked in cinema, and offered all manner of sound advice. A group-taught course in 2001 at the University of Richmond, VA, with my then colleagues, professors Claudia Ferman and Álvaro Kaempfer, was a source of several useful ideas and approaches. Nancy Membrez, at the University of Texas at San Antonio, is another filmmaker in her own right as well as an aficionada and teacher of Latin American cinema. Nancy has been extremely generous with time and effort in reading and orientation, particularly with the chapter on Eliseo Subiela's *El lado oscuro del corazón*. David Wood at UNAM in Mexico City has helped with several readings and comments, and has made various films and written material available to me.

Several authors have provided texts of entire books or articles on film (Latin American or otherwise). These include Vicky Lebeau, Elissa Rashkin, María José Somerlate Barbosa, Glen S. Close, Juana Suárez, and David Ranghelli.

Other people who have read chapters creatively and offered invaluable comments include Freya Schiwy, Linda Craig and Josefa Salmón. Two other people at national cinematic institutions were particularly helpful with readings and comments, as well as providing texts and copies of films. Adrián Muoyo at INCAA in Buenos Aires and Eduardo Correa at the Cinemateca Uruguaya in Montevideo helped with advice and data. Patricia D'Allemand at QMW in London provided useful suggestions on the book's format.

In Bolivia I have been helped in various ways by the director Paolo Agazzi, actor David Mondacca, cinematographer Guillermo Medrano, composer Cergio Prudencio, art director Jorge Javier Altamirano, journalist Elizabeth Scott Blacud, academic Ana Rebecca Prada, teacher/poet Juan Carlos Orihuela and librarian/archivists Patricia Suárez and Marisol Vargas.

Some of the people who facilitated contact with filmmakers have worked on the productions I analyze, while others have provided information concerning local or national conditions of production. These include Carolina Scaglione and Rafaela Gunner (Buenos Aires), Julián Pizá (Mexico), Ricardo González Vigil (Lima), Jose Antonio Elizeche (Paraguay), Janaina Bernardes and Sérgio Pentiocinas (both in São Paulo).

My heartfelt thanks are due to all of the above.

Foreword

by Alfonso Gumucio-Dagron

To review current Latin American cinema through 19 films is a real challenge—one that Keith Richards has taken on with cinematic joy. He has taken the unusual option of analyzing the cinematography of a whole region through the crystal of selected films ("to look at film in its own right"), putting them at the center of the analysis, though far from oblivious of other considerations.

His choice of films is interesting because unexpected, since he has avoided the "usual suspects," focusing on recent works (the oldest is dated 1985) and filmmakers who are mostly better known in their own countries than internationally. He has naturally achieved geographical balance, allowing the reader to discover some countries otherwise nonexistent for the rest of the world in terms of their film production. Many of these films remain unknown in commercial circuits in Latin America, although they are readily available in DVD in the U.S., an added paradox to the choice. In any case, Richards has the merit of revealing them.

Most interesting is that the analysis is grouped under seven sections covering essential themes, and not necessarily the most obvious. From "Pre-Columbian Mexico" (which actually broadly covers indigenous-themed filmmaking in Latin America) to "Poets in the City," a fresh look to Latin American social and cultural reality is offered and Richards succeeds in facilitating a dialogue between the proposed films and the audience/readership, as much as a conversation among the films selected.

The looking-glass is above all that of cultural diversity, recognition that this region is a dynamic and constantly self-transforming entity never frozen within exotic or ethnocentric boundaries. Geography, ethnicity, age, gender—none of these is the main descriptor; culture is. But culture as complexity: a sponge that absorbs conflict and contradiction given that Latin America, like any other region, is a mix of major/minor cultures that have come to share a common space, not often in harmony.

Richards highlights the educational potential of feature films. He joins those who value stories over documentary sources and thinks of fiction film in the same way as those who believe that novels say more about society than history books or academic essays.

The author approaches the subject with an open spirit, from beginning to end. I like that. Contrary to many essays, this one does not force the analysis to fit squarely into a mold that has been elaborated beforehand. Richards did not begin his research with a firm hypothesis that he then tried to prove right all the way to the end. It is clear that he started with curiosity and questions, his perception evolved and his uncertainty grew as he gathered more questions than answers. That is educational.

No less important is how Richards destroys superficial myths and characterizations of

Latin America, and does so by quoting sharp writers and filmmakers who reject romantic, tropicalist or patronizing visions.

Humbly, the author announces that the book is made and structured to support "the teacher of Spanish language and/or Latin American film, literature or social issues." This may be so, but I believe the end result goes much further and the potential readership is wider than initially sought. Certainly the book is structured as a teaching tool, addressed to those not yet familiar with the subject. However, the methodology can help anyone to enter the realm of current Latin American cinema (if the films are available, which ironically is true for the USA but not for our own region).

The analysis of films in each chapter is always preceded by contextual analysis that helps enormously to understand the diversity not only of cultures but of viewpoints. "Who tells the stories" is a constant thread running throughout the book.

If only 19 films have made the list for in-depth analysis, each thematic chapter mentions many other examples that are related, and includes brief descriptions attempting to qualify the range of productions that connect to a specific theme. Richards shows at all times a very solid knowledge of Latin American film production throughout history, only matched by his ability to read the social and political context. This is what I consider knowledge, and not just information. To deliver a text that is easy to read and aims to be an educational support, Richards has gone through hundreds of books and films and certainly spent several years reflecting on them.

The reader is pampered with everything he or she needs: context analysis, film synopsis, biographical notes on "creators," interviews with film directors, film analysis, excerpts from dialogues, textual analysis, linguistic features, references and bibliographies, a brief "for cultural understanding" section with a wealth of historical references, questions for discussion and supporting images which are not merely random illustrations. With so many "bonus features" (like on DVDs) providing insights into the films discussed, what more do we need?

On a personal level, this book has renewed my thirst for the films selected. To see them, whether for the first time or as a revisit, is something that he inspires the reader to do.

Writer, journalist and photographer Alfonso Gumucio-Dagron has worked in five continents on communications for development. Twice exiled from Bolivia by military regimes, he is the author of more than 20 books, which include fiction and poetry as well as works on cultural themes and communication.

Introduction

"Cultural" difference is no longer a stable, exotic otherness; self-other relations are matters of power and rhetoric rather than of essence. A whole structure of expectations about authenticity in culture and in art is thrown in doubt.
James Clifford, *The Predicament of Culture*
(Harvard University Press, 1988), 14.

The perception of any culture as purely foreign, or exotic, often willfully and misleadingly overlooks its closeness to one's own. Latin America is an inevitable cultural influence, particularly in the United States, as well as a physical proximity. As a teacher of Latin American film and literature in the U.S., I sometimes began my courses by asking students the leading question: where is Latin America? The standard reply was that the region began on the southern banks of the Río Grande and stretched south as far as Tierra del Fuego. My first reply might be that there was a Mexican community five minutes' walk from campus. If its members were Latinos, and we were already on the American continent, wasn't Latin America really a lot closer than we might think? Secondly, so-called Latin America (I use the term, if not for its accuracy, at least because of its familiarity) contains many communities of non–Latin origin, either culturally or ethnically. Indigenous peoples still abound (particularly in Guatemala, parts of Mexico, and the Andean countries). The African diaspora in Central and South America is huge, and often Black communities are neither Spanish- nor Portuguese-speaking. There are many other peoples including Mennonites and immigrants from Japan, Korea, several European countries, and the Arab world. The Jewish communities, especially in Argentina, are large and influential.

The term "Latin America" is, of course, a misnomer. Coined in nineteenth-century France to support a geopolitical vision of unity with (and annexation by) "Latin" Europe, it is nevertheless the term used almost exclusively in English. In Spanish, "*América Latina*" is still preferred to toponyms that allude to the colonizer's origin ("*Hispanoamérica*," "*Iberoamérica*") or the existence of indigenous populations ("*Indoamérica*"). An alternative gaining currency in the region is *Abya Yala*, which has come from the Kuna people of Panama and is most often translated as "Mature Land," having the advantage of not specifying any particular ethnic group, project of domination or claim to ownership. Whether it is to be adopted, as part of an increasingly strong project of "decolonization" in the area, remains to be seen. Populations of non-indigenous origin would demand inclusion, but a nomenclature that excludes nobody would be cumbersome indeed. As James Clifford argues, "identity, considered ethnographically, must always be mixed, relational, and inventive" (op. cit., 10).

Several years' experience as a teacher of Spanish language and Latin American culture at universities in both Great Britain and the United States have shown me the power of

3

audiovisual material, in particular the feature film, in education over a wide range of disciplines. I have found film to be of considerable use in teaching language, literature and social issues.

This, of course, is not to diminish the value of film as and of itself—it is arguably to the detriment of film studies that the media is so readily applicable to such a range of material. However, it is disingenuous to suggest that the use of audiovisual sources in some ways dilutes or cheapens the discipline of film studies, since it is the very accessibility of film that makes it such an attractive and universal medium. Film addresses our most prominent senses simultaneously, and does so moreover with narration, creating an illusory reality that, if abused, can distort and misrepresent. Today it is more crucial than ever that we be armed with an awareness of the power of audiovisual media, now omnipresent and consequently taken for granted in our lives. We should be conscious of their array of techniques, able to appreciate them but also on our guard against the possibility of their misuse.

The pedagogical use of film has become increasingly widespread at all levels over the past ten years or so. Its application in Spanish and Latin American studies has much to do with the foreign or exotic nature of the reality being presented, though their strangeness is diminished by demographic and political developments (the European community, Hispanic immigration into the U.S., etc.). Nevertheless, cultural differences can be more fully understood with audiovisual evidence, particularly when a film is set in geographically distant countries. There are numerous reasons for this; first, one can point to the changes (dilution, for some) in Latin American film, from a revolutionary and confrontational aesthetic to one more accessible both to domestic audiences and to those in North America and Europe. Secondly, the increased commercial success of Latin American cinema and its ever-greater availability to audiences in North America and Europe is a development attributable to numerous factors. One of these is simply the greater accessibility of "World Cinema" on the general market, the realization of the marketing potential of non–English language films by distributors, and the change, albeit moderate, in public taste.

Eliseo Subiela's response, when asked by Marcia Orell García (2006, 196) about a thematic change in Latin American cinema, was significant:

> Everything has changed. Fortunately, I think there is an evolution; it seems to me that important things are taking place. We appear to be freeing ourselves from a kind of ideological burden that limited us a lot. I always thought we lacked freedom, that Latin American cinema didn't take to the air like Latin American literature did, but it's acquiring that ability. There are important things happening in Chile, in Argentina, and we haven't stopped dreaming or believing in utopias, but I think time has passed and we have learned, otherwise it would be terrible. We have to talk about the market; we have to talk about industry; in this I think there's been an advance."[1]

As politically aware a figure as the Colombian director Sergio Cabrera speaks in this book of the failures of the militant cinema of the 1960s and '70s to reach and persuade its audience. As Cabrera has said elsewhere, "People go to see a film to be told a story, not to be taught a lesson."[2]

This book is intended to be informative to the general reader, as well as serving the teacher of Spanish language and/or Latin American film, literature or social issues. It sets out to fill gaps in the understanding of realities and issues, such as the logistical circumstances of filmmaking in Latin America, explaining everyday conditions that may seem outlandish from the outside, and the criteria involved in reading and interpreting a film.

The book offers brief critical essays in English on themes into which the individual films are grouped. This is, however, not to limit discussion of those films in terms of a single theme; rather, the student is encouraged to look at the films according to other perspectives, while the theme essays look at their relationships with recent developments in Latin American cinema as a whole.

There is biographical information on directors, writers and occasionally actors, though this data does not seek to be overly influential in considering the films. This, and the historical and social background, sets out to explain their significance and conditions of production. Synopses of the films are also kept brief. Production details and credits are offered on each of the films, while I have used my contacts within Latin American cinema to provide original interviews with directors. Interviews were conducted in Spanish and Portuguese and have been translated into English. Where necessary I give transcriptions from selected scenes: these are to enable close textual analysis of script excerpts. For each film there is a set of suggestions for student discussion and analysis, posing questions that may be adopted or expanded upon by the instructor. In each case there is also a brief section on linguistic and occasionally grammatical features emerging from the script.

The films analyzed in this book are all readily available on DVD[3] in the USA with optional English subtitles (from companies such as amazon.com or facets.org) and have been selected to cover a wide range of issues as well as for their inherent cinematic quality. The text may be used in a number of ways. Combinations of films are possible in order to suit disciplines and approaches to teaching. For example, a course in twentieth-century history would do well to look at *Mi mejor enemigo* and *Iluminados por el fuego,* films easily juxtaposed for their thematic similarity. The instructor may want to discuss important social, historical and political developments raised in these two films and possibly include others recommended in Chapter 20, "Fratricidal Wars and Imperialism." Pre-Columbian history and/or mythology and the conquest can be addressed through *Cabeza de Vaca* and *Eréndira ikikunari* and any of the films suggested in Chapter 1, "The Indigenous Image." These are combinations already suggested in the book's organization into sections, but other permutations are possible. For instance, *Cabeza de Vaca* can be considered as literary adaptation and even as portrayal of a writer. Depictions of prostitution can be compared in *El lado oscuro del corazón* and *En la puta vida.* Jewish themes can be discussed through viewings of *Novia que te vea* in conjunction with the section "Jews and Jewish Culture in Latin American film."

Alternatively, the instructor may want to trace the recent evolution of film in Latin America. A linguistic approach would entail using the films to sample national and regional varieties of Latin American Spanish (in two instances, Brazilian Portuguese). The chapters on *Cabeza de Vaca, Novia que te vea, Perder es cuestión de método* and *A hora da estrela* all discuss approaches to the question of literary adaptation into film.

Iluminados por el fuego and *En la puta vida* both derive from journalistic sources (memoir and investigation, respectively). While *El lado oscuro del corazón* and *Caída al cielo* look at other possible filmic approaches to literary themes, and Chapter 24, "Writers as Characters," deals with other relationships between cinema and literature. Throughout the text, literature is linked to aesthetic trends and techniques and underlying visions of national and cultural identity. Details of content are provided to enable the instructor to make choices of material appropriate to the age or preferences of students. Some of the films included in this book may not be considered suitable for high school audiences.

I mostly discuss feature films, but occasionally there are documentaries or television series that serve to illustrate social, historical or other situations. However, the aim of this book is not simply to use film as a way into other disciplines, but also to offer means of seeing the medium in its own right. For this reason I have included the "analysis" sections that examine film language, the whys and wherefores of directorial approaches (and contributions from other film crew members). Elements we may take for granted are scrutinized and questioned in these sections.

The Cuban poet and narrator José Lezama Lima was one of the region's greatest writers (though not one adapted to the screen, partly because of the difficulty of his work). Lezama Lima, despite taking literary expression to levels almost impossible to transpose to other media, was a film aficionada for whom "the birth of cinema marked a new possibility for human expression. It is in itself a pathway and is enriched by a flood of tributaries without becoming subordinate to any one of them. Cinema exemplifies the eternal human search for unity."[4]

The study of Latin American cinema can help us to comprehend this often misunderstood region, both on its own terms and as a diasporic influence on the rest of the world.

1. The Indigenous Image:
From Caricature to Self-Portrait

The Brazilian filmmaker Sylvio Back contends that an Indian filmed by a white man is an image of the white man, an idea illustrated in his film *Yndio do Brasil* (*Our Indians*, 1969). Back's collage of presentations of the indigenous uses clips from films dating as far back as 1912. The images are left to speak for themselves as expressions of a range of attitudes, from paternalism to outright contempt, that have accompanied genocidal policies ever since European arrival in the region. Brazil's Indians have long been considered unproductive and impossible to assimilate into a modern nation: unlike the Andean countries and Mexico, they have been relatively few in number and widely dispersed, making their incorporation into an industrial or agricultural workforce far more difficult. On a similar note, but in a somewhat different style, Guillermo Gómez Peña's *Borderstasis* (USA, 1998) uses archive ethnographic footage of Indians to challenge notions of exoticism and cultural authenticity.

Robert Stam's *Tropical Multiculturalism* examines developments in allegorical and symbolic treatments of the Indian in Brazil (1997, 7) noting the shift away from the idealized native used to differentiate the new country from its Portuguese colonizers. Stam points out that Brazilian Modernists preferred the image of the rebel and cannibal Tupinambá, "who devoured the foreigner to appropriate his force." Although this vision of the Indian was not included in film at the time, it was later used by Cinema Novo directors such as Nelson Pereira dos Santos.

Tropical Multiculturalism devotes a chapter to the "structuring absence" of Indians in the silent era (until the late 1920s). Stam also provides a condensed version of his analysis (2006) in which he outlines some of the "more salient avatars of the figure of the Indian" (ibid., 205) such as the romantic Indian, the patriotic, the tropicalist, the ethnographic and the activist. The evolution of these types is marked by a gradual acceptance and recognition of the indigenous need for, and right to, self-representation.

That filmed images of Indians are so common in Brazil reflects certain characteristics that set the country apart. One is the huge proportion of Brazilian territory taken up by rainforest, and the crucial role in the national imaginary played by this region and its indigenous occupants. Another is that Brazilian filmmakers have been prepared to confront and present unpleasant realities in the treatment of indigenous peoples. These are stories that are readily sexualized, making use of both the natural sensuality of the environment and making their commercialization easier — sometimes with merely exploitative results, but also resulting in films of quality such as Lúcia Murat's *Brava gente brasileira* (*Brave New Land*, 2000) which maps the shifting relationship between an indigenous people and the early Portuguese presence, both initiated by sexual encounters and (albeit temporarily) concluded by means of them. Also noteworthy are the metamorphoses of the pro-tagonist in various film versions of José Martiniano de Alencar's 1865 indianist novel *Iracema*.[1]

The Brazilian example of cinematic Indian as naïve and undeserving inhabitant of par-adise is, as Stam shows, provided in Humberto Mauro's *O descobrimento do Brasil* (*The Dis-covery of Brazil*, 1937). Here the absence of recognizable signs of "civilization" combines with a lush and beautiful landscape to make this facile image possible.

Elsewhere in Latin America, more austere surroundings and materially opulent cultures have resulted in more complex recreations of the pre–Conquest world. Mexican Juan Mora's *Retorno a Aztlán* (1990), for example, set out to reconstruct this environment, compensating for the scarcity of demonstrable evidence with an imaginative and overtly free recreation by the filmmaker and his crew. Mel Gibson is the director of another such project, *Apocalypto* (2006), which, quite apart from Mora's accusation of plagiarism,[2] has courted controversy amid charges of flagrant, wanton inaccuracy and sensationalism in its depiction of the Maya. Superficial similarities exist between Mora's vision of pre–Conquest indigenous society and Gibson's, but the former is undoubtedly the fruit of more serious research and aesthetic enterprise. Admittedly, *Apocalypto*'s art direction and handling of violence make it a persua-sive "action movie" for those unaware of, or indifferent to, pre–Columbian heritage; much of the Mexican indignation concerning *Apocalypto* was based on a nationalistic "patrimonial" opposition to an alleged U.S. cultural imperialism which misunderstood its neighbor's pre–Hispanic cultural riches. However, the unrelenting brutality of this film typifies Gibson's penchant for stirring outrage, his taste for images of barbarism offset by a spurious message of Christian salvation. The final image of a Spanish ship bizarrely hints at impending relief from the context of mindless bloodletting established during the film. Gibson's vision finds its diametrical opposite, in terms of willful misrepresentation, in the kind of uncritical idyll typified, in the Brazilian context, by André Luiz Oliveira's *A lenda de Ubirajara* (*The Legend of Ubirajara*, Brazil, 1975), a romance in a pre–Columbian setting which sees a new nation founded by lovers from warring tribes.

Paul Leduc's *Barroco* (Mexico/Cuba/Spain, 1989) searches for the origins of Mexican and Latin American identity through various *tableaux vivants* depicting the Maya and the development of *barroco* mestizo (otherwise known as American Baroque) the aesthetic synthesis of European and Indian cultural traditions. This is one of several films in which Leduc eschews the use of dialogue. A filmmaker with similar tastes is Diego Rísquez, whose *Orinoko, nuevo mundo* (*Orinoco, New World*, Ven, 1984) and *Amérika, terra incógnita* (Ven, 1988) recount pre–Columbian and colonial history through stylized baroque images and music.

The exploration of first contacts and early relationships between indigenous peoples and Europeans, seen in *Cabeza de Vaca* and *Eréndira ikikunari*, is also noteworthy in *Jericó* (Luis Alberto Lamata, Venezuela, 1990). Lamata also wrote this story of a priest, sole survivor of an Indian raid, gradually becoming assimilated and "going native." However, the process is fascinatingly disrupted by the arrival of another group of Spaniards, obliging the priest to make the reverse journey in terms of cultural identification and allegiance.

The adaptation of existing writings has provided fertile ground: for example, Luiz Alberto Pereira's *Hans Staden—lá vem nossa comida pulando* (*Hans Staden—Here Comes Our Food Jumping*, 1999) is based on the chronicles of a German sailor who spent nine months as a captive of the Tupinambá people under constant threat of being killed and eaten. Staden, who returned home to write his memoirs, uses the very title to express revulsion at his captors' customs: *True Story and Description of a Country of Wild, Naked, Grim, Man-eating People in the New World, America* (1557). This was a highly successful publication in its time, and it has been both seen as both valid ethnographic testimony and sensationalist posturing. Stam (2006, 225) considers Pereira far too ready to take Staden's word for everything, while the same source (combined with the writings of Frenchman Jean de Léry) was used by Nelson Pereira dos Santos for his celebrated *Como era gostoso o meu Francês* (*How Tasty Was My Little Frenchman*, 1971), a satirical look at the question of cannibalism. This film should be considered not only through the tradition using cannibalism for irreverent allegory (see Stam 2006 and Nagib 2007) but also in the context of the Brazilian Cinema Novo and Nuevo Cine Latinoamericano movements within which various local cinemas found ways to express resistance to colonialism and its legacies. Pereira dos Santos's film represents a creative view of cannibalism that adds to a centuries-old debate upon the subject and its possibilities as cultural metaphor. *Hans Staden*, for Stam (ibid., 226) missed the opportunity of enriching the question further, due to its unquestioning acceptance of the German's protestations. Lúcia Nagib[3] (2007) also considers these two films in conjunction with Joaquim Pedro de Andrade's 1978 film version of the Mário de Andrade novel *Macunaima* as marking crucial trajectories in national identity and cultural politics.

In Mexico, the early years of cinema were informed by the ideas of José Vasconcelos (1882–1959) whose vision of a universal Cosmic Race implied the absorption and assimilation of the native. Many of the earliest silent films with indigenous themes, however sentimentalized they may appear, display a will to balance social and religious conservatism with gestures towards modernity and post–Independence nationhood. Some Mexican examples are *Tabaré* (Luis Lezama, 1917), a romantic drama based on Juan Zorrilla de San Martín's poem about indigenous rebellion against Spanish rule, with the stock device of a love affair between members of the two sides; the Indian leader, Tabaré, falls for his enemy's daughter. Manuel de la Bandera's *Cuauhtémoc* (1919) tells of the last Aztec leader's fate. *Tepeyac* (José Manuel Ramos, Carlos E. González and Fernando Sáyago, 1917) recounts the Virgin of Guadalupe's apparition before the Indian peasant Juan Diego. As David Wood indicates, this film's "strength as an effective national and nationalist historical narrative stems from its linking of two periods: the past and mythical time of Juan Diego — an Indian whose faith in the Virgin who appeared to him on Tepeyac hill permits the incorporation of his race (supposedly barbarous) into Creole civilisation — and the present time that makes history relevant for the public in contemporary Mexico."[4]

In the 1920s several noble but doomed indigenous characters appeared on Mexican screens. Actor/director Guillermo "*El Indio*" Calles's *El indio yaqui* (*The Yaqui Indian*, 1926) proved less patronizing towards its autochthonous subject than contemporary U.S. films, while *Dios y ley* (*God and Law*, 1930) is yet another salutary tale illustrated by a love story; the Indian protagonist renounces his claim to the white woman who loves him, allowing her to go to his Caucasian rival. As Jesse Lerner (2009) indicates, this is a stereotype that proved long-lasting; as other social issues came to be addressed relatively responsibly in film, indigenous characters were characterized as a procession of shuffling, submissive bumpkins.

President Lázaro Cárdenas (1934–40) emphasized the assimilation ("Mexicanization") of indigenous peoples, and director Emilio "El Indio" Fernández and cinematographer Gabriel Figueroa devised a film language (influenced by the work in Mexico of Sergei Eisenstein) that went unchallenged for decades as a vehicle for depictions of the indigenous. These latter, radical in their time, were to be challenged as static and conservative monumentalism in films like Luis Alcoriza's *Tarahumara* (1965), a serious drama about the plight of a mountain people and the efforts of an envoy from the capital to alleviate it.

Irresponsible film caricatures of indigenous peoples and cultures are explored by the critic Carlos Monsiváis (1995, 118) whose list of the "mythologies" of Mexican cinema includes a section, "Atmospheres," featuring elements such as an Aztec past projected with "excessive staging impervious to historical authenticity" as well as representations of Indian heritage in the form of "lost paradises" and "Mexican Gothic." Another Mexican critic, Jorge Ayala Blanco, has repeatedly expressed disdain for what he sees as his national cinema's inadequate and inaccurate portrayal of the indigenous.[5]

In Argentina, unlike countries with established sedentary pre–Columbian cultures, the Indian was usually depicted early on as a threat to the spread of civilization. The nomadic aboriginal of the pampas occupied a place not dissimilar to the Wild West Indian; films like *Pampa bárbara* (Lucas Demare and Hugo Fregonese, 1942, remade in English as *Savage Pampas* in 1966) "constructed a mythical enemy, the Indian, who had to be exterminated, who sowed destruction, until he appears fighting in the raid at the end of the film, devastating lives and destroying forts. Hatred for the Indian was not metaphorical.... Remembrance of the struggle against the Indian deepened a split between the official history of this campaign and the memory of the extermination of the indigenous population, excluded from the film"[6] (Tranchini, 2005, 15).

A more measured approach is seen in *El último malón* (*The Last Indian Attack*, Alcides Greca, 1917), the reconstruction of a rebellion that occurred in Argentina's northwest, in and around San Javier, in 1904. The film shows a degree of sympathy with the cause of the Mocoví people who revolted against what is acknowledged as long-term oppression and neglect. Greca divides his film into six acts, some of which are documentary and anthropological in nature whilst others depict failed rebellion. The final act has the instigator, Jesús Salvador, escaping and living as "chief in the heart" of his lover, the mestiza Rosa Paiqui.

Leopoldo Torre Nilsson's adaptation of the epic poem *Martín Fierro* (1968) contains some harrowing scenes in its depiction of the runaway gaucho's period of refuge among nomadic pampas Indians. This is an unsentimental vision befitting an era of cruelty, with the outlaw-hero's adoption by the Indians a clear identification between similarly marginalized groups.

Gerónima (Raúl Tosso, Argentina, 1986) is the true story of a Mapuche woman's suffering in Patagonia at the hands of the Argentine state. It draws parallels between white invasion and massacre on Mapuche lands during the late-nineteenth-century desert wars, and the process continued by other means under the twentieth-century guise of scientific progress. According to Adrián Baccaro (Satarain 2004, 135) if Gerónima is to be seen as representative of her people it is not as a rebel: "Gerónima may be one of the most fragile characters in cinematic history.... Curiously, today Gerónima's story reveals itself to us as contemporary, although multiplied into millions."[7] Tosso himself (ibid., 167), in an interview with Baccaro, tells how he and his crew gradually gained the confidence of a Mapuche community reluctant to trust outsiders due to the historical reasons given in this film, which still apply in view of the Mapuche's unfinished struggles in both Argentine and Chilean Patagonia.

The taboo theme of inter-racial attraction also appears in Argentina, such as in *La quena de la muerte* (*The Flute of Death*, Nelo Cosimi, Argentina, 1929), as a wealthy sophisticate couple retreats from city excesses in a mountain chalet. The couple meet and seduce mestizo siblings, becoming emotionally and physically involved but also fatally beguiled.

As Ana Laura Lusnich observes (2009, 46), "family and social melodrama makes way for a moral drama in which the abuse of power and racial discrimination are established as central themes."[8]

Bolivia's high proportion of indigenous population has meant that its cinema has (until recently) been largely concerned with rural themes. It developed aesthetics to codify the indigenous world for the comprehension of an urban public, adopting pre–Columbian heritage as nationalist iconography. That this occurred partly due to the initiative of foreigners (Austrian Arthur Posnansky and Italian Pedro Sambarino) shows the local "white" minority's insecurity regarding acceptance of the indigenous majority's rights in a country only recently beginning to feel comfortable with its own native presence. Posnansky's association of indigenous heritage with national identity was apparently notable in his *La gloria de la raza* (*Glory of the Race*, 1926), now sadly disappeared. *Wara Wara* (José Velasco Maidana, 1929), the only surviving film from the silent era, presents a discourse of reconciliation which employs the analogy of a love story between a native princess and a Spanish conquistador. Sambarino's *Corazón aymara* (*Aymara Heart*, 1925) is known to have contained a rather more radical message: for Alfonso Gumucio-Dagron (1982, 72) the film "used romance as a façade to transmit the basic ideal of rebellion and class struggle."[9]

The second phase of indigenous representation in Bolivian cinema occurred with the National Revolution of 1952. Jorge Ruiz's *Vuelve Sebastiana* (*Come Back, Sebastiana*, 1953) tells the story of a young girl from the impoverished Chipaya people living on the harsh plains south of Oruro. Her curiosity leads her to stray to another community, that of the Aymara people traditionally seen as enemies of the Chipayas. Her return represents twin ideals in the political discourse of the time: maintenance of a sense of indigenous community, and integration into national life. Ruiz made other valuable ethnographic documentaries, such as *Los urus* (1951), and though the political project of the then government may have been discredited, Ruiz is still acknowledged as a master in his field.

The city-countryside dichotomy is central to the vision of *Vuelve Sebastiana*, as it is to certain films by Jorge Sanjinés and the Ukamau Group in the 1960s and '70s. This radicalized vision sought to present the indigenous subject on its own terms: uncomfortably urbanized characters seek to restore their cultural integrity in both *Yawar mallku* (*Blood of the Condor*, 1968) and *La nación clandestina* (*The Clandestine Nation*, 1988). The latter, generally considered the best Bolivian film yet made, tells a powerful story of acculturation and attempted reconciliation. Its protagonist, Sebastián, has left his Aymara community to live in La Paz, changing his Indian surname out of embarrassment. His treachery goes still further, and he voluntarily undertakes a punishing expiation. In contrast Antonio Eguino's *Chuquiago* (1976) presents a four-part portrayal of La Paz, including the stories first of Isico, an overawed Indian boy thrown into city life from the countryside, and then the young man Johnny, who denies his native culture and language. Carlos Mesa (1985, 112) sees a continuation between the two; "the culture of those holding power is imposed upon those who have arrived, like Isico, as bearers of indigenous cultural values." However, by the second or third generation, outsiders like Johnny come to "reject not only an oppressive, dead-end situation but also his parents, his language, the culture that gives him identity. Johnny is Isico devoured by the city..."[10] as subsequent generations of indigenous migrants succumb to alienation and delinquency.

Nevertheless Jorge Sanjinés, as both director and theorist (despite less well-received more recent films), has provided the most far-reaching voice in Bolivian indigenous-themed cinema to date. With the Ukamau group, which he co-founded, he has made several films informed by his artistic and political credo, *Theory and Practice of a Cinema with the People* (Sanjinés, 1979). The early expression of his position is explored by David Wood (2006) in the context of the filmmaker's emergence from the ideological influence of the 1952 National Revolution.

Other Bolivian approaches include the compelling *Ajayu* (*Soul*, Francisco Ormachea, 1999) which examines the Aymara view of death and afterlife on an island in Lake Titicaca. Mela Márquez's *Sayariy* (see Chapter 26 on *Caída al cielo*) conveys the shock of indigenous urban migration. Its memorable final scene is an ingenious deconstruction of the interior of a rural Quechua Indian house to reveal the interior of a film studio, leaving the spectator with a feeling of disorientation comparable to that experienced by the indigenous urban migrants themselves upon arrival in the city.

If urban-based cinematographic and audiovisual interest in rural life has become part of Bolivian cultural history, it has far from disappeared. Recently, fiction features have become the province of the true originators of its sources, the native communities themselves, under the auspices of indigenous video organizations such as CEFREC (Centro de Formación y Realización Cinematográfica) and APCOB (Apoyo Para el Campesino-Indígena del Oriente Boliviano). Urban migration and improvements in communication have meant that frontiers between the city and countryside have ceased to be clear-cut. An example of native peoples using video to explain their cultures and voice grievances is *El grito de la selva* (*Cry of the Forest*, Alejandro Noza, Nicolás Ipamo, and Iván Sanjinés, 2008), a feature dramatizing the victimization of communities whose lands are coveted as a potential source of short-term enrichment through forest exploitation. *Qati qati* (*Whispers of Death*, Reynaldo Yujra, Bolivia, 1999) is one of the films described by Freya Schiwy (2009, 46) as illustrating a process of "decolonization of the soul" currently under way in Bolivian indigenous video. An interesting analogous Mexican production is *Corazón del tiempo* (*Heart of Time*, Alberto Cortés, 2009), the first film purportedly made by Mayan Zapatista rebels in southern Mexico and an attempt to launch indigenous debates into a more mainstream film circuit.

The first Ecuadorean feature, Augusto San Miguel's silent *El tesoro de Atahualpa* (*Atahualpa's Treasure*, 1924), combines history with the legend surrounding the last Inca's death at the hands of Spanish conquistadors. The film also presents contemporary injustice as a legacy of the conquest, a position San Miguel followed up with *Un abismo y dos almas* (An Abyss and Two Souls) (1925) which denounced landowners' cruelty in a then semi-feudal rural environment.

Not all Latin American countries recognize their indigenous peoples in cinema. The absence of substantial feature-film representations of the important native populations in countries like Guatemala, Paraguay[11] and Ecuador (with the notable exceptions of San Miguel's oeuvre and Jorge Sanijnés's work in exile, *Llocsi caimanta, Fuera de aquí* [*Get Out of Here!*, 1977]) is at odds with the history and ethnic makeup of those countries, due partly to limited resources but also, at least equally importantly, to an apparent unwillingness to address this demographic reality.

In Peru the Cusco Film School, whose prominent members were Luis Figueroa, Manuel and Víctor Chambi and Eulogio Nishiyama, brought Andean culture into the ambit of the filmable with some twenty productions, mostly documentaries, during the 1950s and early '60s. The admirable Figueroa continues to make films over four decades after the success of the group's one feature, *Kukuli* (Nishiyama and Figueroa, 1961), the first-ever Quechua-language film and a pioneer semi-documentary depiction of native Andean culture. Figueroa followed with important adaptations of novels: Ciro Alegría's *Los perros hambrientos* (*The*

Hungry Dogs, 1976) and the great José María Arguedas's *Yawar Fiesta* (*Blood Festival*, 1980). Another Peruvian filmmaker, Federico García Hurtado, has long been identified with politicized views of indigenous culture and history. His recreation of the 1781 Cusco Indian rebellion, *Tupac Amaru* (1984) is as yet his largest production but others include *El caso Huayanay* (*The Huayanay Case*, 1981) and *Kuntur Wachana* (*Where the Condors Are Born*, 1977). García, as John King (1990, 201) argues, has been heavily influenced by the Cuzco school and by the photographer Martín Chambi: "If Chambi can be said to have 'revindicated' the Indians by focusing on their customs and lifestyle, García would add the dimensions of social struggle, even if he would try to deny his precursors."

Claudia Llosa's controversial *Madeinusa* (2006) courted controversy with its perceived distortion of indigenous culture. For some in its parable of flight from a mythical Andean village, it presents a neoliberal perspective; for others it is a subtle critique of the (possibly neoliberal-leaning) rescue fantasy. However, no such charges were made of Llosa's extraordinary *La teta asustada* (*The Milk of Sorrow*, 2009) which adapts an anthropological study of the effects upon Andean women of abuse during the conflict between the Peruvian military and Shining Path guerrillas.

Among foreign filmmakers who attempt Amerindian themes, some are motivated by genuine interest and sympathy. *Tigrero, a Film That Was Never Made* (Mika Kaurismäki, Brazil/Finland/Germany, 1994) sees the veteran director Samuel Fuller return to a remote area of Brazil where he had researched for a Hollywood production in the 1950s. Fuller, accompanied by another maverick filmmaker, Jim Jarmusch, is saddened to see the changes that have occurred in the intervening decades to a formerly proud and vibrant Karajá people. Such productions tend to follow indigenous populations in crisis: Brazilian rainforest devastation in *The Emerald Forest* (John Boorman, Great Britain, 1995), the invasion and pollution of Indian land in *Altiplano* (Peter Brosens and Jessica Hope Woodworth, Germany/Netherlands/Belgium, 2009). *At Play in the Fields of the Lord* (Héctor Babenco, USA, 1991) deals with the questionable role of missionaries in preparing the ground for environmental exploitation and cultural abuse of previously un-contacted tribes. The desolation wrought by psychotic Guatemalan military anti-insurgency is the theme of *Men with Guns* (John Sayles, USA, 1997).

Other foreign "auteur" filmmakers irresponsibly and inaccurately apply preconceived notions to a Latin American reality distorted to accommodate their visions. Some examples, apart from the above-mentioned *Apocalypto*, are Werner Herzog's *Fitzcarraldo* (1982) and Dennis Hopper's *The Last Movie* (1971) (see Richards 2006).

The phenomenon of Indian video has been explored in studies by, among others, Freya Schiwy (2009), who sees such productions as a new form of empowerment that allows communication with the outside world. Perhaps more important still is they allow dialogue between indigenous populations, once barely aware of each other's existence, who are now able to share and compare vital experiences. It seems, and is to be hoped, that indigenous video is here to stay. Sofía Kenny sees similar developments in two Bolivian tendencies; she cites a greater horizontality in the work of CEFREC, under the directorship of Iván Sanjinés, than in earlier films by the Ukamau Group headed by Sanjinés's father Jorge. Although Ukamau created films alongside the people, it did not allow them full participation, which is a keystone of CEFREC's approach (Kenny 2009, 215–18). The example of the Purépecha (western central Mexico) video-maker Dante Cerano suggests the emergence of a new generation of individual indigenous filmmakers with a personal vision. It remains to be seen whether the collective model introduced by CEFREC will prevail, or a continuance of the auteur model will encroach into indigenous video: perhaps, indeed, the two can coexist.

2. *Eréndira Ikikunari*
(Indomitable Eréndira)

CREDITS: Mexico, 2007; *Produced by:* A co-production involving several national and state bodies (see below); *Script and Direction:* Juan Mora Catlett; *Music:* Andrés Sánchez; *Director of Photography:* Toni Kuhn; *Sound:* Enrique Ojeda; *Make-up:* Julián Pizá

CAST: Eréndira (Xochiquetzal Rodríguez), Nanuma (Justo Alberto Rodríguez), T'shue (Luis Esteban Huacúz Dímas), Timas (Roberto Isidro Rangel), Cuynierángari (Edgar Alejandro Pérez), Tangaxoan (Rubén Bautista), Old Woman of the Oracle (Soledad Ruiz)

Synopsis

Omens warning of conquest, and of the removal and replacement of ancestral gods, are borne out by the arrival of Spaniards in Purépecha lands. Eréndira is a young woman who defies tradition; she despises Nanuma, her betrothed, and refuses to marry him. Nanuma's younger brother, T'shue, secretly loves Eréndira and admires her nonconformist attitude. News of the Spaniards' arrival is brought by Eréndira's uncle, Timas. But the timorous young monarch, Tangaxoan, obsessed with prophecy, resolves to commit suicide rather than fight. Later convinced that the foreigners will not harm them, he and his lieutenant Cuynierángari decide to collaborate. A battle ensues between Tangaxoan's forces, allied with the Spaniards, and those opposed to the invaders led by Timas (who allows Eréndira to fight). Eréndira captures a Spaniard's horse and learns to ride, using it against the invaders in subsequent combat. This intensifies Nanuma's resentment and determination to destroy her. The film's ambiguous outcome alludes to the survival of Eréndira's spirit of challenge in contrast to the defeatism and betrayal represented by Tangaxoan. The protagonist resists the machismo and fatalism of her own culture as much as the threat of foreign invasion.

About the Film

Eréndira ikikunari was co-produced by a number of national and local bodies including the National Council for Culture and the Arts (CONACULTA), Mexican Institute of Cinematography (IMCINE), Fund for the Production of Quality Cinema (FOPROCINE),

Juan Roberto Mora Catlett and Eréndira Productions, Imagen en Movimiento and the Government of the State of Michoacán.

It should be pointed out that this film is only minimally connected to Gabriel García Márquez's short novel *La increíble y triste historia de la cándida Eréndira y de su abuela desalmada* (*The Incredible and Sad Tale of Innocent Eréndira and Her Heartless Grandmother*, filmed as *Eréndira* by Ruy Guerra in 1983). Other than the name, the only similarity between the two is the emblematic nature of the protagonist of both versions. However, instead of García Márquez's (at least initially) passive, somnambulant victim, Mora presents a young woman who vehemently rejects all attempts to oppress her.

Eréndira's defiance is reflected by the film's aesthetic, which is rigorous, uncompromising and eclectic. Mora insists upon the use of Purépecha (a little-known native language) due to its authenticity and sonorous qualities, but combines these elements and sixteenth-century sources with a highly modern use of sound and image. The film was shot in digital format, then blown up to 35mm, a process increasingly used in Latin America for budgetary reasons.

Ana Cristina Ramírez Barreto has suggested that the historical basis for the Eréndira story is shaky: Eduardo Ruiz, a liberal lawyer and writer from Michoacán, wrote the historical document known as *Relación de Michoacán* o *Códice Escorial*. "Ruiz probably conceived Eréndira as an image in negative of *doña Marina* ... her own woman, patriotic, with her own ideas, chaste and childless, in complete contrast with Malinche."[1]

Eréndira is a name originating in the Purépecha (Tabasco) culture, meaning one who smiles, or Princess of the Eternal Smile. As Ramírez Barreto points out, it is a name that appears and reappears at difficult times, a sign of its association with the spirit of resistance.[2]

About the Film's Creators

Juan Mora Catlett was born in Mexico City in 1949 to an artistic background: his father was the painter Francisco Mora Pérez, one of whose friends, Raúl Kamffer, was a filmmaker whose work displays a great interest in pre–Columbian Mexico. Mora Catlett's mother is the African-American sculptor Elizabeth Catlett. After studying at the Film School of the UNAM (Universidad Nacional Autónoma de México), he was awarded a grant to study film in Prague, in the then Czechoslovakia, where he remained from 1969 to 1974. The experience of life abroad, he says, helped him appreciate and understand his own culture. Mora Catlett has worked on a number of films as writer, producer, director, or editor. He combined all these activities on the following projects: *VolArte* (2003), a short film that showcases the paintings of Diego Rivera on a computer-generated "flight" through a collection of his works. *Retorno a Aztlán* (1990) is a re-telling of a pre–Columbian myth, spoken entirely in Nahuatl (the film is discussed below in detail).

Interview with Director Juan Mora (August 2007)

KR: The use of painting is something that can clearly be seen in your films. But in Eréndira Ikikunari *painted images are part of the scenery and take almost a leading role. Did you seek in this way to give a constant reminder of your source for this narrative?*

Juan Mora Catlett. Photograph by Xolotl Salazar.

JM: The use of plastic resources in the images from the codices is a resource that I use to emphasize the non-realistic interpretation of narrations, in accordance with their non–European or non–Western origin. They create a strange image, unusual in the cinema, which make the spectator aware of his/her distance from what is narrated. I also think it is a resource that allows us to maintain the poetic, legendary and mythical nature of the content, emphasizing that this is a poetic metaphor and not a prosaic narrative, such as the public is used to. For me it is important to maintain the indication that this is a myth or a legend, because in that way it is possible to accede to the archetypical interpretation on the part of the spectator (in the Jungian sense). This was proven in several screenings of *Aztlán*, both in Mexico and abroad, where the public spoke not of having seen a film, but of having participated in a sacred ritual. Some young people were even known to have ingested a drug in order to view the film. With *Eréndira*, some spectators have commented to me that they lived it as a kind of rite of passage. Of course this also refers back to the sources — in other words, the codices and the Mexican indigenous plastic arts, appropriately since it's congruent with the material.

Sound is another element that distances the spectator from the first level of the film, from what is immediately perceptible. How do you explain the use of echo and dubbing in the soundtrack?

     The use of sound is different in the two films. In *Aztlán* I tried to create a unitary soundtrack, using the sounds of pre–Columbian and indigenous American musical instruments (which imitate the sounds of nature) in order to create not only the music, but also the ambient of wind, rain, fire and water, just like many of the incidental sounds: the growling of the beast is made with an earthenware conch, the sounds of the arrows with panpipes, etc. In this way I eliminate the conventional categorization of film soundtracks: music, ambient and incidental effects, turning the entire thing into music (if we consider that music is basically organized noise, then we see that any film soundtrack can be considered as a musical composition). The use of classical Nahuatl from the fifteenth century (now a dead language) served to maintain the verisimilitude of the narrative (to have had it spoken in any other language would have been implausible), just like using the plastic qualities of the sound in conjunction with that of the image, to suggest the poetic character of the narration mythical.

With *Eréndira*, I took advantage of the spatiality of Dolby 5.1 and THX systems to go further and position the sounds in the internal space of the spectator (sound at the center of the room, for instance when the narrator speaks, when Eréndira sobs over the death of her uncle, or in the battle scenes). Or the external space (more conventional; in other words the sound seems to come from sources shown on the screen or at its sides), also in spaces that involve the spectator (thunder and lightning, fire, the ambience of nature), or on all sides (the voices of the true gods in the volcano, or of the false gods among the pyramids, to emphasize their supernatural nature (real or apparent). But as this is a non–realistic narration, in this case I used technical resources to emphasize the musicality or artificiality of the sound; in fact I asked the composer to construct it like an opera, and some of the images (the volcano, or the court of Tangaxoan) are sketched out operatically. Indeed there is a lot that's operatic in the mise-en-scène. That is one of the occidental elements I introduce into the narrative form of this film, since it deals with the encounter of the pre–Columbian world with the Occidental. Another of the occidental (or global) elements is the use of electronic music created out of the digitalization and processing of the incidental sounds recorded during the shooting (arrows being shot, human voices, conches, metal armor, clashing of stones, etc.), just like using music to substitute for incidental noises (for example, the flight of the arrows) or to reinforce ambient sounds (the fire of the human sacrifice) as well as speeches or segments of words included in the music in rhythmic form. The musician is a young man who actually works in clubs and has played in rock groups, so is more interested in popular music. It's a union of the archaic with the modern, because myth is atemporal and profoundly human.

You've spoken of presenting a "pre–Columbian cinematographic codex": But if the codices and other Purépecha visual sources don't record the invasion, does that mean it's something you've invented?

The codex from which the image of Eréndira was created is a colonial codex (apparently commissioned by Don Pedro Cuynierángari, the Governor of Michoacán in the sixteenth century as a report to the Viceroy), made by indigenous artisans, where the pre–Columbian (image-based) narrative form combines with a European calligraphic text that puts together a literal translation of testimonies by Purépecha informants. So yes, an indigenous representation of the conquest does exist. Another colonial representation done by *tlacuilos* (painters of codices), mixing their pre–Columbian visual style with European elements, is that of the murals of Ixmiquilpan (highly dilapidated thanks to the ignorance of the priests officiating in the temple, who have even nailed loudspeakers onto the painted surfaces), where the horses are represented as monstrous centaurs with human feet, heads and arms. These images appear at the start of the film (where I had to create, digitally, a version of the temple, due to the deterioration of the real one, placing the murals where I wanted them and making them appear as phantoms, so creating an introductory atmosphere that is myth-

Extras with masks from the dance of the Cúrpitis. Photograph by Xolotl Salazar.

ical, non-realistic) and in Eréndira's dream. Another thing is that, given that it was possible to show an image of the conquest through pre–Columbian eyes (the colonial codices) it was also possible to do it through the eyes of contemporaneous indigenous people, since in their traditional dances and crafts they represent aspects of the conquest (the masks of the dance of the Cúrpitis, which I used to represent the Spaniards as strange, non-human creatures, or the little sculpture of Santiago the Apostle, which is a piece of contemporary craftwork bought in an everyday shop), not to speak of their active participation as actors and advisors on the film.

There seem to be relatively few films about the indigenous world. What place does this thematic occupy in the current Mexican social and political environment?
     Although there is an official discourse to the contrary, the indigenous is seen as backwardness, an obstacle to the development of the projects of the class in power in Mexico, where much of its wealth comes from robbery and from the inhuman exploitation of the indigenous peoples, since the colonial era (just look at Chiapas or the Yucatan peninsula, or the extermination of groups as the Yaquis, Seris or Kukapáhs of Baja California). In this sense all things indigenous are seen with distrust, contempt; it's marginalized or simply ignored; it's the opposite of emphasizing and celebrating the nexus of the Mexican with the European or global. An example: the National Association of Actors (ANDA), a kind of union of Mexican actors, demanded that I pay in dollars the actors who did the dubbing into Náhuatl on *Aztlán*, arguing that as they used a language distinct from Spanish, they had to be paid on the scale for foreign languages, it wasn't until a newspaper accused them with the headline — ANDA considers Náhuatl to be a foreign tongue — that they allowed

me to pay them in Mexican pesos, as agreed with the cast. Another example: the call for nominations for the film to represent Mexico at the Oscars and Goyas[3] indicated literally that it had to be mainly in Spanish (which after all is a language of foreign origin imposed through violence and at gunpoint). This barred the participation of *Eréndira* (spoken in one of Mexico's original languages). It wasn't until I expressed my discontent to the Mexican Academy that they relented and allowed me to enter it; in fact it was even included in the eight films that are to be proposed for both prizes (though I sincerely don't believe it will be chosen either by North Americans or Spaniards). I don't believe this has been done as a conscious proposal; rather it reflects an entrenched custom among the Mexican middle class of ignoring indigenous people or of seeing them as an inferior race of servants (which condemns them to invisibility). My brother-in-law, who is German, said that there are more blond people to be seen on television in Mexico than in his own country. The scarcity of indigenous professional actors was another of the factors that led me to cast local people (several spectators have thanked me for the fact that, finally, dark-skinned people can be seen on Mexican screens).

In Eréndira Ikikunari *the Purépechas display negative characteristics (for many observers) like their machismo, cannibalism, internal conflicts, etc. Nevertheless, the film clearly adopts their perspective. In this way did you want to avoid accusations of idealization of the indigenous?*

The decision to have the story represented by indigenous people was also an invitation to them to express their point of view on the conquest and their culture. For that reason I gave them the script so they could revise it and offer me their observations (namely to the Coordination for the Attention of Affairs of the Indigenous Peoples of the State of Michoacán in Ocampo and to Dr. Ireneo Rojas, director of the Center for Purépecha Studies at the University of San Nicolás de Hidalgo, in Morelia, Michoacán, at first also revised by the specialists in indigenous traditions at the Colegio de Michoacán in Zamora). Moreover, the indigenous interpreters also expressed their convictions and points of view with respect to the values and imperfections of their culture, that correspond to the imperfections of all humanity, without this being in any way detrimental to their human dignity as a people or as a culture. On the contrary, it appears to me an example of their ancestral maturity. For my part it was a respectful approach to their culture (which, as a Mexican myself, is part of my own), trying to overcome my middle-class prejudices, that goes so far as to respect the very nature of their representation (that's why the narration feels slow and at times repetitive, but that's how they tell stories) and not try to adapt it to the modes and models of North American commercial cinema, with the economic risk that this implied for its acceptance by exhibitors, distributors and festivals, above all European. Nevertheless, its commercial run in Mexico City lasted more than four months, almost without publicity, because the public recommended it despite this being the summer, the time of premieres for North American blockbusters, which filled all the theaters (some are premiered with as many as 1,000 copies).

*You've spoken of the encounter with the horse as a moment of beginning of the mixture of races and cultures (*mestizaje*) which implies a certain mutual interest. Given the lack of attraction between the protagonist and the invaders, would it be greatly exaggerated to speak of a form of sublimated love between Eréndira and the animal?*

I think what moves Eréndira towards the horse is firstly a great curiosity, and then a genuine interest (which according to the Argentine gestalt therapist Jorge Bucay, is the base of love, to which can then be added other ingredients like eroticism, tenderness, sexuality, etc.; Bucay presents love-interest as the basis of all human relations). The relationship with the animal is one of tenderness, on seeing its fragility and innocence rather than its apparent monstrosity, at no moment did I intend it to be erotic, if you like it's more maternal: to see someone weak whose strength can grow. It's a white horse (not a mare) because that's how it was registered in the legend. The declaration of Eréndira she will never become the wife of any man, which I thought I had invented, to correspond with her character, and which I later found in another version of the legend — has no sense of sublimation of the sexuality, but of defending her dignity as a person, instead of what is implied by being the wife of a man, an atavistic condition described in Eréndira's first dialogue with her aunt. There are versions of the legend that present an Eréndira who, after the conquest, bathed in moonlight so as to whiten her skin and render herself agreeable to the eyes of a Spanish priest, with whom she had fallen in love and who evidently despised her. For that reason she drowned herself in the lagoon of Zirahuén, turning herself into a phantom that has ever since lured and drowned enamored men. Of course, this part seemed to me to be a colonialist distortion and for that reason I didn't include it in the film.

José Felipe Coria described Return to Aztlán *as one of the two films that provide a link between* El Indio Fernández *and the present. How do you see your representation of the indigenous in the context of previous Mexican cinema?*

At no point did I take references from the representation of the indigenous in Mexican cinema which, in my opinion, always depart from the condescending vision of the middle class. My films are, in that sense, totally divorced from that tradition. I think that's why Jorge Ayala Blanco used the words "unusual representation" to refer to my work.

The figure of Eréndira seems to occupy the interstices between myth and history. Was that liberating as far as the construction of the character is concerned?

I used the combination of myth and official history as a resource to ground the figure of Eréndira, to make her real. To have retained the romantic vision that characterizes Eduardo Ruiz's nineteenth-century version of the legend would, I felt, have been to betray the indigenous vision, sustenance of the legend itself. Of course, official history can be every bit as fantastic as legend, since it was commissioned by the victors, who I think dressed everything up for their own convenience. But despite that, it is a sixteenth-century text which reflects its own way of seeing the world. Given the lack of further information, I applied my imagination and the concepts of Carl Gustav Jung and Joseph Campbell regarding myth; after all, I can enjoy the freedom of art and am not subject to the rigor of science.

Analysis: Makeup and the "Invention" of Pre-Columbian Culture

In the scene (C4, 22m) after the women have rushed to defend the gold against the Spaniards, Eréndira's aunt criticizes Nanuma for not defending his people's heritage. The rest of the scene is described in the original script of *Eréndira ikikunari* (p. 27) as follows:

> ERÉNDIRA, with one hand, wipes off her face paint and with it smears the face and chest of NANUMA. HIRIPAN is scandalized. At once ERÉNDIRA turns around and tries to move away from the enormous NANUMA, who follows her enraged. He grabs her by the hair, shaking her and throwing her to the ground. As she falls, her hand touches a rock and instinctively she throws it at NANUMA, hitting him on the forehead. He falls on his backside. HIRIPAN looks on, fascinated. Everyone is in suspense. When NANUMA recovers he stands shakily and makes

ready to hit ERÉNDIRA, but her AUNT and the WIVES OF TANGAXOAN surround and protect her, brandishing their canes. NANUMA steps back and looks at the WOMEN. HIRIPAN tries to protect his brother. Some NOBLES laugh at the scene. NANUMA realizes and feels ashamed.[4]

The film's makeup artist, Julián Pizá (personal communication, 10 April 2008), confirmed my interpretation that this action violates a code according to which all the warriors have stripes painted on the left side of their face to denote bravery. This code cannot be authenticated, of course: no relevant historical data exists. It was created by the filmmakers, using the sources available (chronicles and contemporary illustrations).

Pizá described his job as to "transfer [Mora's] ideas and intentions into a facial and corporeal plasticity": a "metaphorical interpretation of how the life of the Purépecha people may have been. The reference for all the art direction was the codex *La relación de Michoacan*, besides other oral and bibliographic sources. These served as inspiration; from them I designed the makeup."[5]

Linguistic Features

The Purépecha language is spoken by less than a quarter of a million people in the area around Lake Patzcuaro and the volcano Paricutín in the state of Michoacán. The language has been classified as an isolate, due to its limited and inadequately proven relations with other indigenous languages. Previously known as Tarascan, it has several local variations despite the restricted geographical area in which it is spoken. The prevalence of Purépecha makes the use of Spanish (among the conquistadores) and Latin (by the priest) appear all the more invasive.

For Discussion

1. In *Eréndira Ikikunari*, as in *Cabeza de Vaca*, there is the dissenting voice of the clergy represented by a single priest. What similarities or differences are there between these two views of the church?
2. What links are established between warfare and religion according to indigenous and European conceptions?
3. How is the relationship between woman and horse built up through the film?
4. What are the social repercussions of Eréndira's independence?
5. What effect is gained by the association between Eréndira and the goddess Aratanga?
6. Consider the relationship between types of shot and camera mounting (hand-held, traveling shots etc.).
7. How does *Eréndira Ikikunari* relate to traditional depictions of the Indian in Mexican film?

3. *Cabeza de Vaca*

CREDITS: Mexico/Spain/United States/Great Britain, 1990; *Produced by:* Iguana Producciones, IMCINE, others (see below); *Director:* Nicolás Echeverría; *Script:* Nicolás Echeverría, Guillermo Sheridan; *Music:* Mario Lavista; *Cinematography:* Guillermo Navarro; *Costume Design:* Tolita Figueroa; *Special Makeup Effects Artist:* Guillermo del Toro

CAST: Álvar Núñez Cabeza de Vaca (Juan Diego), Dorantes (Daniel Giménez Cacho), Castillo (Carlos Castañón), Estebanico (Gerardo Villareal), Araino (Roberto Sosa), Mala Cosa (José Flores)

Synopsis

Naufragios, the memoir of would-be conquistador turned accidental ethnographer Álvar Núñez Cabeza de Vaca (c 1490–c 1560), tells a story of loss and rediscovery. Its adaptation in the film *Cabeza de Vaca* opens in 1536 when the protagonist, after eight years' separation from his compatriots, has rejoined Spanish forces in central Mexico. Álvar Núñez laughs bitterly when a young soldier asks about his "suffering" amongst the "savages"; this comment prompts the flashback which constitutes the main narrative.

The following scene is set in 1528, at the beginning of the adventure: two rafts hold the survivors of a storm that destroyed Captain Pánfilo de Narváez's ships in a storm near today's Tampa Bay. Cabeza de Vaca criticizes Pánfilo, in both chronicle and film, for having separated the survivors into two groups, segregating the weak from the strong to prevent the former becoming a burden upon the latter. Pánfilo's reply, that Spain "ends here," proves oddly prophetic. Cabeza de Vaca, who describes himself as leader of the "weaker" group, was one of only four men who managed to rejoin their compatriots after an epic walk of some 11,000 miles from the coast of Texas to central Mexico. The author and protagonist tells how, during the eight intervening years, he was enslaved by indigenous healers, coming to understand their world view whilst himself becoming a shaman and learning several native languages.

About the Film

Cabeza de Vaca was filmed in three Mexican states: the director's native Nayarit in the northwest; Coahuila, to the north of the capital; and Tlaxcala, between Mexico City and Puebla. The film takes advantage of its barren, mountainous desert locations to emphasize the isolation of its protagonist. The film's long and tortuous route towards production and funding is analogous to the odyssey of Cabeza de Vaca himself. Domestic finance was shared between the Mexican Institute of Cinematography (IMCINE), the Fondo de Fomento a la Calidad Cinematográfica, the state governments of Nayarit and Coahuila, and private film producing companies Grupo Alica and Iguana Producciones. Spanish TV and the funding body for the 5th Centenary (V Centenario) made further contributions, as did American Playhouse Theatrical Films and Channel 4 Television of Great Britain.

The film historian Emilio García Riera (1998, 331, 359), tells how Echeverría's project was shelved by Mexican film bureaucracy in 1986 in favor of lesser, and ultimately unsuccessful, projects. Such favoritism ignored the fact that Echeverría had completed all necessary preparations. Once the film was finished, an achievement attributable to the filmmaker's sheer tenacity, its quality and originality were belatedly recognized by most observers.

About the Film's Creators

Nicolás Echeverría was born in 1947 in Tepic, in the Mexican state of Nayarit. He studied painting and architecture and also showed a talent for music from an early age, but eventually opted for a film career as a way of reaching and understanding remote native cultures. He became known as a maker of ethnographic documentaries well before *Cabeza de Vaca*, his first feature film. The project reflects his fascination with indigenous mysticism and ritual, as well as the syncretism resulting from conquest and the spread of Christianity. Echeverría described himself thus in 1992: "My subjects have always been religion, magic, mysticism, pre–Columbian cultures, esoteric disciplines, the taking of hallucinogens: that's the very reason why I found Cabeza de Vaca so interesting" (García Tsao 1992, 88). He made short films on traditional healers such as *Maria Sabina* (1978) and *Niño Fidencio, el taumaturgo de Espinazo* (*Child Fidencio, the Healer of Espinazo*, 1980). However, his interests in other areas of Mexican culture are also visible in documentaries on some of the country's greatest artists. *Sor Juana Inés de la Cruz* (1988), a biography and appreciation of the great colonial poet made in collaboration with Nobel Prize–winner Octavio Paz, looks at the literary patrimony of Mexico and the development of an independent American voice. *Gunther Gerszo* (1999) deals with the work of a celebrated modern Mexican painter. Since *Cabeza de Vaca*, Echeverría has made several documentaries and worked in television before finally directing another full-length feature film, the social comedy *Vivir mata* (*Living Kills,* 2002).

Guillermo Sheridan, who was born in Mexico City in 1950, is a novelist, satirist, academic and author of several books on Mexican literature. He has also written on a huge variety of social, political and other topics. His first novel, *El dedo de oro* (*The Golden Finger,* 1996), was a grimly humorous prophecy on Mexican life in the early twenty-first century; much of it, sadly, has already proved accurate.

For Cultural Understanding

This historical drama must be considered in the context of the early 1990s debate occasioned by the Fifth Centenary of Columbus's first journey, in 1492, to what became known as the Americas. The moment was seized upon by numerous film directors, writers and other artists to present revisionist historical works of varying degrees of accuracy or persuasiveness. Some defended the conquering and colonizing European powers, others the pre–

Columbian indigenous world. *Cabeza de Vaca* belongs in the latter category, along with other Latin American films of the same era in which received views of the Conquest are radically reconsidered. Films such as *Nuevo Mundo* (*New World*: Gabriel Retes, Mexico, 1991) and *Jericó* (*Jericho*: Luis Alberto Lamata, Venezuela, 1991), instead of presenting the natives as uncomplicated victims, examine the effects of the "discovery" on the Spaniards themselves. In the United States a similar will to take a fresh look at relationships with the Native American can be seen in films like *Dances with Wolves* (Kevin Costner, 1990), *Last of the Mohicans* (Michael Mann, 1992), and Terrence Malick's *New World* (2005).

The role of the interpreter as a cultural and linguistic intermediary is paramount in this controversy. The unenviable position of cultural go-between in the Conquest of the Americas brings to mind the Italian dictum *traduttore — traditore*; some of the indigenous "*lenguas*" who accompanied early Spanish expeditions had been captured or given away by their own peoples; the poisoned chalice of translation was foisted upon them and the charge of treachery made when the need for a scapegoat arose. In Cabeza de Vaca's story the would-be conqueror himself is saddled with this responsibility, but for his own survival rather than to serve invasion: he alone comes to understand and translate indigenous languages. The author of *Naufragios* takes advantage of this position to enhance his image before the king, posing as the only trustworthy reference with regard to the interpretation and representation of the natives. Another key issue at the time of the Conquests of the American continent, still relevant in the twenty-first century, is the question of the very legitimacy of language; to what extent is one tongue more valid than another? In the sixteenth century it was thought that the natives simply did not possess intelligible or civilized language; hence it was essential that the Europeans teach them to speak. There was a single valid language, just as there was one true faith. This prejudice is clearly visible in the writings of Columbus as well as those of other explorers and conquerors. An example of this symbolic, rather than communicative, view of language is the *Requerimiento* (Requirement), a document unintelligible to the natives which was nonetheless read aloud to them before any confrontation, demanding their submission to Spanish secular and religious authority. Its recital was a perfunctory gesture theoretically fulfilling the invaders' responsibility to inform and protect the Crown's prospective subjects, according to royal decree. An important historical moment was the 1492 publication of the first Castilian grammar by Antonio de Nebrija (1442–1522), a scholar conscious of the potential of language as, in his words, a "tool of empire." This acknowledgment of the power of language was reinforced by the practice of taking natives to Europe (with or without their consent) and teaching them the imperial tongue so that they might serve as interpreters, often becoming figures of hatred and scorn, viewed from both sides as traitors. Below are two particularly famous and important examples of this phenomenon.

La Malinche was a woman from an indigenous aristocratic background, born in what today is the state of Veracruz on the east coast of Mexico. She was presented as a gift, first to a Tabascan chief, then to the Spaniards, becoming the mistress of Hernán Cortés, the conqueror of the Aztecs. The son she had with Cortés was seen, at least symbolically, as the first *mestizo* child (born of American indigenous and European parents). In his seminal work *The Labyrinth of Solitude* (1950) the poet Octavio Paz suggests that Mexicans view themselves as the illegitimate and abandoned offspring of this legacy, fruit of what may be seen as an illicit union, even rape.

Felipillo, in Peru, occupies a similar position. His testimony was manipulated by the Spaniards under the command of Francisco Pizarro to justify their execution of the Inca

Atawallpa. He is also despised by native Andean peoples as a symbol of collusion with the invaders. Felipillo and La Malinche both represent the figure of "translator-traitor," although they differ in gender and nationality.

The discursive background to *Cabeza de Vaca*, then, is the ferocious ideological battle that raged in the fifteenth century (and its echo in the late 20th) over Spain's role in the "Indies." In this controversy several contrasting figures come face to face: those who opposed their country's right to dominate and enslave the natives include **Bartolomé de las Casas** (1484–1566), the legendary "universal protector," dedicated to saving the natives from his countrymen's abuse. Las Casas inverted the predominant discourse of the era, which classified the Indians as associates of the devil, instead placing in this role the Spaniards, describing their treatment of the new subjects as diabolical. In his key work, the *Brief relation of the destruction of the Indies* (1539), he considered the natives as innocent "lambs" harassed and devoured by the Spanish predators.

Juan Ginés de Sepúlveda (1490–1573) was Las Casas's main adversary in the famous 1550 "Valladolid Controversy" that debated the capacity of American natives for self-government and, consequently, Spain's right to conquer them. Sepúlveda contested the spirit of reform in the Catholic Church, and was instrumental in repealing the New Laws (*Leyes Nuevas*) that curtailed Spanish abuse of the natives. His arguments were based on the notion of just warfare waged against the indigenous in order to save them from their own sins — idolatry, backwardness and tendency towards fratricidal tribal conflicts.

Two contrasting figures in the Catholic Church in Mexico illustrate a similar polarity:

Bishop Diego de Landa (1524–1579), guardian (ecclesiastical authority) of the Mexican peninsula of Yucatan during the 1550s. Landa is known to have burned thousands of sacred Maya codices, or written texts, containing information that now appears irrevocably lost. Later, he altered his opinion regarding the value of the codices and devoted his time to writing his *Relation of the things of Yucatan* (1566), a supposed reconstruction which is inevitably incomplete and Eurocentric in nature.

Fray Bernardino de Sahagún (1499–1590), in contrast, was a Franciscan monk who achieved a profound understanding of native Mexican cultures. His translation into Spanish of the Nahuatl text known as the Florentine codex, in the second half of the sixteenth century, was a rare and invaluable acknowledgment of the value of pre–Colombian cultures. He is considered by the historian Miguel León-Portilla as the father of anthropology in the New World.

This historical epoch cannot be well understood without taking into account the "Black Legend" spread by the enemies of Spain. The protestant powers of Northern Europe (England, Holland, Flanders, etc.) waged a propaganda war against what they saw as the increasing threat of an increasingly wealthy and influential Spain, whose dominion already extended across much of Europe as well as the Americas. What was the position within this debate of Cabeza de Vaca? It would be misleading to associate him too closely with the ideas of Bartolomé de las Casas, whose idealization of the natives presented them as simple innocents. Cabeza de Vaca's *Naufragios*, as Trinidad Barrera (1993, 8) suggests, combines fiction with documentary information in a "happy marriage" that neither hinders the fluidity of the narrative nor calls its credibility into doubt. As the "Black Legend" controversy reappears at the beginning of the 1990s, Álvar Núñez is variously described as pragmatist or idealist, cynic or naïve.

Álvar Núñez Cabeza de Vaca was born to an illustrious and well respected family in

Jerez de la Frontera, Andalusia, probably in 1490. The unusual surname was derived from the site of a battle against the Moors in which the family proved its loyalty to the crown. It was this ancestry, as well as the military distinction he earned in Italy and in the war of the *comuneros* in Spain, that allowed Álvar Núñez to obtain the prestigious position of treasurer of the expedition led by Pánfilo de Narváez that set out to conquer Florida in 1527. Cabeza de Vaca worked in the house of the Duke of Medina Sidonia in Seville, in an atmosphere conducive to the formation of an adventurer. The Duke was acquainted with real adventurers such as the conqueror of Mexico, Hernán Cortés. Several descriptions exist of Álvar Núñez as astute and picaresque, with an instinct for survival and social ascent. Despite this, his life ended in misfortune and poverty: after the epic experience described in *Naufragios* he was appointed governor of the River Plate region. But it seems that he was too keen, for the liking of various local authorities (*encomenderos* and *corregidores*), in his application of the Crown's relatively benign policy regarding the treatment of the natives. These authorities conspired to have him expelled from the colony and sent to Spain for trial in 1545. After a spell in prison, Cabeza de Vaca died in 1557, discredited and impoverished, without being able to clear its name of this disgrace. *Naufragios* is famous for its relatively benign, supposedly objective descriptions of the natives and their culture, religion, languages and medicine.

Interview with Director Nicolás Echeverría (January 2006)

KR: What inspired you to make this film in the first place? Was the story of Cabeza de Vaca already well known in Mexico?

NE: At a gathering of friends in 1982, I heard the story of Gonzalo Guerrero. He and other survivors of a shipwreck were the first Europeans to reach the coast of Mexico (Yucatan, in 1511). That's the source of the first images I used in the film; the drifting raft, the encounter with other-worldly lands and beings, slavery (roles in the common experience between Spaniards and indigenous are reversed, which generates another form of relationship). The knowledge and skills taught by the West become forgotten. What became of the fatherland, love, reason and morality?

In 1984 I replaced the figure of Gonzalo Guerrero with that of Cabeza de Vaca. This had certain advantages — the chronicle *Naufragios* existed, whilst almost nothing was known of Guerrero. I was given the opportunity to invent peoples, dress and customs (something that was impossible to do with the Maya): to invent America. Guerrero became one of the Maya and died fighting alongside them against the Spaniards. Álvar became a shaman, assimilating the knowledge of his captors. I would have had to dress the former (raising production costs), but the latter I needed to undress (more in keeping with the budget).

There are several elements in the chronicle that are not found in the film. To what extent would you say that you constructed the script thinking of "filling the gaps," telling parts of the story that Cabeza de Vaca omitted? In particular I'm thinking of the erotic scenes, the use of hallucinogens, things that Álvar Núñez would not have wanted to disclose to the king.

My film is more of a chronicle of the common man, however fantastic, than a letter to the king.... I was greatly inspired by Haniel Long's essay *The Marvelous Adventure of Cabeza de Vaca.*

There are numerous images and cultural references in the film that do not belong strictly to the historical era—among other elements you allude to a painting by Géricault, and a prehistoric drawing in Britain (the Cerne Abbas Giant). If this is so, with what spirit have you made these references?

Géricault's *The Raft of the Medusa* (1817) was another inspiration; the shipwrecked sailors cling to their raft as if it were the last redoubt of reason.

I understand that getting funding for the project was a painful and difficult process.

That's correct. Making the film was an odyssey in itself.

There is still controversy over the figure of Cabeza de Vaca; some consider him a cynic and an opportunist. For others he is almost a precursor of Las Casas, and this is the image that your film appears to prefer. Did you suppress any doubts in this presentation of the protagonist?

For me Cabeza de Vaca is one of the fathers of *mestizaje*. Neither Indian nor European, he is a new man who thinks in a different way. He is also a precursor of a new mentality and attitude towards the indigenous world. Guerrero, Las Casas and Quiroga are among those similar to him. Others include Antonin Artaud and Carlos Castaneda.

Could you explain something about the relationship between your other films and Cabeza de Vaca? *The link with the ethnographic films is almost self-explanatory but the connection with* Sor Juana, *for example, is less obvious. And that with* Vivir mata *is even less so.*

Vivir Mata was an experiment that blew up in my face, an obsession with making a comedy, something different. It isn't an *auteur* film like the others I have made. I didn't get on with my collaborators.

Could you tell me something about the process of "recreating" the dress, body painting and other cultural practices of pre–Columbian peoples?

The dress was largely inspired by the illustrations of Theodore de Bry (1528–98) for *Historia Americae,* as well as by the need for improvisation encountered by the wardrobe artist Tolita Figueroa (daughter of the famous cinematographer Gabriel Figueroa). Also important was our very lack of resources (hence the nudes, bodies painted with clay), and eagerness to invent another world.

Analysis: From Script to Screen

The frustrated escape is central to the trajectory of the film and its protagonist, defining a transformation in the relationship between Cabeza de Vaca and his captors and a pivot point in the Spaniard's attitude towards things indigenous in general. Where before there was hostility, antagonism and utter scorn, afterwards there is friendship and mutual understanding. The scene also echoes the director's experience in making the film.

The scene begins when Cabeza de Vaca, already a captive, must perform domestic tasks for the healers. While he prepares food, Álvar Núñez is verbally attacked by the dwarf Mala Cosa, whose disdainful shouts are unintelligible to the Spaniard and the spectator alike. Nonetheless, his tone is clearly aggressive and offensive to the European's pride — intolerably so when Mala Cosa spits half-eaten food in his face and the two shamans both explode into laughter.

The original published script by Echeverría and Sheridan has Álvar simply waiting at a distance and calculating his move: the incident with Mala Cosa is included in the film, presumably because it gives a clear sense of outrage with which the audience can identify. The final version sees a humiliated Cabeza de Vaca, both pitiful and comical, entering the water to cool his temper. The attempted escape is thus both desperate and spontaneous. A tracking shot sees him running along the banks of the lagoon (not through the forest, as was originally planned). Staccato music heightens the tension: the rest of the sequence is much as given in the written script, though the animal used (a lizard instead of a beetle) for the spell is changed.

> The witchdoctor blows on the beetle and Álvar feels a gust of wind. The witchdoctor ties a thread around the creature's body and Álvar feels suffocated by a force he does not understand, but he continues running in stretches. The witchdoctor ties one end of the thread to the stake and puts the beetle on the ground. The beetle begins to scuttle in decreasing spirals and Álvar looks for somewhere to keep running. The witchdoctor's chants increase in intensity while the beetle begins to circle the stake. The image will synchronize the creature's movements with Álvar's direction. When eventually the beetle comes close to the stake, Álvar decides upon one last change of direction and quickly executes it. The witchdoctor falls silent. Suddenly the undergrowth nearby opens and Álvar reappears, panting, in the camp. He realizes he has run in a circle and falls headlong next to his companions, gasping with fatigue and exhaustion. At this moment we see the beetle attached to the stake. Mala Cosa unties the beetle and puts it away [Echeverría and Sheridan 1994, 55–57].[1]

The film has a medium close-up of Cabeza de Vaca entering a clearing where the healers wait patiently for him; he collapses on the ground, after running in a futile circle similar to that traced by the lizard. An extreme close-up (ECU) captures the eyes of the natives watching him with a certain scorn that gradually transforms, via curiosity, into sympathy and even affection. Echeverría's introduction to Sheridan's published script (1994, 18–19) compares the protagonist's predicament to his own desperate situation as his film project, at one point fully financed and ready to go, foundered at Mexico City's Churubusco studios[2]: "Destiny tightens its circles: when we try to escape, we die little by little; what impels us to live, to persevere in our liberation, is the illusion of changing, or of resuscitating in the attempt and in that instant."

The following scene does not appear in the published script: here a delirious Cabeza de Vaca speaks as if to himself until he is reduced to a "baby," observed bemusedly by the natives.

> Transcription of ÁLVAR NÚÑEZ's speech after he comes into clearing and falls in front of the stick to which a lizard is tied. A medium-long shot (MLS) of ÁLVAR NÚÑEZ from a slightly raised angle emphasizes his abjection and solitude.
> ÁLVAR NÚÑEZ: "God! What am I doing in this land? In this world, God!"
> (Cut to subjective POV shot of ÁLVAR NÚÑEZ from behind with MALA COSA and HECHICERO in view.)
> "As the slave of a son-of-a-bitch Indian, a witchdoctor besides."
> (Return to original shot Álvar Núñez). "I curse the day I met you, Mala Cosa. Laugh, go on, laugh! Endriago, in my country they'd have impaled you!"[3] Cut to Álvar Núñez who also laughs, hysterically.

We must understand the Spaniard's injured pride, even if we do not sympathize: he is a high-ranking official in a royal expedition, humiliated by people who, according to contemporary belief, do not even have intelligible language. Of course, they have no Spanish and effectively, he is talking to himself. If the futility of this monologue is not lost on him, it nonetheless allows him to believe in his own innate "superiority." He is reduced to invoking the Almighty, his only possible hearer, then launching into a useless and impotent tirade against the dwarf.

The futility of this talk becomes apparent to him, but language is nonetheless his emblem of superiority: "and I talk and talk and talk ... because I am more human than you ... because I have a world, although I am lost, although I'm a castaway. [...] My name is Álvar Núñez Cabeza de Vaca, I am treasurer ... of Carlos V of Spain ... I am from Seville...." These grandiose references, absurdly irrelevant here, give way to far more elementary vocabulary: "This is the ground ... the sky ... the Indians ... a plant ... sand. And what else? What else?"[4]

Language is the conquistador's only badge of identity in such a distant and hostile world. At the end of his rambling he mentions the sea (evoking its maternal connotations of a return to the mother country) and begins to sing what appears to be a lullaby.

This is the *Romance de Abenámar* (a fifteenth-century anonymous poem with several references to Andalusia).[5]

ECU of Hechicero looking now at Álvar Núñez with more sympathy.

Clearly the song (mentioned neither in the chronicle nor the script) serves various purposes within the scene. What allusions and references does it contain that enhance the film at this juncture?

Linguistic Features

The song harks back to sixteenth-century Castilian and beyond. It is the form of Spanish that would have been used by the conquistadores, but the film's spoken dialogue has been modernized somewhat to aid comprehension. The formation of the future ("dárete" instead of "te daré") is a grammatical example of its archaism, and the general construction is rhetorical in nature. As we watch the "performance" of this song we can understand the words (perhaps with the help of the subtitles) but within the scene they have no receiver or interlocutor. Nevertheless expression occurs through body language and gestures, and the healers are not unmoved. In the following scene we see Cabeza de Vaca transformed into a healer, dressed and painted in native style and following indigenous cultural practices.

For Discussion

1. The critic Jean Franco has spoken of a widespread recent change in the representation of indigenous peoples which transforms them "from being 'others' and converts them into multicolored strands in a pluralistic weave." Is this a valid perception, and does it apply equally to *Naufragios* and *Cabeza de Vaca*?

2. In what ways do the book *Naufragios* and the film *Cabeza de Vaca* reflect changing ideas of the origins and the historical formation of Latin America?

3. Do you agree that the increasing interest in Cabeza de Vaca since the 1990s is due "more to 5th-centenary opportunism than to a serious attempt at historical and philological research"?[6] Discuss with reference to the film *Cabeza de Vaca* and/or the chronicle *Naufragios*. (The quote comes from a review by Ángel Delgado-Gómez of *Shipwrecked*; the translation of *Naufragios* by Enrique Pupo-Walker (*Colonial Latin American Review* 3, nos.1–2, 1994, 275–280.)

4. Cabeza de Vaca wrote in *Naufragios*: "I refrain from telling this story in greater length,

because everyone may think [imagine] what might happen in such a strange and bad land...."[7] How does Echeverría's film respond to this invitation to the reader?

5. Cabeza de Vaca says of his chronicle that "though many new things are to be read in it, and things difficult for some to believe, they may believe them without any doubt."[8] Does Echeverría's film also display this quality of restraint?

6. Would you agree with Echeverría's assertion that Cabeza de Vaca was "the first Latin American man and ethnographer"? To what extent do *Naufragios* and *Cabeza de Vaca* present their protagonist as a mediator between two worlds?

7. Compare treatment of the themes of individual history and destiny, and the significance of differing notions of authorship and audience in *Cabeza de Vaca* and *Naufragios*.

8. In what aspects do the chronicle and film reflect the discursive climates of the fifteenth and late twentieth centuries concerning the fate of indigenous American peoples?

9. Are there any parallels to be drawn between the representation of indigenous peoples in Mexican and U.S. cinema?

10. The great Mexican poet Sor Juana Inés de la Cruz suggested: "What remains unsaid explains — tags — what is supposedly silenced."[9] Why do no subtitles appear when the indigenous characters speak?

11. Margo Glantz argues that Cabeza de Vaca "integrates nakedness into brevity": conciseness constitutes a way of "structuring his experience" in an environment deprived of writing and hence (at least according to a European/Western frame of reference) devoid of history. There are various instances in *Naufragios* of Cabeza de Vaca withholding information; he refrains from telling, as the narrator of a fairy tale might do.

12. Cabeza de Vaca's family was well known from battle: the strange name, it's generally thought, comes from a track marked by cow's skull, by ancestor, before battle with the Moors. How does Echeverría represent the Spanish fifteenth-century preoccupation with heritage (*abolengo*) in this film?

13. Margo Glantz associates Cabeza de Vaca's insistence upon his nakedness with his attempt to portray himself as a Christ figure. Is this also true of the film? What other Biblical allusions does Echeverría make?

14. The film employs a degree of cultural eclecticism in its use of recognizable visual elements as well as the obvious Amerindian and Spanish cultural references. What does this set out to communicate to the viewer? Some examples are:

The raft: carrying shipwrecked men in the opening scene; as Echeverría has acknowledged, this is inspired by Géricault's *Raft of the Medusa*.

Mala Cosa: There are several references in *Naufragios* to a being that is feared by the natives as a destructive force and alluded to by the author as "Mala Cosa." How do the book and film differ in their depiction of this being?

Dress and body decoration: In the absence of reliable, detailed documentary information, the makers of this film have had to resort to their own imagination in order to "reconstruct" the look of pre–Columbian cultures.

The drawing in the sand: The scene following the "conversion" of Álvar Núñez shows the three men on a riverbank. The shaman traces a figure in the sand that is reminiscent of a famous prehistoric figure in Britain. Why does it appear in this context?

4. Sexuality and Its Social Dimensions

Carol Donelan defines gender (itself a term recently challenged in Latin America) as "a representation, a sociocultural construct which assigns a position to each individual, both within material society and in relation to the symbolic contract, and therefore in relation to power" (Donelan 1993, 1) but this is to deny the agency of the individual, the possibility of defining gender roles anew.

In Latin America, recent years have seen a relaxation and flexibility in attitudes towards sexual conduct or tendencies previously seen as deviant, such as homosexuality, transsexuality, interracial sex, or promiscuity. This affirmation, of course, is a generalization that depends on several factors: whether the setting is urban or rural, what religious norms and particular national realities are in effect. What is acceptable in the city may well not be tolerated in a remote village. Brazilian mores are generally considered far more permissive than elsewhere in the region. A lingering machismo has nevertheless not precluded an increasing tolerance of difference, and irreverence, which may be expressed in film. For example once-sacrosanct symbols of masculine authority such as the Obelisk in Buenos Aires, is satirized in Argentine films such as Subiela's *El lado oscuro del corazón* (see chapter) and Eduardo Mignogna's *La Fuga* (*The Escape*, Argentina, 2002). *Pizza, birra, faso* (*Pizza Beer Smokes*, Adrián Caetano and Bruno Stagnaro, 2000) has another sarcastic reference to this rather obvious phallic icon, when a youth idly chats about his girlfriend's arousal by the libidinous energies supposedly emanated by the monument.

Films such as *Dependencia Sexual* can be seen as opening up and redefining the normative framework in a debate no longer dominated by a binary concept of gender.[1] Whilst "deviant" sexuality is not yet fully accepted as a cultural issue, and is still largely viewed as a transgression to be "cured" or "treated," self-definition in this area is increasingly inscribed in national constitutions as a basic human right.

Concepts of nationhood predicated on male authority are often mocked: in the Chilean comedy *Lokas*, for example, the camp co-owner of a continent-wide chain of gay nightclubs talks of achieving what one of Latin America's greatest heroes could not: "We'll make Bolívar's dream come true. The unification of America."[2] Javier Fuentes-León's innovative *Contracorriente* (*Undertow*, Peru, 2009) sets a gay love story in the more conservative site of a Peruvian fishing village, where a couple is "outed" through tragedy and set apart via the supernatural.

Queer theory holds that sexuality is not essential to personal identity, that the latter is formed through interaction with existing social norms (themselves imposed). If so, then sexuality is inevitably a social and political element, particularly in environments where rigid gender norms are rigorously maintained.

Sergio de la Mora (2006) has researched the contribution of Mexican national cinema to the edification of a macho norm as part of an unwritten state ideology: film plays an "indispensable role ... in reshaping social identities and modern definitions of the nation"

(2006, 3). What he terms *"cinemachismo"* is defined as "the particular self-conscious form of national masculinity and patriarchal ideology articulated via the cinema and also vigorously promoted by the post-revolutionary state as official ideology" (2006, 2). De la Mora (2006, 3) talks of the post-revolutionary project of imposing a virile nationalism to counter the perceived evils of effeminacy and homosexuality in civil service or artistic circles. He looks at the codification of gender and cultural identities at regional and national level through genres such as the Revolutionary melodrama, the prostitution melodrama, the buddy movie and the *fichera* picaresque comedy subgenre (2006, 3).

The most problematic issue is, perhaps inevitably, homosexuality: this is still a matter of contrasting attitudes, but there is now room for the expression of difference. Two elegant gay love stories by Julián Hernández, *Mil nubes de paz* (*A Thousand Clouds of Peace*, 2003) and *Cielo dividido* (*Divided Sky*, 2006), at times contrast idyllic affection with brutal and hypocritical rejection. *Quemar las naves* (*Burn the Bridges:* Francisco Franco, Mexico, 2008) focuses on the routes taken by a brother and sister left with a large house after their mother's death, the former discovering his true sexual inclinations and having to deal with homophobia.

Alejandra Islas's fascinating documentary *Muxes: Auténticas, intrépidas buscadoras del peligro* (*Muxes: Authentic, Intrepid Seekers of Danger*, Mexico, 2005) introduces the remarkably large and tolerated gay population of Juchitán, in Mexico's Oaxaca state, and the Zapotec indigenous heritage that contributes to it. The word "muxes" is derived from the archaic Spanish variation of *mujeres* (women), and the individuals featured in this film are flamboyantly transvestite in a way that is a declaration of not only sexual preference but also cultural belonging. They proudly wear indigenous women's dress (Indian women in Latin America are much more likely than men to use traditional clothing). Besides this, as the title indicates, these are people who defy gay stereotypes, showing no fear in their activism in issues such as AIDS awareness. Another documentary dealing with gender issues in the surprisingly liberal state of Oaxaca is Maureen Gosling and Ellen Osborne's *Ramos de fuego* (*Blossoms of Fire*, Mexico, 2000) which investigates Juchitán's reputation as a matriarchy (albeit open to various interpretations) and its lesbian population.

Doña Herlinda y su hijo (*Doña Herlinda and Her Son*, Mexico, 1985) is one of several enterprising comedies by Jaime Humberto Hermosillo which look at the theme of sexuality in an oblique and provocative way. Doña Herlinda is a well-to-do lady whose son is about to get married when his true (gay) sexual orientation becomes apparent. She pragmatically reaches an accommodation that keeps everyone happy, including the gay partner, whilst preserving the secret. Hermosillo's musical comedy *De noche vienes, Esmeralda* (*Esmeralda Comes by Night*, 1997) is based on an Eva Poniatowska story about a wife who has five husbands. When denounced to the police, she smilingly insists that she loves them all. The exasperated inspector gradually comes to accept her vision: love, and its sexual expression, is not necessarily finite or exclusive.

Wilhelm Reich linked mental well-being with sexual health, but did not accept the validity of non-heterosexual behavior. Homosexuality is often seen as a provocation even if not presented in any intentionally challenging way: gays are a marginalized group, almost everywhere forced into an antagonistic position vis-à-vis the prevailing power structure. In Cuba, controversy over the alleged repression of gays is seen as paradoxical given the island's social progress in other areas. Néstor Almendros and Orlando Jiménez Leal's *Mauvaise conduite* (*Improper Conduct*, France, 1984), a film denouncing the ill treatment of gays through alleged state homophobia, met with the approval of gay activist Paul Julian Smith and the dismissal of Michael Chanan, a long-time supporter of revolutionary Cuba, in a revelatory polemic (Smith 1996, 64). Conversely, Smith rejected *Fresa y chocolate* (*Strawberry and Chocolate*) Tomás Gutiérrez Alea's famous 1992 exposition of gay rights on the island, (1996, 91) as "persistently and willfully sexless" signaling a refusal by gays to be inaccurately or inadequately represented in what was seen elsewhere as a belated and conservative response to *Mauvaise conduite*.

Homosexuality is compared, in social terms, to poverty by the gay dressmaker in Juan Carlos Desanzo's *Eva Perón* (Argentina, 1996) as he reminds Eva that "the poor and the faggots are always in agreement."[3] Both groups are condemned to oppression from the oligarchy's machos. The equation includes Eva herself, stigmatized as a whore by her implacable enemies on the right, as the dressmaker concludes: "To be gay, to be poor, to be Eva Perón, it's all the same thing in this pitiless country." Significantly, Eva's perceived political crimes are viewed in terms of sex, one of few means of social ascendance for a working-class woman and simultaneously a stigma seized upon by her enemies.

Perceived sexual deviance contributes to a broader picture of criminality and rebellion in Karim Aïnouz's *Madame Satã* (*Madam Satan*, Brazil, 2002). Barbet Schroeder's adaptation of Fernando Vallejo's partly autobiographical novel *La virgen de los sicarios* (*Our Lady of the Assassins*, Colombia, 2000) narrates a gay, middle-aged intellectual's return to his native Medellín, and his affairs there with two young men involved in gang-related violence. The bizarre succession of love and death is endemic in an environment where "enamorarse" (to fall in love with someone) is also a slang term for the desire to kill.

The link between criminality and homosexuality is seen in a different light in Marcelo Piñeyro's *Plata quemada* (*Burnt Money*, Argentina, 2000), based on the true story of a robbery in Buenos Aires in 1965 by a gang that included an inseparable gay couple, Nene and Ángel, known as the twins (*los mellizos*) and tolerated within the group for their efficacy as thieves, though also subjected to some mockery. David William Foster has criticized the film for its prudish representation of gay eroticism: a straight sex scene is filmed with full nudity, but participants in a comparable gay encounter keep their underwear. Nonetheless, credit might be given to Piñeyro's film for its depiction of gay protagonists within a brutal environment which is far from the effete stereotype. Nene and Ángel may not be examples of orthodox machos but are nevertheless convincing and complex characters, both individually and in tandem.

An effeminate gay figure appears in Héctor Babenco's English-language *Kiss of the Spider Woman* (Brazil/USA, 1985), an adaptation of the famous novel by the Argentine Manuel Puig (1932–1990), who explored his own sexuality in his writing through his fascination with the romantic and fantastic capacities of cinema. In this novel the gay prisoner Molina is used by the authorities to spy upon his cellmate Valentín, a political prisoner whose ideological rigidity is matched, at least at first, by his unwavering heterosexuality. As Molina wins his cellmate's confidence, a revealing dialectic develops, the two interchanging ideas on politics, sexual tendencies, and visions of reality nurtured by art and fantasy. William Rowe and Vivian Schelling, in examining the gender implications of viewing and reading in Puig's work, point out (1991, 217) that this novel, unlike Puig's earlier *The Buenos Aires Affair* (1973),

> explores a different use of popular media, as a counter-manipulation to dominant machista values. These are the terms of discussion Puig's work suggests, a good deal more useful than the notion of audience passivity or than what the autobiographical protagonist of Puig's first novel was able to learn: that treachery is a characteristic of female attraction and, by implication of films.

Puig's novels are known for their incorporation of cinema narrative: Molina "tells films" to pass the time, at least symbolically escaping from his confinement. Valentín objects to Molina's passive and non-analytic film narrations, romanticizing Nazi propaganda and identifying with the leading lady's infatuation with some Aryan beau. More complex are the real films that Molina narrates — low-budget but intense and ingenious "B" movies by Jacques Tourneur (*Cat People*, 1942, and *I Walked with a Zombie*, 1943) that probe Freudian themes of repressed and sublimated sexuality not incorporated into the film. Neither, unsurprisingly, is there a space in the film for Puig's mixture of true and invented theories about homosexuality. William Hurt's controversially camp portrayal of Molina is central to the story's development, as his tellings of films help spin a "web" around Raúl Julia's macho revolutionary. Puig, himself a homosexual, was not presenting frivolity as inherent to gays; rather he suggests that the uncompromising ideologue Valentín and the non-politicized Molina have much to learn from one another. Babenco, in a television interview,[4] talked about the duality with which gender is traditionally portrayed: the male character, not associated with compassion, is contrasted with the tenderness seen as a female preserve. Babenco tells of getting ideas for the character of Molina from witnessing his daughter listening to her girlfriend: a spectacle akin to Puig's teller/listener.

Female homosexuality is less inevitably bound up with crime or rebellion: the feature-length documentary *Lesbianas de Buenos Aires* (Santiago García, Argentina, 2004) offers a serious and sympathetic examination of lesbian life in the Argentine capital without objectifying its three main subjects, nor belittling them with any pity.

Géminis (Albertina Carri, Argentina, 2005) is a disturbing look at the effect of brother-sister incest upon a high-class Argentine family whose treasured self-image of openness and integrity is shattered. Discoveries of secrecy, suspicion and malicious gossip exacerbate the transgression itself. Similarly, grim repercussions of incest appear in one of the three stories that form Cristián Galaz's otherwise comic *El chacotero sentimental* (*The Sentimental Teaser*, Chile, 1999).

Hermaphroditic representation is less common in film. Sally Potter's 1992 adaptation of the Virginia Woolf novel *Orlando* expounds a diachronic and transgender thesis rather than a biological one. But *XXY* (Lucía Puenzo, Argentina, 2007) is a tale not only of sexual awakening but of nascent self-awareness. The title refers to the chromosome composition necessary for hermaphroditism: the film shows a relationship between two adolescents leading to self-discovery on both sides. The "girl" Alex (an aptly chosen androgynous name) has her first sexual encounter with Álvaro, who in the process becomes aware of his own true sexual inclination. As the parents face peer pressure to subject their daughter to an operation to ensure her womanhood, young Alex defines her/his own position, eventually insisting that the choice need not even be made. The film defends the right to self-definition beyond binaries, stating the validity of hermaphrodite sexual identity. Asked why she made the film, Puenzo replied: "Because sexual awakening, and the mark of identity that comes with it, it the most universal theme in the world. It's the stamp of sexuality upon identity, beyond homosexuality or heterosexuality.... The film chooses to speak about an intersexual, but it also deals with the moment when we cease to be children and choose our identity"[5] (García 2007, 34).

Sergio Toledo's *Vera* (Brazil, 1987) is an absorbing study of transsexuality, psychological rather than physiological, focusing upon a young woman's yearning to be a man. Her cross-dressing leads her into some awkward situations that nonetheless reveal the inherent absurdities in stereotypes. Toledo's subdued but never scientifically detached direction commendably maintains a compassionate but never maudlin eye upon Vera's subjectivity.

Arturo Ripstein's *El lugar sin límites* (*Hell without Limits*, Mexico, 1978) adapts the novel by Chilean José Donoso, with the result described by María Lourdes Cortés (1999, 144) as "the metaphor of Manuela, of whom [Donoso] wants to erase the limits of a body-space of transgressions."[6] Ripstein "invites [us] to read this 'place without limits' as an everyday inferno, placing Manuela's body-hell as the axis of the filmic text."

Sexuality and Nationhood

Heterosexual identities are also defined, albeit in a chaotic manner, in Gerardo Chijona's *Un paraíso bajo las estrellas*. Here, it is ethnicity that is ultimately of interest, however problematized due to the story's riotous and unrestrained sexuality. But although there are factors that can be attributed to Latin America as a whole, this film is specific to Cuba, both in terms of sexual mores and national makeup.

Tropical eastern Bolivia, far more sexually open than the country's Andean west, is the setting for one half of Rodrigo Bellott's *Dependencia sexual* (*Sexual Dependency*, 2003). The rest of the film was made in the USA, a fact due partly to circumstance, but one used by Bellott to draw an analogy between national, political relationships and their individual, sexual counterparts.

"Straight" sexuality in an offbeat context is a feature of the work of maverick Mexican director Carlos Reygadas, who specializes in films that challenge audience expectations, not only in cinematic form and aesthetics, but also content. Perceptions of what is valid material to be shown on the screen, to a non-porn public, is stretched by films like *Japón* (Japan, 2002) in which the protagonist has consensual but oddly dispassionate sex with an old lady, or *Batalla en el cielo* (*Battle in Heaven*, Mexico, 2005), which features graphic intercourse between the unlikeliest partners. Reygadas's third film, *Luz silenciosa* (*Silent Light*, 2007), is set in Mexico's Mennonite community. The illicit affair depicted among this puritanical group is filmed, if not as explicitly as in his previous films, with an intensity and obtrusiveness that makes the viewer an unwilling voyeur, participating in the main character's anguished self-confrontation as he grapples with his faith and conscience.

Sexual Mores and Commodification

Alejandro Agresti's *Una noche con Sabrina Love* (*A Night with Sabrina Love*, Spain/Italy/France/Argentina/Netherlands, 2000) is a critical but not condemnatory look at the commercialization of sex. It follows a provincial youth, Daniel, who wins a contest and journeys to Buenos Aires to claim the eponymous prize. Sabrina turns out to be far more than a commodity, and the encounter leads to revelation that typifies director Agresti's interest in observing human values the preserved in bleak and incongruous situations.

Crime delicado (*Delicate Crime*, Beto Brant, Brazil, 2005) is an experimental feature film that explores relationships between power, sex and art through its story of the relationship between a theatre critic and a young woman amputee who models for a painter's erotic visions (those of the real painter Felipe Ehrenberg who acts, paints and explains his own work). The plays upon which the critic comments are also investigations of sexuality, yet another facet of what is a fascinating and multilayered exposition of sexual norms and modes of representation.

Chile is ostensibly one of the most modernized Latin American countries in terms of infrastructure and economic advancement, yet its official attitudes towards sexuality reflect a deep, underlying conservatism. Since the turn of the century several Chilean films have emerged to challenge received ideas about connections between sex, morality and the church. The comedy *Sexo con amor* (*Sex with Love*, Boris Quercia, 2003) sees the libidinal urge as a healthy manifestation frustrated by spurious pseudo-moral postures. Similarly, *Mujeres infieles* (*Unfaithful Women*, Rodrigo Ortúzar Lynch, 2004) uses humor to raise the question of women's sexual needs and machismo's failure even to acknowledge them. Refusing easy interpretations, it is a sex comedy with social content, avoiding sensationalism largely through its very setting in the superficial media world of Santiago. The main catalyst for self-examination is the arrival of a Spanish actress, far less repressed than the Chilean women who show her around town. The dichotomy of Chile emerges through the story of a TV station investigating infidelity, supposedly through social interests but clearly for less noble reasons, opening a debate with surprising conclusions. *La Sagrada Familia* (*The Sacred Family*, Sebastián Campos, Chile, 2007) and *Gente decente* (*Decent People*, Edgardo Viereck, Chile, 2004) both explore the hypocrisy that still reigns in sexual matters, examining connections between the power resulting from wealth and what might be seen either as sexual freedom or libertinism. Gonzalo Justiniano's comedy *Lokas* (*Krazies*, Chile, 2008) is a satirical look at macho attitudes towards the perceived threat of homosexuality, following its Chilean protagonist through a Mexican jail term and seeing him take his son back to Chile to live in an irregular family and work situation that forces the heterosexual father into a more tolerant outlook. The ingenious *Muñeca* (*Doll*, Sebastián Arrau, Chile, 2008) has a homosexual protagonist whose self-image is inexorably redefined as his erstwhile lover's prank lands him in a bizarre situation.

In Peru, sexuality has been aired cinematically in comedies like *Un día sin sexo* (*A Day without Sex*, Frank Pérez Garland, 2005) and *Mañana te cuento* (*I'll Tell You Tomorrow*, Eduardo Mendoza de Echave, 2005). Armando Robles Godoy's *Imposible amor* (*Impossible Love*, 2000) treats the subject in a more philosophical, even mystical light. Francisco Lombardi's *No se lo digas a nadie* (*Don't Tell Anyone*, 1998) adapts a novel by gay writer and TV presenter Jaime Bayly on the pressures to conceal homosexuality at all costs within upper-class Lima society.

Another Gonzalo Justiniano comedy that tackles sexual politics is *El Leyton* (Chile, 2002), in which the eternal confrontation between fidelity and promiscuity is played out in a Chilean fishing village. This adaptation of the story *La red* (*The Net*) by Luis Alberto Acuña, uses the fishing metaphor of entrapment to show hypocrisy as a dilemma that applies to both sexes.

Eliseo Subiela's *No mires para abajo* (*Don't Look Down*, Argentina, 2008) is a tale not of sexual awakening in the normal sense, but of initiation into erotic sensibilities. The departure from the norm here is that the "educator" is a young woman, Elvira, who has in turn been prepared by her learned therapist grandmother. Eloy, the young man she initiates and prepares sexually for the rest of his life, is thus brought out of depression following his father's death. The title refers both to the above and to his reciprocal teaching her to walk on stilts: fear hampers fulfillment in both activities and looking down, metaphorically or literally, can result in a disastrous fall.

Whether explored in the light of gender, social change, or cultural or mystical issues, sexuality is becoming an increasingly important subject in Latin American cinema and treated with ever greater maturity, responsibility and respect for difference.

5. *Un paraíso bajo las estrellas* (Paradise beneath the Stars)

CREDITS: Cuba/Spain, 2000; *Produced by:* Wanda Visión (Madrid), ICAIC (Cuba); *Director:* Gerardo Chijona; *Script:* Gerardo Chijona, Luis Agüero and Senel Paz; *Music:* José María Vitier, Carlos Faruelo, Carlos Fernández; *Cinematography:* Rafael de la Uz, Adriano Moreno, Raúl Pérez Ureta

CAST: Sissy (Thaïs Valdés), Sergio (Vladimir Cruz), Mabel (Daisy Granados), Cándido (Enrique Molina), Promedio (Litico Rodríguez), Armando (Santiago Alfonso), Olivia (Amparo Muñoz), Sonia (Jacqueline Arenal), Josefa (Alicia Bustamante), Master of Ceremonies and several other cameo roles (Luis Alberto García)

"Un paraíso bajo las estrellas" is the slogan used by the Tropicana, one of the longest established and most famous cabarets in Cuba, near central Havana.

Synopsis

Sissy comes from a solid and respectable (White) family background in Havana. She yearns to follow in her mother's footsteps and become a singer and dancer in the Tropicana. But her truck driver father Cándido, himself once a nightclub singer, opposes this ambition. This is partly due to his rivalry and hatred for the club's (Black) choreographer, Armando, who has libidinous designs on Sissy and so is keen to recruit her to the fold. Sissy defies both men, staying at the club but resisting Armando's overtures, which means she is relegated to the troupe rather than being the main dancer.

Sissy meets the handsome Sergio through an accident which results in Sissy's parents suspecting the two may be brother and sister. Sissy and Sergio fall in love, blissfully unaware of the suspicion. Cándido, horrified at the possibility of incest (and the consequent revelation of his own infidelity), makes Sissy suspect that Sergio is unfaithful. In revenge, she flirts with Armando who, in return, allows her to fulfill her dream of singing at the Tropicana. However, he is keen to exact his "price."

After Cándido also suffers an accident, and Sissy falls pregnant, the family reunites and numerous secrets are divulged when Olivia returns from Spain. All of this makes for an unlikely and amusing dénouement.

About the Film

The theme of unwitting incest is common in Greek and Nordic myth and not, as Roberto Fandiño (2002, 209) suggests, simply the territory of soap operas. Of course, *Un paraíso bajo las estrellas* (Henceforth *Paraíso*) is by no means a tragedy and the incest is never consummated. But the possibility of it is suggested, and with an added interracial element.

About the Film's Creators

Gerardo Chijona, who was born in Havana in 1949, studied English literature at university before entering the film world as a critic. He began working in the archive at ICAIC (Cuba's film institute, Instituto Cubano de Artes e Industrias Cinematográficas), working his way up as assistant director and documentarist before making his first feature film, *Adorables mentiras* (*Adorable Lies*) in 1992. This film was controversial, not because of any ideological opposition to, or divergence from, Cuban communism, but because of its depiction of a society that had drifted away from revolutionary ideals. On the other hand, *Paraíso* won immediate popularity with Cuban audiences, if not entirely with national critics. Chijona sees his main preoccupation as portraying the changes in Cuban society, which he describes as follows:

> Cuban society, as is well known, underwent a number of changes and transformations during the 1990s which nobody has been able to escape. The economic crisis from which the country still suffers has been reflected in spiritual life, in human behavior, in relationships between people. *Adorables Mentiras*, my first full-length fiction, which still provokes considerable controversy in Cuba, was written and filmed when the crisis was just beginning. Despite this being a comedy, acerbic and with occasional touches of black humor, it was described by some as "painfully prophetic," since it reflected in a quite flagrant manner the double standards, hypocrisy and falsehood of the world in which the characters were living, characters which at the time seemed exceptional.[1]

Chijona views his third feature, *Perfecto amor equivocado* (*Love by Mistake*, 2004), as a continuation of *Adorables Mentiras* in both theme and tone. *Paraíso* maintains the critical stance towards society, but does so with a humor that is far more anarchic, absurd and, at times, slapstick.

Luis Agüero was part of the group that founded *Lunes de Revolución*, an influential cultural supplement in the newspaper *Revolución* after 1959. For several years, before and after the revolution, he was a chronicler of cabarets and other shows found in Havana nightlife at the time. He was a great friend of the prominent dissident writer Guillermo Cabrera Infante (1929–2005) who lived outside Cuba for 40 years. Like Cabrera Infante, Agüero became disaffected with life in Cuba and now lives in the USA.

Senel Paz, who collaborated with the script, is a well-known writer who also worked on Gutiérrez Alez and Tabío's acclaimed 1992 film, *Fresa y chocolate*, which was based on his short story *El lobo, el bosque y el hombre nuevo*. He also co-scripted Gerardo Chijona's *Adorables mentiras*.

José María Vitier, the composer whose work on *Paraíso* won the 2000 prize for best film score from the Asociación Cubana de Autores Musicales, is one of the most renowned of Cuba's living composers. He also provided the score for *Fresa y chocolate* in 1992.

For Cultural Understanding

Several cultural strands intertwine in Chijona's film. Perhaps the most important is Cirilo Villaverde's nineteenth-century novel *Cecilia Valdés*, crucial in the definition of a

Cuban national identity. Its tale of love between a stunning mulatto woman and a respectable white man was revolutionary at a time when issues of ethnicity and interracial sexual attraction were taboo. *Paraíso*'s reference to unwitting incest clearly alludes to this novel, in which Cecilia and her lover are also suspected of having a common father.

This process of ethnic and cultural convergence, set in motion by colonization and slavery, finds theoretical expression in the 1940s in the term "transculturation," coined by the Cuban sociologist Fernando Ortiz (1881–1969). Ortiz viewed this phenomenon as not only positive but inevitable, a question not of superiority of one culture over another but of a gradual and progressive interaction resulting in a culture recognizable as intrinsically Cuban. This was already visible in the early twentieth century, particularly in music: Ortiz identified the song form known as *son* as a blend of African and European elements.

Afro-Cuban Santería is now a well-established and widely practiced religion, but was once repressed and clandestine. Other versions of this faith can be found in Brazil, Uruguay, Colombia, Mexico and several other Latin American states.

The Spanish influence on Cuba can be seen as not just a historical and cultural process that ended with the island's independence in 1898. It is also economic; Spain has had an important role in trade with Cuba during the "Special Period." The same period has paradoxically seen the introduction of "dollarization," the use of U.S. currency in Cuba, which is commented upon in Chijona's film.

Popular culture has a considerable input, through the incorporation of soaps (*telenovelas*) the television genre derived from the *radionovela*, which largely developed in Cuba (see interview with Chijona).

From Imperfect to Adult Cinema — Cuba and the Special Period

Cuban cinema before the 1959 revolution was characterized by the earnest endeavor of a handful of enthusiasts, rather than any coherent collective effort classifiable as a movement or industry. The renowned cinematographer Néstor Almendros (1930–1992) has pointed out that Cuban film, despite its auspicious beginnings, failed to grow because of an inadequate local market and competition from Argentine, Mexican and Spanish productions (Almendros 1992, 57).

The three decades of film before the revolution reflected the extent of foreign interest in the island. Apart from sporadic co-production with Mexico, the early 1950s was mainly a period in which Hollywood used Cuba as a handy exotic or Hispanic location. This was the era of U.S. economic penetration, when Cuba was a holiday destination for visitors from the north. Casinos, nightclubs and brothels proliferated as unscrupulous local politicians collaborated with some of the least desirable elements from the U.S.

Film and Cabaret

A large proportion of the films made during this era were set in the nightclub ambience, making use of the island's status as the cradle of musical developments in the Caribbean, an image used by these films to heighten the escapist sensuality and hedonism of films like *Week-End in Havana* (Walter Lang, 1941) and *The Big Boodle* (Richard Wilson, 1957).

Almendros sums up the usual locally produced fare as "Cuban folklore musicals made with scarce resources, based on mambos, congas, cha-cha-chas, etc., guaranteed commercial success due to proven formulae" (ibid).[2]

Cabaret themes and settings largely waned after the revolution; as Chijona points out, cabaret culture is now kept alive mostly for the European tourist market, and has lost its intensity and contemporary relevance. The theme reappeared only in satirical or allegorical mode, such as in *La bella del Alhambra* (*The Beauty of the Alhambra*, Enrique Pineda Barnet, 1990).

The Impact of the Revolution

Most critics agree that Cuban cinema began as a recognizable entity with the Revolution, whose first cultural measure was the creation of the Cuban Film Institute ICAIC. This state organization used many creative and technical personnel who had worked in the hitherto fragmented film activity, some with revolutionary sympathies such as ICAIC cofounders Tomás Gutiérrez Alea and Julio García Espinosa.

Most agree that the outstanding Cuban film since the revolution is Gutiérrez Alea's *Memorias del subdesarrollo* (*Memories of Underdevelopment*, 1968) whose protagonist, Sergio, is a middle-class malcontent unable either to commit to the Revolution or to leave the island. This is complicated further when his becomes embroiled in a troublesome affair with a working-class girl. Sergio is no revolutionary hero, but his skeptical nature lends the film a perspective from which to examine the changes in Cuban society and his place within it, looking back at the Bay of Pigs invasion and contemplating the crucial moment of the 1962 Missile Crisis.

Film as Reflection and Self-Examination

Since ICAIC's inception Cuban film has had a unique relationship with popular consciousness, encouraging spectator evaluation rather than offering facile views or vapid "happy endings." Cuban cinema becomes self-referential and intertextual, films entering into dialogue with one another. The audience is protagonist in Octavio Cortázar's *Por primera vez* (*For the First Time*, 1961), which simply filmed people in a remote village seeing a film for the first time. A reference to this film in turn by the itinerant film projectionist in *El elefante y la bicicleta* (*The Elephant and the Bicycle*, Juan Carlos Tabío, 1993) reinforces its foundational status. There are also hints of this in *Alicia en el pueblo de Maravillas*, where the social merits of a cartoon is discussed by "committee," as well as in films dealing with the role of art and modes of representation. Even in *Amor vertical* (*Vertical Love*, Arturo Sotto Díaz, 1998) makes an oblique reference to Gutiérrez Alea's 1962 *La muerte de un burócrata* (*The Death of a Bureaucrat*) in the use of a cavernous hall crammed with pettifogging officialdom — now openly hostile, even Mafia-like, rather than merely smug or inefficient as in the original. Tabío's *Plaff* (*Too Afraid of Life*, 1988) repeatedly reminds the viewer that it is a film, albeit one that shares its characters' everyday Cuban logistical problems. Finally, Gutiérrez Alea's valedictory *Guantanamera* (1995) alludes to his previous filmic comments on Cuban reality.

Theorizing the Changes

Cinema in 1990s Cuba, faced with the body blow of political isolation and economic hardship dating from the period of Perestroika in the URSS and the fall of European communism, inevitably involved a degree of self-examination. However, such a process was already in evidence in the mid- to late 1980s, and indeed has been an essential element in Cuban films ever since the creation of ICAIC.

Tomás Gutiérrez Alea's notion of *dialéctica del espectador* (spectator's dialectic) advocated a cinema where the filmmaker entered into a conscious dialogue with the public.

Julio García Espinosa's theory of imperfect cinema lamented the simulation of a seamless alternative reality in classic cinema, arguing that film should display and even celebrate its artificiality as a means of stimulating the viewer to question reality rather than become lost in the kind of fantasy realm promoted by Hollywood.

The concept of third cinema envisioned a new cinematic language replacing the "first" or classic mode and the "second" or European-style individualist "auteur" cinema. This was a cinema created for, and in close collaboration with, the people.

Rectificación de errors: In the mid–1980s Cuban officialdom called for a program of recognition of errors and "negative tendencies" and their "rectification." New concepts emerged in Cuba, as well as a return to some others formerly discarded, in response to the crisis of socialism in Eastern Europe.

Cine pobre: Humberto Solás, one of Cuba's most celebrated filmmakers, became the figurehead of this movement. More than an aesthetic, it is aimed at using the new digital media to make filmmaking a possibility for those who would not normally get the chance.

Cine perfecto: This was, of course, a response to García Espinosa's idea of imperfect cinema, arguing that its opposite might ultimately prove more revolutionary.[3]

Cine incómodo: Orlando Rojas spoke in an interview (*Cine Cubano*, 130) of the need for an "uncomfortable cinema" aimed at provoking audiences into questioning their reality.

Herejía sistemática: a phrase coined by Joel del Río, "systematic heresy" is seen as a means of sustaining a perpetual revolution through which socialism could constantly renew itself and vouchsafe freedom of thought. This is a prerequisite of ***cine adulto***— a mature cinema for a discerning audience.

The "Special Period": The austerity of the "Período Especial" hit Cuban cinema hard. Production plummeted, especially of documentaries: co-productions and services to foreign producers became the norm. Faced with a lack of state finance, ICAIC had to become self-funding with earnings ploughed back into other projects. Further blows came with the deaths of two of ICAIC's founders. Santiago Álvarez was Cuba's foremost maker of documentaries, while Tomás Gutiérrez Alea was simply the island's finest filmmaker. His legacy of social criticism within the revolution contributed to the above-mentioned concept *cine adulto*. Key films of the Special Period include *Alicia en el pueblo de Maravillas* (*Alice in Wondertown*, Daniel Díaz Torres, 1989) became the watershed film of the decade, a test case for artists and filmmakers that reconfirmed the role of cinema as crucial in the process of social change. The controversy surrounding *Alicia* overshadowed the polemical potential of other films and made it practically a scapegoat in this regard. It was conceived in 1987, during the rectification of errors period, but was released into a very different set of socio-political circumstances. Nonetheless its creator, Daniel Díaz Torres, continues to make films in Cuba. *Papeles secundarios* (*Secondary Roles*, 1989), by Orlando Rojas, was a provocative view of Cuban society and the state of the Revolution, represented in microcosm as a group of theater actors attempting to reform, emphasizing individualism, victimization, and nostalgia for more exuberant and idealistic times. A scene where one actress reminisces about her lover, a writer frustrated by official limitations who left for U.S. in 1973, was the first such mention of such difficulties in Cuban cinema. *Papeles secundarios* largely evaded controversy due to being eclipsed, in terms of notoriety, by *Alicia*. *La vida es silbar* (*Life Is to Whistle*, 1998) shows director Fernando Pérez's compassionate humor and non-judgmental vision at its least sentimental. His hermetic, idiosyncratic vision foregrounds Havana in a role enhanced by the photography of Raúl Pérez Ureña. Its protagonist is Elpidio Valdés, a name that resonates as a historical character in animation films by Juan Padrón. Elpidio is a sculptor abandoned by his mother, Cuba Valdés; his fruitless search for her is also a quest for *cubanidad*—the elusive national essence. Pérez's poetic whimsy was seen in some quarters as abstruse and self-indulgent—but he has maintained this line with *Suite Habana* (2003) and *Madrigal* (2006).

Younger Cuban directors to watch out for in the early twenty-first century include Juan Carlos Cremata Malberti, whose *Nada* (*Nothing More*, 2001) and *Viva Cuba* (2005, co-directed and co-written with Iraida Malerti Cabrera) both offer innovative and occasionally ironic views of life on the island. *Tres veces dos* (*Three Times Two*, 2004) offers three views of love affairs by Esteban Inchausti, Lester Hamlet and Pavel Giroud: the latter's *La edad de la peseta* (*The Silly Age*, 2006) is a hard-edged and surprising view of childhood.

An Email Conversation with Director Gerardo Chijona

When I wrote to Gerardo Chijona in 2006, I asked how his film had been received, in Cuba and elsewhere. It had been accused of "cinematic prostitution" by Roberto Fandiño (see bibliography) which seemed an absurd exaggeration, as if it were flaunting its wares to Western audiences (there is a reference to dollarization, when Cándido comes back to life, but this is ironic). After what happened to Daniel Díaz Torres with the controversy surrounding *Alicia en el Pueblo de Maravillas* (*Alice in Wondertown*, 1989) I suggested there couldn't have been much energy or space left for this kind of problem.

Chijona replied that the film was a hit in Cuba, premiering at the Festival of New Latin American Cinema in Havana and winning the public popularity prize. During its first year of exhibition, with twelve copies, it pulled in two million viewers. There were no fanatical criticisms of this film, as there had been with his previous feature *Adorable Lies*, a controversial and quite aggressive questioning of some aspects of Cuban orthodoxy. It's always a lot easier, Chijona pointed out, to use humor as a way of taking on certain polemical aspects of Cuban reality with a critical spirit. *Paraíso* was first shown in the U.S. at the Sundance Festival (with a critical article in *Variety* saying that it was the most important Cuban film to open in the country since *Fresa y chocolate*[4]) and from then on did very well, touring festivals in North America such as San Francisco, Los Angeles (AFI), Montreal, and Toronto. This reaction had surprised him, since the USA is the home of the musical comedy and standards are high; nonetheless, at every festival in North America people were laughing at what Chijona calls "the same goofy things" as the Havana public.

I asked about *Cuando termina el baile* (*When the Dance Is Over*), his documentary on the Tropicana, and how it had been turned into *Paraíso*. Had he already been thinking of the feature film when he made it? He answered that when he made the documentary he was, indeed, dreaming of doing something more ambitious in the Tropicana — making the most of the exuberance of the cabaret and the people in it. In fact, the documentary deals among other things with the way the women working there were discriminated against by Cuban machismo. When the opportunity of making a full-length feature presented itself, he immediately had the "crazy" idea of doing a musical in the Tropicana. He cited the Hollywood Golden Age adage that you only graduated as a director when you made a Western or a musical; he could hardly make a western in Cuba, so...

The story for *Paraíso* was at first rejected as too complex, and certain aspects of the script were used in *Adorable Lies*. The success of this film meant that *Paraíso* could, eventually, be made — though "for reasons that had nothing to do with cinema and plenty to do with politics, I had to wait a good number of years to make the film."

A perennial question, but one I felt compelled to ask, was about the everyday realities for filmmakers at this time (the Cuban Special Period. This also brought us on to the topic of co-productions, and whether he had forged his own strong links with Spain, or these had come from ICAIC's influence.

Chijona reminded me that *Paraíso* was co-produced with a Spanish company called Wanda Visión and with collaboration from both the Spanish TV company Canal Plus and from the state-owned TVE (Televisión Española). In Cuba, as elsewhere in Latin America, co-production is the only way to get projects off the ground: the foreigners (Spanish, French, Germans) put up the money and ICAIC contributes the infrastructure (laboratory, photographic teams, lighting and sound, transportation, and naturally the technicians and creative people are pretty poorly paid. But it's the only way to film, because the subsidy that the Cuban government used to pay ICAIC (with which as many as ten features a year used to be made) for the production of fiction films is suspended due to the virulent economic crisis the country is living through.

Gerardo also reminded me that the Tropicana is still going: in his view it will long remain the mother of Cuban and Latin American cabarets. The place is still just as it was when it was inaugurated over fifty years ago and the show still features traditional Cuban music, along with the by-no-means-traditional *mulata* women who make up the dance troupes. Today it's a place almost exclusively for tourists, who most of the time come to see the show as if they were in a living museum.

The tourist chain controlling the cabaret was very enthusiastic about the project and decided to close for one week, for the first time in the club's history, in order to film the musical numbers. The film, fortunately, had very good distribution in Europe, which is where most tourists visiting the cabaret come from.

Then came some discussion about certain details of *Paraíso*: where had the theme of unwitting incest been taken from, apart from being a central theme of Cirilo Villaverde's novel *Cecilia Valdés*? The film's antagonist Roberto Fandiño likened it to a soap opera (not necessarily either untrue or an insult), but of course there are examples of this delicate theme in many mythologies. What is different in this film is that it also brings in the question of ethnicity.

He pointed out that in fact there is more than one case of incest; apart from the one we are faced with, which moves the story along and proves to be nothing of the sort, there is another, subsumed incest that is almost consummated at the end of the story. The incest in his film originated, as I had suggested in *Cecilia Valdés*, as a fundamental pillar of the nineteenth-century Cuban novel (and, probably, a good part of the 20th).

But for him, much more than in literature, incest became a pillar of the Latin American *telenovela* from its outset. The first *radionovela* written in Latin America, the mother of all subsequent *radionovelas*, was written by a Cuban at the beginning of the 1950s. It was entitled *El derecho de nacer* (*The Right to Be Born*) and its author, Félix B. Caignet, was a Cuban musical composer from Santiago. There, too, the incest theme was present.

With *Paraíso* the team had taken all the topics and themes common to the Latin American melodrama and *telenovela* and subverted them, "dynamited" them and inverted them, forcing the public to see the material from a comic angle and have fun with all the clichés they might have cried over in their homes. The tale of incest, taboo in any society, was wrapped up as a musical, based upon the "life's a show" concept. As everything that happened on screen was part of that show; the team could take all kinds of liberties with the narrative, ranging from farce to complete delirium, and showing Cuban reality from this other perspective.

Chijona talked about making the most of what he called a "sack crammed with plots and subplots," as a chance to pillory the underlying racism in some sectors of Cuban society; although the system in Cuba legally guarantees equal rights for everyone, a mere decree does not necessarily eliminate distortions in some people's minds, or in aberrations like racism. That, of course, was the reason behind the "monster" joke, in the case of the black baby girl.

However, Chijona stated that a Cuban public is perfectly able to understand this veiled criticism as an antiracist joke. He was surprised to find that, in the United States, some black people felt offended at someone daring to make a joke about such a serious subject; they called it politically incorrect and left the cinema thinking he was a racist.

This led on to another controversy: the use of Thais Valdés to play Sissy. How much did this (the choice, and its rejection by some) have to do with her ethnic origin? Naturally, as Chijona pointed out, if this had been a realistic film, the protagonist would have had to be a younger mulatto woman — and a real cabaret dancer. But *Paraíso* wasn't realistic, and its maker could allow himself all the license he wanted. Thais Valdés had been a part of the project from the beginning, because of her prowess as an actress, besides which she was capable of learning to dance and turning herself into a cabaret star. In order to justify the racial tangle that develops in the story, it was not only necessary but even indispensable to have a blonde Sissy. (Thais Valdés isn't a natural blonde and her hair had to be dyed). This made even more unlikely (though not biologically impossible) her being the illegitimate daughter of a black man — Armando, the choreographer.[5]

I put it to Chijona that one of the most difficult problems in teaching Cuban film or literature in the USA is that any film, book, or other work that criticizes the situation in Cuba is inevitably taken as supporting the received image of the country as deprived of freedom, etc.— instead of something very different, that the capacity for self-criticism in Cuba is testament to a high degree of maturity.[6] What would you say to those who are reluctant to relinquish the "official" U.S. image of your country?

His response was that it's always easier to explain, to a non–Cuban audience, that it's easier to live in Cuba than to explain what it's like to live there. Unfortunately for the artists who try to work in their country, everything to do with Cuba is inevitably politicized from one side or another. Artists are always worse off, because if they make historical films or something not set in the present day, then they are dubbed cowards, cheapened artists, or spokespersons of the regime. If they make films that critically take on crucial themes about contemporary Cuban society, then they are seen as instruments of the regime, a regime that allows them to do these things just to cleanse the government's image and project a false picture of a country with complete freedom to confront the negative aspects of its society critically.

The best thing, according to Chijona, is to simply ignore such ill-informed comments, whether from inside or outside Cuba; just try to tell your story as best as you can and, above all, as authentically as possible. He considers that the Cuban public, for whom of course Cuban films are principally made, will never forgive a lack of authenticity or any kind of coarse manipulation of their everyday reality. This is the opinion that really matters to all Cuban filmmakers as is the fundamental reason for them to make films. This naturally doesn't discount the possibility ("because we aren't crazy and we want to reach other audiences") that one's own perspective on what may be a very Cuban story might nonetheless just be universal enough to reach other people around the world.

Analysis: Intertextuality in Film

If we apply Gérard Genette's notion of *transtextuality* (a term he preferred to the more usual *intertextuality*) to *Paraíso*, then both the *metatext* (upon which it comments) and even the *hypotext* (upon which it is based but which it transforms) would be literary: both roles would be played by the novel *Cecilia Valdés*, which at one point is even mentioned in the film.

As Gerardo Chijona has pointed out, *Paraíso* also has its antecedents in radio melodrama. But there are other, cinematic, sources, among which are the many dance films set in Cuba (see above). There are even nods to Busby Berkeley in the choreography. These antecedents, in radio and film, could be attributed to Genette's *architextuality*: the position of the work within a genre or set of genres.

However, *Paraíso* is not simply a product of intertextuality but also consciously plays with the phenomenon. It ostentatiously quotes from at least two film "classics": the cradle sequence (C8: 1h 10m) is a quote from Polanski's *Rosemary's Baby* (1968) and the lost key scene (C8: 1h 17m) echoes Hitchcock's cigarette lighter in *Strangers on a Train* (1951). This latter is openly acknowledged: when Sergio puts his arm down the drain to retrieve the errant key, Mabel remarks, "Shit! I've already seen this in a film!"

Chijona told me: "Of course, [the cradle] is one of several examples of the homage to good genre cinema that I always include in my films, just as the drain scene is, as you point out, homage to Hitchcock."[7]

Michael Iampolsky, whose theory of intertextuality in film uses the metaphor of blind Tiresias constructing and maintaining visual memory in darkness, sees a limitless chain of quotes that absorbs all other arts and often invents precedents. "The initial characteristics of the quote — its corporeality, its inability to dissolve into the logic of narrative — disappear to the extent that we are able to construct its intertexts. The quote is then said to be integrated into the text" (Iampolsky 2008, 251). However, *Paraíso*'s quotes do not dissolve but are intentionally obtrusive, comic references clearly transformed by their context: the horror that greets Sissy's baby is a parody of the Cuban terror of Black ancestry, whilst Chijona's drain impedes the prevention of incest, not a frame-up for murder.

Linguistic Features

Some of the basic characteristics of pronunciation in Cuban Spanish are aspiration of the final *s* to something akin to an *h* sound. This can mean that to an untrained ear the *s* disappears altogether, which makes it difficult to discern singulars from plurals.

The omission of consonants (such as the first *l*, for instance in *los, las*) is common in working-class speech (mostly but not exclusively Afro-Cuban). It mainly occurs at the ends of words (hence "tó" = "todo") but can also be found at the beginning or middle ("*¡Cierra sojo y tapa boca!*" = "*¡Cierra los ojos y tapa la boca!*" or "close your eyes and cover your mouth").

The diminutive "*-ico*" is preferred to the "*-ito*" form used in most parts of Latin America (e.g., "*taburetico*" from "*taburete*," stool).

Unsurprisingly given the island's history, popular Cuban speech is packed with phrases and vocabulary originating in West African languages. Santería argot naturally includes many examples of Afro-Cuban speech patterns. However, in *Paraíso* much of this was invented for comic effect. An example is the phrase "*tanto vitití y tanto lepe lepe*": as Chijona explains, "This sentence isn't mine but Luis Agüero's — he was an expert in Santería. It survived all the versions of the script and I know it means absolutely nothing, it was pure invention by Luis, who was always joking around with Santería"[8] (personal communication, 25 August 2007).

For Discussion

1. Would it be true to say that, although *Paraíso* is a comedy aimed at entertainment, it nonetheless discusses certain aspects of Cuba's social and political life?

2. To what extent would you agree with Roberto Fandiño's assertion (2002, 208) that *Paraíso* betrays the principles of ICAIC in an opportunistic preference for "a gratuitous and prostituted commercialism"?

3. How different is the image of Cuba presented in Chijona's film from that projected by the U.S. and other western media?

4. How does the idea of transculturation apply to *Paraíso*?

5. "It's a world of institutional prostitution, which comes from on high and doesn't reach the lowest and most dispossessed social spheres until it has destroyed all good manners and social rules."[9] Is this opinion from Florida-based Cubanet a fair assessment of the world depicted by *Paraíso*?

6. What does this exploration of interracial incest tell us about Cuba? Could you name a U.S. film that treats a similar subject in anything like the same way?

6. *Dependencia Sexual* (Sexual Dependency)

CREDITS: Bolivia/USA, 2003; *Produced by:* Rodrigo Bellott, Gerardo Guerra, Ara Katz, Greg Leonarczyk, Christopher Casanova; *Director:* Rodrigo Bellott; *Script:* Rodrigo Bellott/Lenelle N. Moise; *Original Music:* John Dobry, Jeremiah Vancans; *Directors of Photography:* Rodrigo Bellott/Daryn Deluco; 35 mm: 105 minutes (rated: ?)

CAST: Jessica (Alexandra Aponte), Sebastián (Roberto Urbina), Choco (Jorge Antonio Saavedra), Adinah (Ronica V. Reddick), Tyler (Matt Guida)

Synopsis

Sexual Dependency is made up of five stories, distinct but interlinked. Between Santa Cruz de la Sierra (in Bolivia's tropical eastern lowlands) and Ithaca College, NY, the lives of characters from wide-ranging social backgrounds interact.

1. "MY BABY IS A WOMAN NOW": Jessica, a pretty girl from a poor background, is seduced by the far better-heeled Fabián, who has gatecrashed her friend's 15th birthday party to pick up a girl.
2. "YOU GODDAMN WHORE": Sebastián, a somewhat naïve young man, visits from Colombia. He is met at the airport by Fabián, his cousin, and driven around the city until well into the night. Finally he is coerced into his first sexual experience in a brothel.
3. "THE BLUEST EYES IN THE WORLD": Stereotypical and feted macho lover Choco is about to travel to study in the U.S. After a jealous outburst against his model girlfriend, he seduces a Brazilian woman to impress his friends. He arrives at his U.S. student residence to find he is no longer the alpha male but rather is met with indifference, even scorn.
4. "MIRRORS": a monologue by a young black woman, Adinah, tells of self-recognition as a child, followed by sexual self-awareness and ethnic self-acceptance. These are all issues that are faced by other characters in the film and rendered by the images of Choco and the BoSD billboard which occasionally occupy half the screen. The narration of rape also has its correlation elsewhere.
5. "ANGELS AND BILLBOARDS": Tyler models with a girl for the underwear ads at right of screen, a contrast with football training at left. This sets the tone for several instances of hysterical anti-gay phobia and macho posturing, culminating in a dénouement that exposes the hypocrisy behind the façade. The final images hint at the sociopolitical structure underpinning the pretence.

About the Film

That the title of *Dependencia sexual* is so easily translated — almost symmetrically — is no coincidence. The film was conceived as manifesting a series of irreconcilable dualities, binary contradictions, rendering a double bind of representation and perception. Bellott, who had planned a short film about a girl's 15th birthday party for his thesis at Ithaca College, was advised to avoid both stereotyped views of the United States from a Latino viewpoint and vice-versa (personal communication, 25 March 2008). This got him thinking about ways to avoid clichés and resulted in the idea of two cameras, working simultaneously on the same subject, representing Bolivian and U.S. perspectives. Writing in tandem with a Black Haitian/North American woman, Lenelle Moise, both linguistically and culturally enhanced this dual perspective.

About the Film's Creators

Director **Rodrigo Bellott**, a native of Santa Cruz de la Sierra, in Bolivia's eastern tropical lowlands, was born in 1980. At 16 he moved to the United States for a formative period of several years during which he gained a strong political consciousness, becoming aware of African-American, Latino, and gay issues; an awareness he says would have been unlikely to have come from living in the wealthy Equipetrol district of Santa Cruz, the setting for

Rodrigo Bellott. Photograph by Billy Feldman.

three of the stories in *Sexual Dependency*. It is a period which he considers key to the conception of this film, made as part of his studies at Ithaca College, New York, between the ages of 21 and 25. Bellott has made other feature films: he had critical and box-office success with a blend of social commentary and comedy in *¿Quién mató a la llamita blanca?* (*Who Killed the Little White Llama?*, 2006). *Perfidia* (*Perfidy*, 2009), a feature-length film which uses only one actor and three lines of dialogue, has yet to appear on Bolivian screens. *Rojo amarillo verde* (*Red Yellow Green*, 2009; the title refers to the colors of the national flag) is a film made with two other Bolivian directors featuring three stories that obliquely reflect national reality.

Uncompromisingly innovative, Bellott is a staunch defender of younger filmmakers with fresh ideas and aesthetic approaches such as the Bolivian Martín Boulocq and the Chilean Matías Bize. He is also forthright in his ideas on film:

Cinema, just like all applications of art, is experimental by nature and principle — in the sense that the results (the aims) are not known; only the elements and structure, the causes but not the effect, since it depends on human experience, individual, unique, uncontrollable, thus constituting a political, technical, formal, aesthetic, emotional and personal search[1] [Suárez, 2007, 69].

Bellott's public image is that of a talented polemicist, as adept at marketing and getting projects financed as he is at conceiving and making films. Well before his 30th birthday, he had became a kind of youthful elder statesman, representative of a younger generation of filmmakers in Bolivia and a defender of innovative cinema in Latin America. Along with the aesthetic innovations come the technical, not only in terms of filming itself but also in the forging of economic relationships and making of contacts necessary for films to be made. Even the reduced costs of digital technology require financial support, and Bellott has outspokenly insisted that younger filmmakers take full advantage of new technology, such as the internet, to sell themselves and their ideas. He has little sympathy for what he sees as the eternal Bolivian excuse — lack of funds.

Lenelle Moise is a Haitian-born writer and performer/actress, based in the USA, whose work often explores themes of a social nature. She has written plays, poetry and essays on matters akin to those aired in *Dependencia sexual*. Her range of concerns is broad, though race, sexuality and gender issues are crucial issues in her work.

For Cultural Understanding

Santa Cruz is the richest city in Bolivia, remote from the Andean highlands and far lower topographically. The city has long been resentful of what it sees as La Paz hegemony, during a history of neglect in which a journey from the highlands to the tropical *"oriente"* was a matter of several days. Now Santa Cruz has prospered, mostly through oil and soya, but also through less legal means. Many people resent having to contribute to the coffers of a nation from which the city was once marginalized. Since the 2005 election of indigenous president Evo Morales, the *Oriente's* relationship with La Paz has fluctuated between outright hostility and uneasy coexistence, depending on the level of intensity in the region's campaign for autonomy — a somewhat deceptive banner used by the local oligarchy in order to maintain its own hegemony, as well as undermining the Bolivian government.

An example of the city's social divisions comes only 5 minutes into the film, when a boy trying to clean the windshield of the SUV driven by Fabián is greeted with a racist insult.

Ethnically, Santa Cruz is a mix of indigenous migrants, white people (often relatively recent arrivals from Europe) and mixed race. The wealthier class is almost exclusively white, such as the young people who gather outside the Burger King. However, this elitism is seen to be completely parochial when Choco reaches the USA and is suddenly marginalized instead of feted.

Sexual references abound in this film, though representation of the sexual act is entirely absent: the inference is that sex is as much to do with perception as physical reality. That sexual identity is socially determined is placed beyond doubt by scenes such as the rabid anti-gay sentiments shown both in Santa Cruz (the pelting of transvestites with eggs) and on the university campus (the incident with the black gay in the locker room). The incessant bragging of sexual conquest among the *camba* rich kids and their insistence that Sebastián lose his virginity, suggest an underlying insecurity. Michael Sofair examines the use of sexuality as a vehicle for a neocolonial impulse:

Implicitly, *Sexual Dependency* ties the reorganization of social conflicts within the West around identity politics to the process whereby capitalism has, through globalization, not so much been projected outward as assumed a new world scale. One consequence is that the tensions surrounding sexuality pervading the American stories cannot be simply psychologized, because we see them channeled into production of the billboard, an instrument of cultural power over the Third World. And, viewing the same dynamic from the "other" Third World perspective, if issues like sexual freedom — of which the billboard offers a false image — seem to give content to Westernization, its reality is the propagation across the globe of economic relations which are veiled behind such content [Sofair 2006, 54].

As the Bolivian critics Santiago Espinoza and Andrés Laguna point out, (2009, 124) Bellott's debut is "Bolivian cinema's first attempt at reflexión about sex, about how relationships are shaped from it, about how it influences our daily lives on a sociocultural level." But further than this, "it sets out more universal, more human reflections.... It's the first film to portray the other side of sex and of the erotic; the less idyllic side, the one that hurts, that creates anguish...."[2]

Interview with Director Rodrigo Bellott (May 2008)

KR: Did you have any problem structuring your film in two halves (in narrative terms, visually and geographically)?

RB: The script wasn't a problem; in fact it was very clear: we had the five acts, five very clearly structured stories, and I wrote the script at that time like a conventional script. Only that at the moments when the same action was happening, we did only the action that occurred on, or was happening on the left or on the right. But at any moment when there were simultaneous actions or parallelisms of different spaces, then I did use two columns, but the script was quite traditional in that sense. There were even some scenes in which I knew there'd be no written dialogue and it would be completely improvised, but it's very well marked in that scene's pivot points, the actions are clear. I didn't want to work with a storyboard, so every time I was about to shoot a scene, I and the director of photography, with the actors present, would set out to do the scene with a lot of freedom, which was very important. We didn't impose anything on each other, except that we would coordinate moments with the camera. The script was very flexible both as a text and for the use of the actors and technical crew.

So what is seen on the screen wasn't prepared beforehand?

It was prepared in the sense that, the 15th birthday party is written as if it were linear, a single screen, because the action is the same, there were simply two directors of photography and two simultaneous cameras so we had the option of pointing the cameras simultaneously at distinct places, but it was the same scene. But that wasn't in the script, it was direction; what the spectator was going to see isn't there, what actually was in the script were the pivot points, this happens, the high society kids come in, and Jessica dances with one of them. But the rest wasn't in there, and the whole of Adinah's monologue is informed by the other four stories, so there's a correlation; I provided her with all the key criteria of the other four stories so that she could incorporate them. The monologue is much longer in the script than in the film, I had to cut a lot of it [12 minutes remain from almost 20], for example, the whole story of how Adinah conceals her sexuality as a lesbian.

Was it your aim to comment upon the relationship between Latin America and the USA as parallel to personal and sexual relations?

Yes, from its conception it was a film about very passionate opposed binaries, no? Binaries of class, camba-colla,[3] third world-first world, English-Spanish, man-woman, everything we wanted to do in the film. It was precisely to talk about binary opposites... From there came the idea of the two pairs of eyes, photographed simultaneously, and we'd both have autonomy and freedom to point the camera wherever we liked, and the public should also have the option of choosing which is the American screen and which is the Latin vision. And from there comes the personal part, the film that was my own experience. I had lived 16 years in Santa Cruz de la Sierra and then my formative and educative years in New York, a long period during which I didn't speak Spanish. So it was like a political identity that was formed in the United States, very distinct from what I had in Equipetrol. And it was a conflict of mine that I had to fight and learn to handle — what am I, more Bolivian or more gringo?[4]

In Sexual Dependency there is a homosexual rape, anti-gay violence, plenty of repression of that tendency: didn't you consider giving a more positive face to the gay world?

At various moments I thought of censuring myself, no? I wrote it when I was 20 and had to edit it at 25, so it's a film that suffers from a palpable adolescence. At the same time I think that's okay; it's one of its great qualities. It's an adolescent film, not only for or about adolescents but *made* by an adolescent in the sense that there is no filter; it's a direct address to the emotions that I experienced, and the things and circumstances that I happened to live through. The Equipetrol part is the best understood here in Bolivia but also living over there, in New York, I came up against a lot of that. I identified a lot with African-Americans, Latinos, and met Lenelle, who is lesbian, and is tremendously active politically. And I happened to live through a lot of that in the time of Matthew Shepard,[5] in the United States, I was at the university during the time of several hate crimes, not against me personally but as a community. We were, and are, a generation in a tremendously active context politically, demanding rights. So I lived through that kind of experience and had many friends besides. My first roommate in Ithaca was a football player, and the other was a wrestler. And on the other hand being with Lenelle, talking about being Latino, about color, about marginalization and difference, studying the concepts of queer theory, otherness, postcolonialism, concepts that impregnate my film, talking about that, so it isn't a pose, neither invented nor represented, but something I lived through and that I witnessed, not personally but very close.

It doesn't have to be explicit, you feel it.

Of course. So that was the side of New York I lived on, Adinah's and Tyler's side. I know the characters, people, circumstances, the locker room situation, when the black gay comes in, I lived that, I was in the lockers, at one side, you know? All these are small anecdotes that go into making a big film. It's a big story that is fictionalized, made up of small things that have happened to us, to me and to Lenelle, who also contributed a lot to the construction, not only hers but also Tyler's.

Didn't you think of putting in even one moment of tenderness between gays?

There is one moment, which is when he helps his roommate, he gives him his first kiss, it's the only flashback in the whole film. And there are also moments of a less victimized homosexuality, less violent. I've never been interested in weighing up, balancing things:

that's why I didn't want adults, either, in the film, at various times they criticized me at the university itself, that there are no adults in the film and in fact there *was* a story of adults, the sixth story, but I only got to film half of it. I realized when filming that it was another film. It's an example of that adolescence, of not seeing both sides and of not being objective, of being more emotional; that's what the film has, isn't it?

Reading some commentaries, I was struck by the annoyance that the divided screen seems to have provoked (above all in the U.S.). What do you put that down to?

It's very simple: people aren't used to operating multifacetically, simultaneously, above all when it has to do with a Hollywood film language, that has a way of being read, that's why there's little cinema in the United States with subtitles. Indian cinema, Asian cinema still have trouble entering, because they respond to a different language. And that is changing but not in 2003 when my film came out. I don't want to say my film is innovative or aggressive or anything, simply that the public wasn't used to it.

The problem with *Sexual Dependency* is that it's a film that can't be categorized as *art house*. That was one of the problems that we had in distribution. It doesn't fall easily into any category. It was the American movie in Spanish but also in the other half is in English, and it was very New York. It was about sexuality, but it didn't show sex; it had *gay and lesbian* content but wasn't a gay or lesbian film. It wasn't an African American film but its strongest character is African American. It's art house, but it has a much more traditional structure, so where does it fit? People don't have the facility to articulate that, so they grab the double screen as an excuse to say, "Ah no, this film doesn't come into the tradition of films I'm used to seeing." Especially the majority of people who had a problem with it, they're not people who've had a film education. The most aggressive type of cinema they've seen is David Lynch, if indeed they've seen David Lynch. So you have to take it with a grain of salt. It isn't a film like *Four Weddings and a Funeral*. I knew what I was getting into and I knew the risks with distribution. As an author, I set myself challenges that are interesting for me as an author, but that are quite obstructive and difficult for the audience. The bilingualism and dual screen in *Sexual Dependency*, the multiple screen and specifically Bolivian language in *Who Killed the Little White Llama?* and the absence of dialogues and action in *Perfidy*. But I'm not interested in making another kind of cinema. I believe that now more than ever the public is opening up to non-mainstream films. At the time *Sexual Dependency* was released, it was a big obstacle but I think that despite that, it fulfilled expectations and opened spaces I never thought I'd open.

Far exceeding expectations, no?

By a long way, and I'm still surprised by how deep an impression the film made among critics and film programmers in places where I never dreamed it would be seen. It has a cult following in places like Burma, Denmark, Israel, so I'm at ease, I couldn't ask for more.

There are many musical registers and connotations: hip hop, electronic, ambient music with acoustic guitar and piano, Chabuca Granda, rock, electronic kitsch, disco, saya, morenada. How did you conceive the musical multiplicity in Sexual Dependency *in relation to the visual language and narrative?*

The ambient music in *Sexual Dependency* wasn't so multiple because it's a single theme composed by John Dobry. But the diegetic music was more dictated by what was playing in Santa Cruz at the time in which *Sexual Dependency* is set.

Was Camba Motherfucker *composed for the film?*

No, it's a piece that was playing a lot on the radio in Santa Cruz. The kids loved it and it worked very well. The only thing I did was, there were a lot of Argentine *cumbias* that are usually played at 15th birthday parties that I couldn't get, so I had to create a false one.

That cheesy one, isn't it?

Sure, it has that mawkish quality from northern Argentina, that was having its heyday, but it was still like *cumbia*...[6] I wrote one of the songs, the more danceable *cumbia* when Jessica is dancing with Fabián; I wrote it, it's pretty kitsch. And well, one of the pieces of incidental music in New York was composed by Jeremiah Vancans, also for Tyler's party, the frat house party. It's one of Jeremiah's groups, semi-rock, hip hop, jazz, and things I heard over the five years that I was at university. And the rest of the pieces were contributed by John Dobry but all the arrangements were done by Jeremiah. I think he managed to capture the sound and the feeling we needed. It has a sound, a texture, very much of an adolescent band, which I liked, and which worked with the film. It doesn't sound like the London Philharmonic and I liked that, for another film it wouldn't have worked. And the rest are small songs by friends, who were forming their groups at that time and who gave me their songs as gifts.

What about the song Cardo y cenizas (Thistle and Ash)*, by Chabuca Granda?*

RB: The Chabuca Granda piece was the most complicated of all the music because it's sung by my aunt, Vilma Frías, who is with the group Contrapunto, which I grew up with. Putting that composition in was a bit complicated but I think it's very emblematic of that moment for Jessica.

Where do you begin, with image, narrative...?

Narrative, always narrative. Then the image, and then music. But I'm not one of those people who are able to write in a process. I write when it's clear to me what my pivot points are.

Analysis: The Split Screen and Its Implications

Sofair (2006) has spoken of this film in terms of "*The Split Screen of Globalisation,*" a political reading very much in keeping with the ideas expressed by Rodrigo Bellott. Theory regarding split-screen techniques has largely concentrated on aspects of films or characters such as duplicity, schizophrenia, narcissism, the compulsion to become another: qualities and syndromes all in some way integral to *Sexual Dependency* and the vision it seeks to present a world essentially split, hence the persistent use of the divided screen throughout the entire film.

As Sofair points out (2006, 48), some of the dualities represented by the split screen would be obvious were they not also linked by the intricate narrative cross-referencing. At the 15th birthday party, the dual image accentuates the girls' fretting over their appearance.

But the duality is used in several other ways, including the more conventional — the two young women conversing in the SUV (C15) are shown through their respective sideview mirrors as a novel two-shot.

Differing perspectives on the same event, such as the haranguing of Jessica by her father (C4) in which the dimensions of the two parts of the screen change: the right-hand side in which the girl is notionally situated shrinks from half to about one-third, using close-ups to further suggest the intimidation she suffers. In C9, the boys' swaggering approach to the Burger King forecourt is an only slightly divided image, which we might see as representing a schizoid tendency. And Adinah's monologue is accompanied at one point by the image of what she is recounting. Elsewhere there is alternation between blurred shots of the wallpaper (what she sees, her mental state) and almost symmetrical double shots as she intones different passages from the monologue.

In C33, the split screen is momentarily suspended as the macho pretence of the football players is dropped. Here, though, the technique does not represent duplicity, but its very opposite: this is precisely the moment at which the fraud disappears, and the characters' hidden desires emerge.

Linguistic Features

The Santa Cruz dialogues in *Sexual Dependency* have much to do with exclusion and the preservation of status. Jessica's father and brother establish their moral superiority by using words like *"grilla"* (slut) and *"cunumi"* (scum). The richer youngsters' use of slang displays another form of misogyny, one in which women are simply to be used and discarded — as Fabián does Jessica. This is language as bravado, bringing the comfort of belonging to a closed group, a tight linguistic community which is shattered for Choco when he arrives in the New York campus to be greeted with thinly disguised scorn (by a Black woman) because of his deficient English. The fact that he is treated thus by a person doubly marginalized in the U.S. is a reminder of the scale of values that operates between the third and first worlds.

For Discussion

1. Do the sexual encounters represented in *Sexual Dependency* justify the title? What do they have in common?

2. Is the fate that befalls Choco at the end of the film nothing more than a "gratuitous climax," as Michael Sofair alleges?

3. What kind of relationship between U.S. and Bolivia is suggested in this film?

4. Is Bellott's split screen simply an indulgence, or is it backed up by a coherent aesthetic?

7. Madame Satã

CREDITS: Brazil, 2002; *Produced by:* Isabel Diegues, Mauricio Ramos, Walter Salles; *Director:* Karim Aïnouz; *Script:* Karim Aïnouz, Marcelo Gomes, Sérgio Machado, Mauricio Zacharias; *Music:* Marcos Suzano, Sacha Ambaor, Waldir Xavier; *Cinematography:* Walter Carvalho; Casting: Luiz Henrique Nogueira

CAST: João Francisco dos Santos/Madame Satã (Lázaro Ramos), Laurita (Marcélia Cartaxo), Tabú (Flávio Bauraqui), Vitória (Renata Sorrah), Renatinho (Felipe Marques), Amador (Emiliano Queiroz)

Synopsis

João Francisco dos Santos is seen in this film in various contexts which, if they do not define a conventional linear narrative, nonetheless provide a coherent portrayal of the character, his human and cultural environment, and the myths he engendered and inhabited.

João models himself on numerous female personae, real and fictitious. As well as his fascination for Josephine Baker and Scheherezade, and his adoption of the name from De Mille's *Madam Satan*, he invokes the Amazonian princess Jamacy (who significantly becomes fused with the creature she fights) and the Mulata de Bulacoché. Director Karim Aïnouz has described him as "a still unexploited myth of Brazilian culture, a marvellous synthesis of Josephine Baker, Saci Parerê, Jean Genet and a Robin Hood of the tropics."[1]

About the Film

Maeve Mascarenhas de Cerqueira and Marta Enéas da Silva[2] see *Madame Satã* as very much a part of the *"retomada"* (resumption) in Brazilian film that occurred in the late 1990s after several years of stagnation, a time of renewed activity as well as the refreshing adoption of new subject-matter and aesthetic approaches after years of relative neglect and underfunding of the cinema.

Madame Satã won prizes at Havana, Huelva (Spain), São Paulo, and Toronto (all in 2002) and was nominated at several other festivals.

About the Film's Creators

Karim Aïnouz was born in 1966 in Fortaleza, in the northeastern Brazilian state of Ceará. He studied architecture in Brasilia and did postgraduate film studies at the University of New York. His other important projects have also dealt, in various ways, with the relationship between northeastern Brazil and the metropolis. In *O céu de Suely* (*Love for Sale, or Suely in the Sky*, 2006), a young woman raffles herself in order to raise funds to escape the small town in which she lives. *Viajo Porque Preciso, Volto Porque te Amo* (*I Travel because I Have To, I Come Back because I Love You*, 2009) is the story of a geologist, sent to survey water resources in the northeast, whose journeys there parallel his emotional situation.

Paixão Nacional (*Irreversible Metabolic Shock*, 1996), is a nine-minute short that deals with a gay man's deathbed ruminations on his country's sexual hypocrisy.

Aïnouz has worked in television, on the 2008 series *Alice* which again concerns an outsider obliged to acculturate, as a provincial young woman is forced by family circumstance to face up to life in São Paulo. He has also co-written screenplays for successful Brazilian films such as Sérgio Machado's *Cidade Baixa* (*Lower City*, 2005) and Marcelo Gomes's *Cinema, aspirinas e urubus* (*Movies, Aspirin and Vultures*, 2005).

Lázaro Ramos was born in 1978 in Salvador, Bahia. Having made a name through theatre work at an early age, he got his break in cinema through *Madame Satã*. Lázaro Ramos has called for roles for black actors as doctors and lawyers, even though, as Sylvie Debs (2007, 69) points out, his success has mostly come from playing marginalized figures.

Marcelo Gomes and **Sérgio Machado**, who worked with Karim Aïnouz on the script of *Madame Satã*, are established filmmakers in their own right.

Marcélia Cartaxo is best known for her portrayal of Macabéa in Suzana Amaral's *Hour of the Star*.

For Cultural Understanding: The Representation of Blacks in Brazilian Film

João Francisco dos Santos (1900–1976) who became Madame Satã, was in many ways a product of the decades following the abolition of slavery in 1888. A short biography by Rogério Durst[3] portrays a flamboyant and resolutely unconventional figure who destroyed, among other myths, that of the weak, delicate homosexual. This ambiguous character spent over a third of his life in jail, killing a guard despite a reputation as a model prisoner, later returning to become a celebrated carnival figure and cabaret artiste.

He took his name from the main character in Cecil B. DeMille's musical *Madam Satan* (1930) a tale of betrayal, deceit and seduction.

João's quest for validity and authenticity, both in real life and art, leads to this "performance" before the mirror in what appears to be both rehearsal and performance, with the character as both artist and public. Photograph by David Prichard.

Linda Craig describes

him as "an African-Brazilian child of former slaves and an overt homosexual who hustled and pimped in Lapa, a poor but bohemian area of Rio de Janeiro. Slavery did not come to an end in Brazil until 1888, and life continued to be hard for Brazil's black population as a result of a policy of *branqueamento* or 'whitening,' which encouraged European immigration as a means of 'civilizing' the largely mixed-race population. There were few options for African-Brazilians and many lived on the margins of society, scraping a living however they could. Within the urban centres, there appeared the famous figure of the *malandro*, hustlers, delinquents and pimps who lived on their wits and often fell foul of the law." As Aïnouz points out in his DVD commentary, this period saw the emergence of black urban culture in Brazil (as in other countries with former slave populations). Numerous Brazilian films deal with slavery and its aftermath.

In 1988 João Carlos Rodrigues,[4] inspired by the inversion of colonial perceptions in Jean Genet's play *The Blacks*, classified black stereotypes or archetypes in Brazilian film. He saw these as largely deriving from Orixás (divinities from *Candomblé*, the African religion transported from the Yoruba kingdoms to the New World) and in *Umbanda* (a blend of Catholic, Bantu and indigenous elements). His categorization includes what he calls "Old Blacks" of both sexes, itinerant keepers of an oral tradition and comparable with Uncle Remus. The "Black Mama" refers to the traditionally long-suffering and resigned wet-nurse to white children, a figure less common in modern Brazilian cinema. His "Martyr" is classically personified by a shepherd child, one subjected to cruelty. This type has persisted since slavery, and Rodrigues sees its epitome in the miraculous slave girl "Saint" Anastácia, a national cult. The "Black with a White Soul" defies political correctness but reflects the social reality of black people, often seen as traitors, receiving a good education and becoming integrated into dominant white society: an example is the upwardly mobile protagonist of *Xica da Silva* (Carlos Diegues, 1976).

The "Noble Savage" has some of the attributes of the younger Oxalá; dignity, respect and strong will. Rodrigues sees such figures, with almost superhuman leadership qualities, in another Diegues film, *Quilombo* (1985) and in *Chico Rei* (Walter Lima Jr., 1985); both films deal with solidarity in the responses of enslaved people to their lot.

The "Rebellious Black" is a bellicose version of the Noble Savage, often engaged with some utopian enterprise.

The "Sensual Black" stems from the stereotypical insatiable sexual appetite; clearly a projection of white fears and displaced guilt, this figure is also gender-ambivalent, prone to bisexual and even homosexual characteristics. Here the influence is visible of another Orixá, Logun-Edé, who for six months of the year is a man, and six months a woman.

The "Malandro" is another stock figure that typifies the inter-war period: for Rodrigues this is another figure that is distilled from various Orixás. Rui Guerra's *Ópera do Malandro* (1986), based on the eponymous musical by composer Chico Buarque's, itself is derived from Berthold Brecht's *Threepenny Opera*.

The "Favelado," or Slum-Dweller, is depicted as honest, hardworking and keen to avoid violence and the authorities. An example of what Rodrigues sees as a paternalistic and ingenuous vision can be seen in *Orfeu Negro* (1959) by Marcel Camus. Naturally the Favelado could not be portrayed indefinitely in this fashion: a counterpart to this image of idyllic, picturesque poverty might be the child assassins of *Cidade de Deus* (Fernando de Meirelles and Kátia Lund, 2002).

The "Crioulo Doido" is a difficult category to either translate or encapsulate, but it can be summed up as a "Crazy Black," a parody of things connected with depictions of

Black people by Whites. This is a figure Rodrigues describes as at once comic, sympathetic, ingenuous and childlike.

"Mulata boazuda" (Appetizing Mulatta) is a sensuous, erotic figure that draws upon the stereotype of mulatto women across much of Latin America. This archetype is subject to racial "whitening": as Rodrigues points out, it has more recently been played by Sônia Braga as Jorge Amado's Gabriela (*Gabriela cravo e canela*, Bruno Barreto, 1983).

The "Musa" (Muse) is a figure that largely emerges from black representation: an example is Eurídice in *Orfeu Negro* or, indeed, in Carlos Diegues's remake *Orfeu* (1999).

On the other hand Sylvie Debs has traced the changes in depictions of marginalized groups, both people from northeastern Brazil and the Black population, seeing a parallel between the two. Early policy was to create an image of a "civilized" country with as little Black representation as possible. Debs argues that there is currently more of a tendency to put a Black actor where a White could have gone. An example is *O homem que copiava* (*The Man Who Copied*, Jorge Furtado, 2005) which again stars Lázaro Ramos but in an entirely different role, free of any residual anger or stigma.

An Interview with Director Karim Aïnouz

KR: There are repeated references to famous or mythical figures that include various film stars, the dancer Josephine Baker, Scheherazade and others. Would it be right to say that this is to emphasize Madame Satã's multifaceted personality?

KA: I think so, in reality I used Josephine Baker because that was part of his [Madame Satã's] life, not only in the sense of how he fantasized with her music, her work, but also during his life. He adopted seven kids, something also very similar to what Josephine Baker did with her Rainbow Tribe, so she was an important feminine figure in the construction of his personality. Scheherazade was an introduction of mine, bringing in a character who, in order to survive, had to invent a new story every night. For this reason the tale of *The 1001 Nights*, hence the two characters, despite having distinct relations to Madame Satã's life, I think serve the same purpose: he was a character who was always changing, reinventing himself, not only artistically but also in a practical way. He used to change his ID card, so that every time he changed identity he went back to being a first-time offender, in that way his sentence was less harsh than if he had appeared as a recidivist. These are questions that I was attempting to transmute into the dramaturgy; they are very important in talking about his personality.

Most of the people you interviewed in the street (in the DVD extra) know about Madame Satã; to what extent is he still a symbol in Rio de Janeiro and Brazil as a whole?

I don't think he was, in reality he was a guy who was recognized in Rio, but in São Paulo I don't think he was well known, not because of himself as such, but rather because there was a very famous nightclub called Madame Satã in the '80s that defined an era, so in São Paulo when the name Madame Satã was uttered it was more for that reason; he wasn't exactly a myth, known across the whole country. I hope the film has helped people know a bit more about him. That was also one of the reasons for making the film.

Is it true that your basic working data were fictitious?

In reality I based my work on both true facts and fictitious elements. I heard about many things that he talks about in his biography. I went to check if they were true, and some stories that he quoted and so on, and some of these stories were true and some were false, stories that he invented and that he would say had been in the news and so on, and when you looked in the newspaper, it wasn't true. So this was really the moment when I began to understand that the film would have to celebrate that capacity he had of invention, of reinventing himself, a myth that he invented, so the film was based as much on true facts as it was also based on this strength that he had in inventing falsehoods.

Madame Satã is ready to flee from everyday reality but also to confront its injustices. Do you see that as a paradox?

I don't know if I see it as a paradox exactly, more as a survival strategy. I believe that what is sympathetic about him is that he had all these elements of a victim, not psychologically but physically. I believe that maybe the reason he had this way of inventing things and recreating himself and suchlike, was because in day-to-day life he had to face very palpable questions. I think that, rather than a paradox, this was a real survival strategy. I don't know if it's really survival, what I find appealing in Madame Satã is that he's not exactly a survivor, he's a guy who lived. The word survivor is a little more threatening; I think this was a way he had of staying alive.

Lázaro Ramos is an extraordinary actor, but he must have been challenged by the emotional demands of such a role. How did you direct him?

Look, the funny thing that happened with Lázaro was that I had chosen another actor, and more or less two months into filming this actor could no longer do the role and I was faced with the situation of choosing another actor; for me, the actor and the character had already fused, we had already worked together and I had to find another actor. Lázaro was an actor who I had tested back in the beginning of the casting process, and he was very young, he was still unknown, and one of the important things in my work with the other actor was that we had got to know each other and everything. Lázaro and I didn't know each other; we'd only seen each other a couple of times before he accepted the role. We began to work together, which meant he had to have very great trust in the director, so as to be able to go to those emotional places that the character required. I don't believe it was at all easy for him. It wasn't easy for me either. We were getting to know each other in the process, and coming to trust each other. At the time Lázaro made the film he must have been about 23 years old, which means a kid, doesn't it? I mean, when you think about his age, and the maturity that the role required, I believe I had a lot of luck with those ironies that happen in life, having lost the other actor and gained Lázaro. And there was something that I believe was very difficult for him, which were the scenes of pain. I think that for me it was important that the character really suffered, that one looked at his face and felt that. I believe that was really one of the biggest challenges for Lázaro, given that we had so little preparation time to make the film.

You often use reductions in framing (doorways, windows, etc.). What effect are you looking for with this resource?

Reductions in framing, in reality when you do that, in some way you're making explicit a certain theatricality of the cinema, the proscenium arch with a frame within a frame. I also believe it's a way of talking about the character. The question of contrast itself was important for me, as an attempt to translate the character. It was important that the image should be well contrasted, and that it should appear as a fiction within a fiction, [reflecting] a little of what I told you about the character, without necessarily constructing a distancing mechanism.

Was it difficult to recreate the era, beyond costumes and scenery?

It was very difficult because we didn't actually have a budget with which to make the film with those open shots that give you a broader geographical design, so as to describe the city, describe the space itself which that historical moment entailed. So we had to really think and spend a long time preparing. I think one of my biggest concerns there was to avoid making a period film, a Costume Drama. I was very focused, along with the producer and art director; we were very concerned. We spent a long time reflecting on how to make a film that is set in a given era but where that would not be exactly the most important thing, where what was important was the experience of the characters. Another very important thing for us was to research that era, make a very careful study. I think it's important to remember this is a very intimate film, despite dealing with a guy who became a hero. We were very concerned about the type of materials they used in that era, the materials used to make clothes around that time, to make furniture, for example, in the old days there was no *prêt-à-porter*. People even used to make their own clothes, and re-fashion them. There wasn't even plastic. Another thing that was important was how people lived; that place where he lived with Laurita and Tabu and the child, a little like a commune, a place you invent so as to live together and share. We did research into what the place was like in those times, whether they had water, a garden, outside space. Despite this not being a film where we had grand shots and so on, we made a film that really tried to represent everyday life at that time, and from there you can draw various conclusions, like the clothes they made, that he made. He also had the possibility of customizing, inventing fantasies. So all this was the fruit of historical research, but at the same time we took great care not to become hostages to that, so that all this was used to serve the dramaturgy.

This character doesn't obey any stereotype, whether racial or sexual. Was it this quality that attracted you as a filmmaker?

The unlikely partnership and friendship between bar-owner and former boxer Amador and cabaret artiste Madame Satã is disrupted by the turning point of a homophobic and racist attack. Photograph by David Prichard.

It was — really as a filmmaker what struck me most about him was the fact that he was a warrior, that he always lived his life, despite all the difficulties, with a lot of happiness, I believe also a lot of pain, but a good deal of joy, too. Another thing was that I think he played with his stereotype. He was a guy who was also in keeping with his own time, he was an individual in the abolition of slavery. In 1888, he was the son of a slave who was brought up in a post-slavery ambience and inaugurates an individual freedom in this way, in the matter of liberty itself, and that struck me. He never fell into these pitfalls that could have turned him into a stereotype, and I found that very appealing.

Analysis: The Close-Up: Affective or Informative?

The opening sequence of *Madame Satã* certainly does not exclude the film's credits, which have a diegetic role: as Karim Aïnouz tells us in his DVD commentary, they were carefully crafted to convey the world of tawdry illusion that his protagonist partly inhabits. This cabaret mood, supported by the off-screen sound of an applauding cabaret audience, is abruptly shattered with the sound and light of an old-fashioned flash bulb, jolting us into the fictional "here and now." Our first sight of the protagonist is as the delinquent João Francisco dos Santos (the off-screen prosecutor's voice mentions yet another alias, Benedito Emtabajá da Silva) but once this passage ends we are restored to the world of night-club spectacle. This opening alternates between implacable state objectification and categorization, on the one hand, and vicarious pleasure and reflected glory on the other. João's employer Vitória sings a version of Josephine Baker's *Nuit d'Alger* and is in turn imitated, João miming the lyrics as she performs (inhabiting her borrowed words as he later puts on her clothes). A little further on, Vitória's evocation of Scheherazade establishes a context of escapism and survival — elements not only compatible but mutually necessary. Thus the character's tendencies — criminality, escapism and metamorphosis — are neatly encapsulated.

Aïnouz tells us that this shot was originally intended only to end the film; instead the scene is split and is bookends to the narrative. A scene in which João is beaten by police is discarded (presumably as superfluous: the prisoner's condition and the context give us the necessary information). The director describes this as "like a mug shot," but this is only the immediate appearance. Behind the institutional aspect of this image, bolstered by the prosecutor's words, the character moves and reacts, barely perceptibly but significantly. What Aïnouz describes as the film's prologue allows him to "strip" the protagonist, offering a glimpse of bleak reality before we are again plunged into the cabaret. A significant ingredient of this scene (albeit a background element) is that the off-screen prosecutor is voiced by Eduardo Coutinho — one of the Brazilian filmmakers most influential in redefining boundaries between fiction and documentary. This is partly Aïnouz's design here, as he juxtaposes bald historical data (the verbatim police report) and evidence of the character's spirit.

But what is gained by moving the passage to the film's opening? This introduction of the character is reminiscent of the development, by Gilles Deleuze, of Sergei Eisenstein's idea of the close-up — as not merely another form of image but "an affective reading of the whole film." In his *Cinema 1*, Deleuze posits his notion of the "affection-image" and talks of the close-up having two poles, mobile and fixed. This use of close-up is very much rooted in its time and context, thanks to the off-screen commentary, but it also has what Deleuze calls the "power to tear the image away from spatio-temporal coordinates in order to call forth the pure affect as the expressed" (1986, 99).

We could also see here the two types of close-up which Deleuze saw as hallmarks, respectively, of D. W. Griffith and Eisenstein: the former being "organised for the pure and soft outline of a feminine face" and the latter more apt to express inner deviance and complexity (1986, 91).

The return to the same shot at the end also moves into evasion, when the judge's voice is replaced by that of João and, again, the evocation of Jamacy. As Antonio Rodrigues has pointed out with particular reference to these opening and closing shots (2008, 100–101), Aïnouz's concentration on smaller spaces heightens this intimacy, acting as a "magnifying glass" for the characters.

Aïnouz's DVD commentary describes the image of João in the police station as a mug shot "that stays in time," and it is significant that he stresses the temporal. His concern for the treatment of time is evident in an interview (Avellar and Sarno 2003, 34) in which he makes the distinction between a film merely informing its audience about a character and making it viscerally *feeling* that individual — sharing with the viewer a contemplative position he goes as far as to describe as "almost sublime, religious" (ibid., 32). This can be seen in films Aïnouz mentions as influences, such as the work with fixed cameras of Derek Jarman and Andy Warhol. He is also intrigued by Chantal Akerman's 1993 *D'Est* (ibid., 34) which features a three-minute travelling shot taking in the eloquence of silent faces on an Eastern European city street. Aïnouz seems to be looking for the same intensity as in Akerman's film, which, despite its lack of actors and narrative, would be difficult to describe as a "documentary." Aïnouz is concerned about the difference between an audience merely being *informed* about a character or real person, and being made to *feel* that person. He has arguably achieved both effects with the "prologue" to this film.

Linguistic Features

Naturally, this film's dialogue mostly uses an approximation to the slang and thieves' cant of early–twentieth-century Rio de Janeiro. As already explained, the *malandro* (gangster, crook) is an important figure emerging around this time, both in reality and in the Brazilian popular imaginary. Thus there are many references to violence and criminality:

- Canhota = left hand: by extension, the fist.
- Evapora (literally "evaporate") = "beat it."
- Meganha is a term that comes to refer to a policeman, perhaps of São Paulo origin rather than Rio, and roughly equivalent to the archaic "copper."
- Pau de fogo (literally "fire-stick") = revolver.
- Azulou (went blue) = got scared.
- Gatuno = crook, thief.
- Balela = piece of news or information of dubious veracity.

Inevitably, there are also several allusions to sexuality:

- Belezura = an attractive person, more likely applied to a woman.
- Danadinha = a woman of "easy virtue."
- Cassete = penis.
- Maricagem = affeminate comportment in a man, seen as denoting homosexuality.

For Discussion

1. Which of João Carlos Rodrigues's stereotypes or archetypes of black figures can be best applied to *Madame Satã*?

2. What (at least according to the characterization of Madame Satã given by Aïnouz) would João Francisco dos Santos have found interesting in DeMille's *Madam Satan*?

3. How, and to what extent, is the *1001 Nights* theme woven into *Madame Satã*?

4. What is revealed about this character by the fact of his taking Josephine Baker as a role model?

5. How would you interpret the scene in which Laurita compares João to Rodolfo Valentino, Johnny Weissmuller, and Gary Cooper (all white) then he curls up like a baby — in the next scene he's holding baby ... all kinds of manifestations.

6. Would you agree with Edgardo Dieleke's view that, unlike *Cidade de Deus* where "the spectator is led to identify with the narrator, in *Madame Satã* this identification is consistently rejected"?

8. The Child as Paradigm in Latin American Film

Childhood is often seen as a state akin to the experience of watching films, by virtue of the cinema's supposedly primal condition. The child's perceptual openness is compared to that of the cinema spectator, exposed to an array of visual and aural stimuli. Another analogy is that the cinema is in relative infancy, still learning a language of its own and surrounded by relatively "grown-up" art forms with which film has an array of often paradoxical dealings.

The relationship between film and childhood has been amply explored by Vicky Lebeau (2008), who looks at images of the child from British Victorian photographs onwards, asking what adult sensibility requires of childhood through the moving image. Lebeau looks at four categories: firstly, the "privileged access to the perceptual" that cinema, which is not bound by words, has in common with infant sensibility. Secondly she looks at the elusive intangibility of infancy in adult attempts to recapture childhood. Thirdly, the adult's often transparently disguised sexualized image of the child is viewed as "one of the dreads of modern cultural life." And finally, she looks at the ways in which images of children's suffering and death are used and/or exploited in cinema.

Childhood has always been fertile soil for the filmmaker, permitting the exploration of perceptions half-buried by adult sensibilities and the use of untrammeled and imaginative perspectives in so doing. Considering the wealth of possibilities offered by the child's viewpoint to the cinema, the combination has been remarkably little studied to date. In one of the few books devoted to the subject, Pol Vandromme observes that memories of childhood have provided cinema with its most abundant supply of themes, asking: "How is it possible to revive an attitude, a gaze, a gesture? Only with the image can we reanimate or conserve those signs from the past, so longed-for and imprecise" (Vandromme 1960, 13).[1]

However, this rich source consists not just of memories but of projections and inventions of childhood that inflect upon and illuminate adulthood. Children can be presented as inhabitants of a hermetic, magical world, or as painfully and vulnerably subject to a reality created, and differently experienced, by their elders. They can also serve as intermediaries, revealing the truths of this reality that the obtuse adult refuses to acknowledge.

In Latin American film, a vein of unflinching examination of unprotected childhood in the most pitiless circumstances owes much to Luis Buñuel's *Los olvidados* (*The Young and the Damned*, Mexico, 1950). The Spanish visionary's portrayal of street life in Mexico City was influential throughout Latin America; Francisco Millán Agudo (2004) argues that Buñuel paved the way for the radical cinema movements that followed. This claim is difficult to substantiate (it should be remembered that Millán Agudo's book was published in Buñuel's native province of Aragón) but the importance in Mexico of this exiled surrealist is beyond doubt. If, as Millán Agudo claims (2004, 40), Buñuel's motivation was not ideological, it nevertheless sprang from revolutionary aesthetic and leftist sympathies. If Buñuel was only a loosely affiliated surrealist, it should also be remembered that this was an artistic tendency, that not only supported anti-colonial liberation but also embraced elements of child sensibility. Manuel Alcalá (1973, 112–113) points out that Buñuel's virulent opposition to the prevailing order and what he termed "bourgeois morality" led him to create characters with whom it is impossible to sympathize. The gang leader Jaibo is a vicious bully and opportunist "at the margins of all normativity" ("al margen de toda normatividad," 113) but it is difficult to identify even with the seemingly blameless Susana. Another *Los olvidados* scholar, Libia Stella Gómez, has spoken of the effect upon Buñuel of Mexican reality, its inherently surrealist qualities (an observation also made by surrealist leader André Breton) coalescing with the filmmaker's own obsessions, with the result that a personal vision could, at the same time, become a social document (Gómez 2003, 21). While Buñuel himself was skeptical about the social impact of cinema, this film was received with telling outrage in Mexico due to its refusal to sentimentalize poverty, and above all its depiction of the brutalization of children who, in turn, brutalize. In his memoirs, Buñuel (1982, 243) recalls and rebuffs the indignation of an indignant crew member, adamant that the film's depiction of a mother's rejection of her son could never happen: "A few days before, I had read in a newspaper that a Mexican mother had thrown her small son from the doorway of a train." One film that directly acknowledges a debt to *Los olvidados* is Leopoldo Laborde's *Sin destino* (2002) which openly replicates the early scene of a furtive Taibo on the street. But if Laborde's film updates Buñuel's concerns to include sex and drugs, it fails to carry the Spaniard's poetics and clarity and refusal of value judgments into the present day.

One of the seminal films of the New Latin American Cinema has genuinely impoverished children as its central image. *Tire dié* (*Throw Us a Dime*, Argentina, 1960) was a collective project undertaken by students at the documentary school of Santa Fe in northwest Argentina. The project was led by the institution's founder, Fernando Birri, one of Latin American cinema's most revered figures. Marginalized inhabitants on the city's outskirts were the subject of the documentary, whose most memorable moment is the daily arrival of a train which carries relatively well-off passengers into fleeting proximity with the poor as it passes through the shanty town. Birri himself describes the scene:

> The passengers react to the spectacle in various ways: some make comments, others display indifference; some throw coins, others scraps of food or candies; some appear sorry or angry, whilst others mock, obliging the children to run several yards before finally throwing them, or not, a coin[2] [Birri 2007, 27].

This is the most moving sequence in *Tire dié* because of the contrast between its rawness and immediacy and the children's innocence. However, it is not the film's only significant moment: the begging has been contextualized by the social and economic information provided by the introduction, and explained by interviews with parents and other adults who are shown scratching a living around and beneath the bridge. These people display only intermittent political awareness and anger: their acquiescence is shared by the laughing children, for whom the "*tire dié*" activity is a game. Like *Los olvidados*, this film avoids sentimentality, but requires no injection of the surreal in order to convey an indelible sense of the bizarre.

Birri's formation has more to do with Italian neo-realism than surrealism (he studied at the Centro Sperimentale in Rome during the 1950s and went into mixes of documentary and fiction after *Tire dié*). His film is more akin to De Sica's *The Children Are Watching Us*, or *Sciuscià*, in its close observation without injections of outlandish, expressive elements à la Buñuel.

Buñuel's influence is unmistakable in Patricio Kaulen's *Largo viaje* (*A Long Journey*, Chile, 1967), an examination of poverty with an expressive insistence on the grotesque and cruelty. The eagerly awaited birth of the boy-protagonist's younger brother is an indicative scene: the baby is stillborn, and the wake, over which the tiny corpse presides as an "angel," degenerates into a drunken revel beneath the gaze of the divine/deceased child.

Childhood in an institutional context is the theme of Leonardo Favio's *Crónica de un niño solo* (*Chronicle of a Boy Alone*, Argentina, 1965) which tells its fictional story against the austere backdrop of an orphanage. This continues a subversive tradition of probing the institution as microcosm and agent of repression, going back at least as far as Jean Vigo's *Zéro de conduite* (*Zero for Conduct*, France, 1933) and continued by Lindsay Anderson's *If* (UK, 1968). *Machuca* (Andrés Wood, Chile, 2006) is set in a privileged Santiago school in the early 1970s, when the Salvador Allende government's policy of democratizing education means bringing in children like Pedro Machuca and his sister Silvana from outlying shanty towns to mix and share with the middle-class incumbents like Gonzalo. This experiment is nipped in the bud when Pinochet's coup restores hierarchy and newly severs links between social classes, but not before Gonzalo has established a friendship with Pedro and Silvana. The contact, which is prohibited but not forgotten, reveals the profound ethnic and social divides in Chilean society.

Discussions of childhood almost inevitably raise questions of the family or its absence, and this too can be used metaphorically. The position of the child in a decadent, aristocratic family setting appears in *Julio comienza en Julio* (*Julio Begins in July*, Silvio Caiozzi, Chile, 1977) whose protagonist, on the eve of his 15th birthday, is set to follow an unscrupulous landowner father (also named Julio). This is a hard-edged, perceptive examination of the formation of oligarchic mentality.

Often children are in search of a family of which they have been robbed by violence or parental irresponsibility. In *Valentín* (Alejandro Agresti, Argentina, 2002) a resourceful, intelligent and sensitive child is alone in a search for solutions to, and a way out of, the problems that beset his fractured family. *Quiéreme* (*Love Me*, Beda Docampo Feijóo, Spain/Argentina, 2007) sees a child foisted upon the grandfather who had been unaware of her existence before; at first reluctantly, they join forces to repair their lives.

Héctor Babenco's *Pixote: A lei do mais fraco* (*Pixote, the Law of the Weakest*, Brazil, 1981) was one of the most influential films to examine the desolating effects of urban deprivation upon the family and, by consequence, childhood. In one memorable scene Babenco's motherless protagonist is suckled by a prostitute, an image offering only fleeting spiritual and physical sustenance. The young leading actor, Fernando Ramos da Silva, was famously shot dead after returning to his previous life. Deborah Shaw (2003, 142–157) has compared *Pixote* with Walter Salles's *Central do Brasil* (*Central Station*, Brazil, 1998) as a demonstration of how children are used to represent opposing national visions: corruption, immorality and hopelessness on the one hand, a sense of national renewal through spiritual and moral redemption on the other.

Salles also looks at the family in *Abril despedaçado* (*Behind the Sun*, Brazil, 1999), this time as repository of destructive rural tradition which children must either reject or obey, defining themselves in the process.

The theme of children stolen by the military during the Dirty War, or robbed of their parents, remains potent in Argentina. Since Luis Puenzo's groundbreaking *La historia oficial* the theme has become ever more itimately treated by a new generation. *Los rubios* (*The Blondes*, Albertina Carri, Argentina, 2003) concerns the absence of parents from a daughter's viewpoint: according to Gustavo Noriega (2003, 26) "*Los rubios* concerns the fury and sorrow of a daughter whose parents, their experiences and their bodies, have been snatched away from her forever."[3] *Cautiva* (*Captive*, Gaston Biraben, Argentina, 2003) deals with another aspect of this social laceration: the attempt to repair the damage by reuniting stolen children with their true families. The issue is also powerfully raised in the documentary *Nietos, identidad y memorial* (*Grandchildren*, Benjamín Ávila, Argentina, 2004). In Marco Bechis's Italian-Argentine coproduction *Figli/Hijos* (*Sons and Daughters*, 2001) a young Argentine woman travels to Italy in search of the twin brother from whom she was separated at birth by the military who "disappeared" their mother. *Voces inocentes* (Luis Mandoki, Mexico/USA/Puerto Rico, 2005), like *Paloma de papel*, deals with children's direct experience of war — in this case, the civil conflict in Central America.

A remarkable debut by Andrea Martínez, *Cosas insignificantes* (*Insignificant Things*, Mexico, 2008) manages to interweave the fortunes of discrete families, different social backgrounds and generations without recourse to facile plot devices or coincidences. The interactions are illuminating, particularly those between children and the adults who by turns shape, deform, contradict and parallel their own subjectivities.

The mobilization of the image of children is visible in the opening to Elia Schneider's *Huelepega: Ley de la calle* (*Glue Sniffer*, Venezuela, 1990) which echoes the radical strategies of the 1960s–1970s in inviting its audience to discuss and comment upon the material they are about to see. This is followed by text and statistics on a catastrophic situation which the state had utterly failed to improve. The central character, Oliver, has fled from an abusive father-in-law to a life, literally, in the sewer: his mother does not oppose this situation, instead excluding Oliver from the home. Such children are marginalized from the margins themselves, and are hunted by the death squads hired to "cleanse" urban areas, particularly in Venezuela, Colombia, Guatemala and Brazil.

A more optimistic tone in the Venezuelan context has appeared with Alberto Arvelo's *Tocar y luchar* (*To Play and to Fight*, 2005), a documentary complement to Hoogesteijn's *Maroa* that explains the work of the Fundación del Estado para el Sistema Nacional de las Orquestas Juveniles e Infantiles de Venezuela youth orchestra (known locally as the System) begun by José Antonio Abreu, the social significance of the project and the enthusiasm it has generated, not only among Venezuelan children but also among many of the world's leading musical figures.

Víctor Gaviria made his celebrated *La vendedora de rosas* (*The Rose Seller*, Colombia, 1998) using child actors chosen from the streets of his native Medellín, where he won their trust during a long period of preparation that meant sharing living space and experiences. The children escape from their squalid reality by glue-sniffing; in the film this means their entry into a magical realm of religious imagery, a mysticism rendered by Gaviria's incorporation into the Medellín slums of Hans Christian Andersen's story *The Little Match Girl*. If Gaviria thus imposes a certain vision, John Beverly (2003, 16) nevertheless argues that his work genuinely speaks for the most vulnerable elements of society — its street children — through not only filming their reality but effectively adopting, and speaking from, their position.

Like *Pixote*, Gaviria's films offer no solutions, instead raising questions to which answers must be provided by social institutions or individuals. Any sense of inviolable moral rectitude the filmmaker may have cherished, as observer or reporter, has been destabilized since the

'70s. An example of this, for Ismail Xavier (Nagib 2003, 52), is José Joffily's film *Quem matou Pixote* (*Who Killed Pixote?*, 1996) dealing with the assassination of the aforementioned boy actor Fernando Ramos da Silva. The police are blamed, but the role of cinema in the young man's life is also seen as detrimental. Nevertheless, Lúcia Nagib's assertion that in *Pixote* "television is a source of lies" (Nagib 2003, 53) is only partly true: the TV presents both the institutional director's versions of events and those of the inspector who opposes him).

Other films about street children include the complementary pair *Gregorio* (1985) and *Juliana* (1988) through which the Peruvian collective Grupo Chaski looked at opposite gender viewpoints on urban migration and street life. Augusto Tamayo's *Anda, corre, vuela* (*Go, Run, Fly*) followed these up by putting the two main characters together, adding the factor of Shining Path's presence in marginalized areas. Urban poverty and deprivation is exacerbated by the constant possibility of arrest by frustrated authorities unable to identify members of this shadowy guerrilla group. Lautaro Murúa's *La Raulito* (*Little Raoul*, Argentina, 1975) concerns a street girl who poses as a boy, for the purposes of easier survival rather than through any conflicts of gender identification.

El polaquito (Juan Carlos Desanzo, Argentina, 2003) focuses on a thirteen-year-old boy who survives in and around Constitución station in Buenos Aires performing tangos made famous by the singer whose name he has adopted. His anxiety to emulate his hero illustrates a child's hurry to reach adulthood and independence: here, it is also expressed by the desire for fatherhood. The storyline for *El cielito* (*Little Sky*, María Victoria Menis, Argentina, 2004) was taken from the newspaper report of a young man of 21—who had himself been abandoned as a child—taking a baby whose parents were no longer capable of caring for him. The film opts to leave questions of the country's political or social situation latent, but its choice of subject matter is significant in view of the nation's experiences during previous years. This interaction between child and adult explores the desire to nurture in a society which has seen that need abused and frustrated.

Vuelve Sebastiana (*Come Back, Sebastiana*, Jorge Ruiz, Bolivia, 1953) is an example of a child protagonist employed to represent ethnic identity and further the ideal of cultural integrity. One of the first productions following the 1952 Bolivian National Revolution, this blend of fiction and documentary sought to promote the integration of Indian peoples into a new concept of nationhood. Sebastiana is a young Chipaya shepherd girl who wanders from her community in search of fresh pasture. Before the reaffirmation of cultural identity implicit in the return to her community, she befriends an Aymara boy, whose people are traditional oppressors of the Chipayas. This childhood imperviousness to ancestral enmities is allied to a spirit of reconciliation and renewal, a combination also visible in *Paloma de papel*. Israel Cárdenas and Laura Amelia Guzmán's *Cochochi* (Mexico/UK/USA/Canada, 2007) charts the misadventures of two indigenous Raramuri brothers from northwest Mexico through their differing attitudes to education and acculturation. One of them wants an education in Spanish and the other to continue a traditional life. This proves to be only the beginning of their disagreements; things become even more complicated, and illuminating, when their grandfather asks them to deliver medicines to a far-off village.

Contrasting portrayals of children faced with the consequences of dictatorship are seen in Marcelo Piñeyro's *Kamchatka* (Argentina, 2002) and Cao Hamburger's *O ano em que meus pais saíram de férias* (*The Year My Parents Went on Vacation*, Brazil, 2006). The Argentine film presents its story of a couple on the run shortly after the 1976 coup through the perspective of one of their young sons, making use of voiceover as the boy, Harry, comes to digest his parents' dilemma. Harry receives their guidance, but does not heed it: an unresolved aspect of the dénouement comes in the consequences of his rashness. The Brazilian film, on the other hand, eschews the adult perspective (revealing the director's track record in children's films such as *Castelo Ra Tim Bum* (*Castle Ra-Tim-Bum*, Cao Hamburger 1999), as ten-year-old Mauro makes his own sense of the world into which he has been thrust. His parents, fleeing from Brazil's dictatorship in 1970, leave him in a Jewish-Italian neighborhood of São Paulo where he makes his own way (not the one they have prepared for him) marked both by the political repression and by Brazil's victory in that year's World Cup.

Of course, not all Latin American films about childhood concern hardship: *2 filhos de Francisco—A história de Zezé di Camargo & Luciano* (*Two Sons of Francisco*, Breno Silveira, Brazil, 2005) is a feel-good biopic for fans of this highly successful country music duo, tracing their origins from poverty in the northwest (actually Goiás, closer to Brasilia) of Brazil. The younger brother died and was replaced by another. The film does give some idea of life in the Sertão at that time. It shows the brothers' vulnerability, both in childhood and during growth into adulthood and fame, without being excessively adoring.

Visions of childhood accessible to all age groups include Lisandro Duque Naranjo's *Los niños invisibles* (*The Invisible Children*, Colombia, 2001). Reminiscent of *El silencio de Neto* in some ways, this again features three young friends during the passing of an era — the introduction of television in a conservative small town, seen against a political backdrop in which a vociferous Marxist barber is conspicuous. The children's invisibility, sought in order to win a girl, involves defiling the sacrosanct, and provides effective glimpses into the seduction of blasphemy and transgression.

Children and Migration

Viva Cuba (Juan Carlos Cremata Malberti and Iraida Malberti Cabrera, Cuba, 2005) is a child's road movie and love story. A boy and girl are forced to run away by their respective mothers' politically founded enmity, a question to which childhood is immune. If the theme of runaway children is not new, the political tinge and allegorical content lend an unusual hue.

This theme of displacementis often brought about by adults: the child protagonist of *La misma luna* (Patricia Riggen, Mexico, 2007) resolves a problem created by the border situation, his parents' separation, and the egoism of a father who has chosen not to take responsibility. *Padre nuestro* (also known as *Sangre de mi sangre*, Christopher Zalla, USA/Argentina, 2007) follows two youngsters who smuggle themselves from Mexico to New York, where one of them searches for his father. *El viaje de Teo* (*Teo's Voyage*, Walter Doehner, Mexico, 2008) is another film concerning child-parent reunions and separations as a boy is taken to the border to await his chance and ponder the consequences of crossing over. The protagonist of *Cruzando* (*7 Days*, Mando Alvarado and Michael Ray Escamilla, USA, 2009) is another estranged son, an adult soon to become a parent. He has a short time to cross the border before his own father is executed. This theme of offspring caught at the frontier has been taken up in numerous coproductions, such as Cary Fukunaga's *Sin nombre* (*Without Name*, Mexico/U.S., 2009), Alejandro González Iñárritu's *Babel* (France/U.S./Mexico, 2006), and German director Marco Kreuzpaintner's *Trade* (Germany/U.S., 2007). The linked issue of child prostitution is raised in *Password: Una mirada en la oscuridad* (Andrés Heidenreich, Costa Rica, 2002).

In view of the region's still-increasing population, concern both to provide services (education and health) and to decrease dangers (sexual abuse, drugs, crime), it is likely that Latin American cinema will maintain a strong focus on the child for some time to come. It is also possible that the infant gaze will continue to be a strong documentary and metaphorical position in the region's national cinemas.

9. *El silencio de Neto*
(The Silence of Neto)

CREDITS: Guatemala, 1994; *Produced by:* Magalí Capi, Abigail Hunt; *Director:* Luis Argueta; *Screenwriters:* Luis Argueta and Justo Chang; *Music:* José and Maurice Gallegos; *Cinematography:* Ramón Suárez; *Art Direction:* Ana Solares; 35 mm: 106 minutes.

CAST: Neto Yepes (Óscar Javier Almengor), Ernesto Yepes (Herbert Meneses), Elena Yepes (Eva Tamargo Lemus), Eduardo Yepes (Julio Díaz), Rodrigo (Pablo Arenales), Nidia (Indira Chinchilla)

Synopsis

The setting is Guatemala in the 1950s — a time when the country is experiencing rapid social and political changes. The government of Jacobo Árbenz (1913–1971), who was elected in 1951, is attempting to free the country from its "banana republic" dependence on U.S. domination. Neto Yepes is a twelve-year-old boy from a middle-class family in Antigua, whose curious obsession with holding his breath is an unfortunate consequence of his asthma. His conservative, authoritarian father is a complete contrast to his uncle Ernesto, a freethinker who visits the house occasionally between his frequent journeys around the world. The two brothers exert opposing influences on Neto; the father restricts his movements whilst the uncle instills in the boy a sense that anything is possible. Both men, moreover, are in love with Neto's beautiful mother, and represent opposite political tendencies. The uncle supports Árbenz, whom the father considers reckless. In 1954, when Washington sponsors a military coup to nip the Árbenz experiment in the bud, Neto is placed in an individual crisis to which he must find his own resolution.

About the Film

El silencio de Neto has won awards and recognitions at several festivals including Sundance, New York Latino, Puerto Rico, New England, Huelva (Spain) and Biarritz (France).

Luis Argueta (2005, 43–75) has described his film's tortuous 20-year "genesis," from its conception in 1970 to completion almost a quarter of a century later. The project began when he was studying at the University of Michigan and exchanged ideas with a visiting Guatemalan writer, Víctor Perera. Argueta then met his eventual collaborator, Julio Chang, with whom he lost touch for eight years. After a chance re-encounter with Chang the project was reborn. The process is also traced in Rafael Valdeavellano's 2005 documentary *Los orígenes del silencio* (*The Origins of Silence*) which interviews people involved in the film.

About the Film's Creators

Luis Argueta was born in Guatemala City in 1946. He was recently listed by *The Guardian* newspaper in Britain as one of Guatemala's "living national icons"[1] for his contribution to the country's cinema. He graduated in industrial engineering at the University of Michigan, but soon turned to studying cinema and making films. Still living in the U.S. by the late 1970s, Argueta managed to begin making films in his homeland: *Navidad guatemalteca* (*Guatemalan Christmas*, 1976) is a seven-minute short about the devastating effects of the 1976 earthquake. The award-winning *El precio del algodón* (*The Price of Cotton*, 1976) concerns the ecological effects of pesticide on the southern coast. *Por cobrar* (*Collect Call*, 2002) traces the fluctuating fortunes of a young Guatemalan seeking a relative, and a job, in New York.

His latest project is *abUSed: The Postville Raid* (*abUSados: La Redada de Postville*, USA 2010), a documentary about an infamous Iowa immigration raid in May 2008. Argueta lives in New York, where he works in advertising and runs the production company he founded, Maya Media Corp.

For Cultural Understanding

From its inception as a republic, Guatemala was governed by a succession of military regimes with varying degrees of authoritarianism. This ended in 1944 with the overthrow of General Jorge Ubico, under whose rule the United Fruit Company had become an entrenched presence. The first elected president, Juan José Arévalo, had to deal with disputes between the company and its workers and handle the ongoing dispute with London over Guatemalan claims to British Honduras (now Belize). Arévalo's successor, Jacobo Árbenz, presided over a moderate but left-leaning government (1951–54) instigating an agrarian reform which included expropriation of lands cultivated by United Fruit. Other U.S. interests were also challenged, until invasion by a force of U.S.–trained expatriates culminated in the overthrow of Árbenz in June 1954. It is against this backdrop, with the question of rights to self-determination, that Luis Argueta's film is set.

The influential Argentine filmmaker and historian Octavio Getino (2007, 197–198) identifies the "Golden Age" of Guatemalan film activity as beginning in earnest after General Ubico's overthrow in 1944, when the new government enabled a string of educational documentaries and the first feature film, *El sombrerón* (*The Big Hat*, Eduardo Fleischman, 1950). With the toppling of Árbenz, U.S. banana companies were reinstated and Mexican companies invited to make commercial films. Pelimex, for instance, used local director Rafael Lanuza to make productions such as *Superzan y el niño del espacio* (*Superzan and the Space Child*, 1973) using Guatemalan locations and some local technical staff. On the other hand, there were also moves toward a genuine national cinema with the creation of institutions such as the *Pro Arte Guatemalan Cinematographic Association* (1968) and the Cinemateca Universitaria Enrique Torres (1970) as well as activity among students making militant documentaries, mostly in Super 8. Another important development was that film people trained in the U.S. began to return to Guatemala, among them Julio Chang and Luis Argueta. *Neto*, as Getino confirms, was one of Guatemalan cinema's most important productions (ibid., 198–199).

Cinema in Central America has always been marginalized, subject to both political and cultural vagaries and receiving almost no state support. María Lourdes Cortés (2006b), one of the region's foremost film scholars, outlines these difficulties:

> The fact of being a strip of land in which various geopolitical interests have intervened has produced fragmentation instead of integration between countries, the absence of communication and a tendency to look outwards, towards the alien and the foreign. It has been a region invaded not only by Marines, but also by seductive Hollywood images. Central American audiovisual activity has had to emerge from the rubble of wars and natural disasters, dodge dictatorships and invasions and, above all, compete with screens crammed with the dominant cinema's ever impeccable images.[2]

Ironically, as Cortés points out, it was largely as a consequence of civil wars and devastation that the need was recognized for a Central American cinematography with its own visual language.

Cortés talks of "Central Americans' need to build their own mirror, to reflect their multiple identities and recognize themselves on their own screens."[3] She, for one, is optimistic that this need can be fulfilled.

Interview with Director Luis Argueta

KR: One striking element of Neto *is the almost exclusive use of the house as a setting. Was this down mainly to budgeting reasons (difficulty in reproducing the historical era) or to the need to represent the childhood and family ambience?*

LA: The reasons for choosing the house as the main setting are twofold (although it would be interesting to "measure" the time devoted to each of the others: school, countryside, street, etc).

Mainly it's a response to the fact that, as kids, we spend most of our time at home. Budgetary concerns will always be present in any production, of course. But I never felt that we were limiting ourselves. We used the exteriors we considered necessary. The family house, apart from its authentic value to the historical situation, is a metaphor for part of society as a whole. There are different points of view and political orientations; behavior in relation to silence outside the house found its echo and concrete expression within. On the other hand, my family house was very similar to Neto's. This house was the most difficult location to find. I was very clear about what I wanted and was never content until I found what we now see in the film.

The treatment of ethnicity is something that raises questions, above all given the level of racism and ethnic violence during the 1980s. It's interesting that Nidia uses the phrase, "We are all Indians," but she seems less indigenous than, for instance, the priest. Was that a conscious attempt to show the heterogeneous nature of the Guatemalan population?

Racism is a phenomenon that is barely discussed now but that, together with ethnic violence, has existed since colonial times. Nidia wears the costume of the people of Cobán, an area of Guatemala with considerable German presence. The phrase used by Nidia ("in Guatemala we are all Indians") has the dual objective of underlining the mixture in the

Guatemalan population and provoking the Guatemalan reaction of self-exclusion, similar to that adopted by Neto when he replies: "Except for me." I consider that the division between the ladino[4] (*mestizo*) group and the indigenous population is perfectly illustrated during the birthday party. For a brief instant we see the image of two indigenous women and their children silhouetted in the doorway of the house, looking inside. Although the door is open, the barriers that separate these two worlds, not only ethnic but also social and economic, are insurmountable.

The way of using music is a significant part of both the historical and geographical setting. This suggests the importance of radio, which besides music brings in elements like the series Los Tres Villalobos. *Was it your intention to give a Pan-American flavor with this?*

The intention of using music as setting responds principally to a conscious desire to reproduce a historical reality. In 1954 radio was everybody's form of communication and entertainment in Guatemala (television didn't arrive until 1957).

It was never my intention to give anything a Pan-American flavor. We were simply reflecting a national reality (which at the same time had a lot in common with other national realities in Latin America). *Los Tres Villalobos,* which originated in Cuba, was a program that went out in Mexico, Venezuela and Puerto Rico. On the other hand, newsreels like *Guatemala Flash* and stations like Radio Panamericana are two elements that are totally Guatemalan.

The intersection of a childhood vision with the adult world is especially strong.

Besides responding to my vision and memories this had the metaphorical object of signaling the country's loss of innocence. In particular the spirit encouraged by Uncle Ernesto, the balloon as a symbol of independence. The film takes place during the 24 hours between nightfall on 19 October 1954 and the evening of the 20th. That date marks the tenth anniversary of the October Revolution of 1944. That balloon, besides its symbolism of independence and liberty, is homage to said revolution, and a celebration of the tenth anniversary that never occurred because of the invasion.

How did you live the political context as a child? What was the impact on your generation of the Árbenz era?

My experience was much like Neto's. My father held an official post in the government. He was the local authority, we lived just half a block from a barracks, and we moved to my uncle's house (in Guatemala City, not in Antigua like Neto). There were differing political opinions among family members and friends. There was an atmosphere of suspicion, a general anxiety. The school I attended was closed because its directors were forced into exile because of their political and pedagogical ideas. Planes were flying overhead and dropping leaflets, classes canceled, the constant buzzing caused by the clandestine transmissions experienced by the film's characters, we lived through all this very intimately. It's also important to note that my generation was four years younger than Neto's, and that contributions to the fiction of the film include not only childhood memories but also later research on the history of the era. The loss of innocence is a phenomenon that we experienced both as children and as a country.

You've presented a social panorama full of secrets and hypocrisies. On an intimate level, perhaps the most striking thing is the suggestion that Neto is the son of Ernesto. Would it be true to say that this is in some way metaphorical?

What you describe corresponds both to the historical situation and to the characters' emotional state. This society was being initiated in democracy but its political and socioe-conomic structures were so rigid and stratified that they produced distrustful individuals, fearful of being misinterpreted.

The suggestion that Uncle Ernesto is the father of Neto is definitively metaphorical. Neto is the spiritual son of the uncle. An influence I could cite is John Boorman's film *Hope and Glory* (1987) in which the protagonist's father and the father's best friend are both in love with his mother.

What did you want to communicate with the emphasis you place on the unhealthiness of silence?

The incapacity for self-expression produces individuals that are introspective, fearful, with no ability to conceptualize complex thoughts or question their historical or personal situation. Neto's asthma is a physiological manifestation of this lack of freedom. At the same time it's a metaphor for a repressed and self-censoring society.

How do you see the future of Guatemalan or Central American cinema?

The current situation in Guatemala and Central America has evolved substantially since I made *The Silence of Neto*. On the one hand, in Guatemala, various features have been produced —*Donde acaban los caminos* (*Where the Roads End*) (on celluloid), based on the eponymous novel by Mario Monteforte Toledo with a Mexican script and director (Carlos García Agraz, 2004); *La Casa de Efrente* (*The House across the Street*, Tonatiúh Martínez, 2003) and *Las Cruces* (*The Crosses*, 2005), both video, transferred to celluloid, by the Casa Comal collective with Guatemalan directors and producers (Elías Jiménez/Rafael Rosales) and cinematography (Daniela Sagone) and a Puerto Rican scriptwriter; sponsored by Swe-den, *Lo que soñó Sebastián* (*What Sebastian Dreamt*) (video, 2003), based on the eponymous novel and directed by its Guatemalan author, Rodrigo Rey Rosa; and *Evidencia invisible* (*Invisible Evidence*) (video, 2003), written and directed by the Guatemalan Alejandro Castillo. Two shorts, *La muerte de Diógenes* (*The Death of Diogenes*) and *Amorfo. te busqué* (*Amorfo, I Searched for You*) by Mario Rosales, Guatemalan resident in New York, and a series for Internet,[5] *Sweet Delilah* by Mendel Samayoa. All these productions seek to reflect the history and situation of Guatemala; they were shot in Guatemala and have enjoyed a good response from the public despite limited distribution. The *Festival Icaro* has become an annual event that presents productions on a Central American level (principally) and Latin American that goes from documentaries, shorts, institutional films, music videos and com-mercials. *CINERGIA* is a support fund for production which has fomented Central American cinema for three years with a fund of just over $100,000 per year. Digital video and non-linear edition in computers is in part responsible for the proliferation of productions. There are film courses at universities; the university film center in Guatemala continued its efforts to salvage twentieth-century films and filmic materials with a small budget and a lot of tenacity. The film historian Edgar Barillas has produced a couple of very important videos in which he presents the urban development of Guatemala seen through film. There is sup-port from the ministry of culture for the formation of a film institute. The Guatemalan institute of tourism has supported productions from outside that have gone to Guatemala to film. The most recent case is *Looking for Palladin* (USA, 2008, video blown up to cel-luloid) by Andrzej Krakowski. This English-language production, with renowned actors like Ben Gazzara, Thalia Shire, and Ángela Molina, has the participation of local actors and uses local sets. This production used mostly Guatemalan technicians and crew (lighting and equipment other than camera). An essential element for all cinema is distribution. There is currently a favorable attitude toward national productions on the part of local exhibitors.

DVD is a new form of distribution (I have "revived" *The Silence of Neto* by producing a DVD that, besides being subtitled, has a documentary presenting the story of the film's creation and production as well as two versions with commentary "by the director," one in Spanish and the other in English. The fact of being able to use the Internet and electronic commerce has meant that a lot of people who had heard of the film can now see it by buying it through the Internet. The success of having been able to reach a public that is interested in our films led me to create a website in order to distribute Guatemalan and Latin American cinema, music, literature and art. The same phenomenon, the popularization of the Internet and the not-so-distant possibilities of downloading entire films and watching them on the computer is something not to be taken lightly.

All this brings us to consider not only the form in which not only Guatemalan film is distributed and seen. We are in a true revolution as regards access to audiovisual content. In Hollywood the expression "platform agnostics" has been popularized and is the object of much discussion. *Platform agnostics* refers to the spectators that "consume" audiovisual content whether in a cinema, on TV, on their computers, or on an iPod. However, I consider that the future of Guatemalan cinema will be directly proportional to the state's creation of organizations today to adopt a serious and aggressive attitude in creating a regional market and penetrating international markets.

Analysis

The scene of the resignation of president Árbenz (C9) is central to understanding both the historical moment and the family's internal dynamics. Perhaps for this reason the camera maintains distance, never entering the house during this sequence. The event brings the family together physically, but clarifies political differences, especially between Ernesto and his mother.

What is the effect of constructing the scene in this way? Luis Argueta's commentary argues that the three-shot structure without camera movement serves to emphasize the content of this edited version of Árbenz's speech. Argueta wanted to capture the sense that the entire country was hanging on the president's words, (he even played the recording during the shoot). However, strictly speaking he violates orthodox film language by using fade-ins (generally used to mark far longer time-lapses) instead of clean cuts. Is this valid? Is the filmmaker under any obligation to follow rules?

At first we see a long shot of Elena sitting outside, a scene prettily lit from within and from the veranda. Ernesto appears in the foreground to our right, just as Eduardo crosses the doorway in the background. The caption *27 de junio de 1954* comes up. This lends the scene a certain documentary authority, anchored in the historical moment a sense reinforced by the Árbenz recording. The composition gives a sense of stillness, with luxuriant vegetation framing the doorway which is central; a pillar divides the frame almost in half. Ernesto stops by this pillar, half-hidden in the semi-darkness. Eduardo comes out and calls Elena to come and listen before summoning everybody. At this, Ernesto moves from this shadowy place, and soon his mother appears. Finally Neto trots into view from behind the camera. The three women are visible through the doorway; we are not told what the men's reaction is.

These fades *are* elliptical, they denote advances in time but only brief ones (to enable cutting of the speech). They also allow an approach to the doorway that avoids using a dolly that, Argueta explains, was too noisy. As he says, at this moment what is heard is more important than what is seen. As well as the president's words, we hear Ernesto's sarcastic remarks (which seem to go unheard) about the non-use of land that is to be restored to its former owners.

The camera finally enters the house when Ernesto opens his trunk to put his puppets away. This marks the end of an episode for Guatemala: the extension of a metaphor, to cite Argueta once more, for the divisions within the country.

Linguistic Features

Despite certain regional differences, Central American Spanish shares certain characteristics. One of these is the familiar third-person pronoun *vos* instead of *tù*. There is vocabulary shared also with Mexico and Central American countries: *platicar* (to speak), *chula* (pretty), *babosada* (drivel). Other terms are more specifically Guatemalan, such as *ishta*, a pejorative term for "Indian," or *pichirili* (shall we go?: *¿nos vamos?*). Such perceived impurities preoccupied nineteenth-century scholars keen to preserve the integrity of the nation's heritage such as Antonio Batres Jáuregui, whose *Vicios del lenguaje: Provincialismos de Guatemala* (*Vices of Language: Provincialisms of Guatemala*, 1897) overlooks the fact that even in their countries of origin, languages absorb outside influences and change.

For Discussion

1. What other issues are introduced along with the theme of sexual awakening?
2. How do we see Neto change during the film, and how are things presented from his viewpoint?
3. What are the various purposes served by the radio?
4. Are the balloon and the puppets mere playthings, or can we give them a broader interpretation?
5. When and under what conditions is English heard?
6. What are the most important differences between Neto's father and his uncle Ernesto?
7. How is the subtext of racism represented?
8. What is the dramatic function of opening with the death of Uncle Ernesto?

10. *Maroa*

CREDITS: Venezuela/Spain, 2006; *Produced by:* Maroa was a co-production between Macu Films (Venezuela) and Tornasol Films (Spain). The executive producers were Diana Sánchez, Gerardo Herrero and Solveig Hoogesteijn; *Director:* Solveig Hoogesteijn; *Script:* Solveig Hoogesteijn, Fernando Castets, Claudia Nazoa; *Music:* Nascuy Linares; *Director of Photography:* Alfredo Mayo

CAST: Joaquín (Tristán Ulloa), Maroa (Yorlis Domínguez), Brígida (Elba Escobar), Ezequiel (Luke Grande), Carlos (Enghell Alejo), Cabeza de Periódico (Víctor Cuica)

Synopsis

Maroa is an 11-year-old girl from in one of the deprived neighborhoods of Caracas — an environment which, according to statistics, produces an average of 130 violent deaths every weekend. Illiterate and neglected, she becomes involved in gang life and petty crime like many children in her situation. Her only family life comes in the shape of her abusive grandmother Brígida, who lives by selling lottery tickets, reading fortunes, and cheating anyone she can. The girl's life is changed when she gradually becomes aware of classical music and its capacity to open horizons beyond her daily intake of rap, *changa* and other musical expressions of life in the poor neighborhoods or *ranchos*.

Maroa joins a youth orchestra directed by a Spaniard, Joaquín, who takes an interest in her despite initial conflict in their relationship. He is drawn into her troubled life outside the class, incurring problems of his own. Two factors are to further complicate Maroa's fragile existence — the death of her grandmother and recurrent conflict with a corrupt and violent policeman.

About the Film

Maroa takes on one of Venezuela's most severe social problems — the situation of its street children. This is counterbalanced by what the film presents as a solution — the national orchestra system. As the music teacher Joaquín says in the film, the orchestra is "a salvation, a first-class therapeutic instrument."

Maroa won awards in Venezuela (CNAC), Spain (IBERMEDIA), France (Fonds Sud) and Germany (Filmburo Nordrhein-Westfalen) which allowed its script to be developed and filmed. It has won the Audience Award at the International Festival of Latin American Cinema in Biarritz, France, and was Venezuela's nomination for both the Oscars and the Spanish Goya prize.

Hoogesteijn has attributed the conception of her film to the first time she witnessed a performance by one of Venezuela's youth orchestras. The pride and empowerment visible in a group of children from obviously humble backgrounds is a phenomenal achievement now recognized worldwide — even in countries that do not share Venezuela's political orientation. Hoogesteijn describes this as "the defeat of despair through music."[1]

About the Film's Creators

Solveig Hoogesteijn is one of the most important figures in Venezuelan culture. She was born in Stockholm in 1946, of Dutch and German parents who moved to Venezuela a year later. At age 21 she went back to Germany, studying film in Stuttgart.

For her "thesis" at film school in 1975 she insisted on returning to Venezuela. The result was the documentary *Puerto Colombia*, made with a Venezuelan crew of four and a tiny budget. Next came a short based on the Gabriel García Márquez story, *El mar del tiempo perdido* (*The Sea of Lost Time*, 1977). This project had a crew of seven and more money. *In Manoa* (1980) is an earlier exploration of the social role of music, making friends of two boys from extremely diverse social backgrounds.

Her most successful and best-known film is *Macu, la mujer del policía* (*Macu, the Policeman's Woman*, 1988) which struck a chord with Venezuelan audiences through its implacable gaze at life in the *ranchos* or marginal areas of Caracas, where it was shot on location. The film achieved the highest box office success of any Venezuelan national production at that time[2]: a total of 1.3 million spectators. Nevertheless the film, made entirely with Venezuelan cash, was completed on a budget of only $70,000 — a fact received with disbelief during one conference in the U.S. where she was told it was only enough to pay for "transportation for a U.S. documentary." The theme of incest and child brides struck a chord — though she insists this is rather a film about power, with the girl Macu (short for Inmaculada) taking control of her own life. This uncomfortable topic returns, albeit more obliquely, in *Maroa*. The script for *Santera* (1994) was distorted, by Hoogesteijn's own admission, in order to write in a part for the Spanish actress Laura del Sol. The title refers to a practitioner of the Santería religion of the African diaspora in Latin America, and the film's protagonist is a mysterious and troubled black woman from the coast who must come to terms with this background whilst in a Caracas jail.

Yorlis Domínguez was the child chosen to play Maroa after Hoogesteijn, who had looked at 250 girls for the part, spotted her in the street and saw the "mixture of innocence, sensuality, violence and musical genius"[3] she was looking for. There is a parallel between Maroa and Yorlis, who found a way out of her own psychological problems and her family's financial difficulties through acting.

Tristán Ulloa is a well-known Spanish actor who was brought in to satisfy the conditions of the co-production agreement but in far happier circumstances than *Santera*.

Elba Escobar, who plays Maroa's grandmother, is one of the most celebrated actresses in the history of Venezuelan cinema. In her youth she played glamorous roles before moving into telenovelas and radio.

For Cultural Understanding

The situation of Venezuela's street children is the theme of *Huelepega: Ley de la calle* (*Glue Sniffer*, Elia Schneider, 1990) which opens with a plea to the audience to take the content seriously and to interact with organizations working toward a solution. It explains too that the situation worsened during the second half of the twentieth century despite Venezuela being one of Latin America's richest countries. Gustavo Balza's *Caracas, amor a muerte* (*Caracas unto Death*, 2000) deals with the subject of underage sex and abortion. Several films by the founding father of modern film in Venezuela, Román Chalbaud, have also touched upon the subject of childhood delinquency and street life.

Venezuela's phenomenally successful Simón Bolívar Youth Orchestra System was the brainchild of José Antonio Abreu, who trained as an economist as well as being a composer. Abreu's visionary work has been recognized with a string of international prizes. His project, aimed at social education through the collective responsibility involved in orchestra playing, is explained in the documentary *Tocar y luchar* (*To Play and to Fight*, Alberto Arvelo, Venezuela, 2005) which draws homage from some of the most outstanding figures in world music, and features performances led by the national orchestra's charismatic young conductor, Gustavo Dudamel. *The Promise of Music* (Enrique Sánchez Lansch, Germany, 2008) is a documentary made for television that also probes the orchestra's success.

Interview with Director Solveig Hoogesteijn

KR: How authentic is your representation of music in Venezuela as a way out of poverty and delinquency?
    SH: Giving children who live in a marginal environment — which means not just material poverty, but also the loss of spiritual and moral values — the possibility of getting to know art, in this case music, of learning an instrument, which is something that gives them discipline. Being away from the temptations of the street during the evening, but receiving classes every afternoon of the week, opens up a real life alternative for these children.

It's not important that they know if they are going to become professional musicians. It's the experience itself of learning about the difficult lives of the composers they interpret, an experience that provides them with examples of how they have to struggle to achieve things in life. It's the experience of playing in an orchestra from the beginning of their musical education, which gives them the experience that means working in a group — that is to say if I play well, but the kid next to me plays badly, if I don't help him or her, then the end result, the performance of the orchestra, will be bad. I'd be better off helping that kid, the child reflects. This experience is the first step towards the formation of a citizen who understands what it means to cooperate with a collective.

Studies have demonstrated that those children who study music in orchestras not only improve their schoolwork, and are more motivated towards achieving success, their families also change. To have the experience as spectators, seeing their children play on stage in theaters and other places they had never previously set foot in, fills them with pride and reinforces the self-esteem of the entire family.

In this sense, it's a social program of incalculable merits and truly enormous success.

You've dealt before with the theme of pedophilia, whether real or latent: however, in Macu *it's a central part of the narrative. Do you think it has equal weight in* Maroa?

Pedophilia isn't a theme in *Maroa*. The seduction attempted by an 11-year-old girl, who comes from a background in which we have the highest number of child pregnancies in all of Latin America, is nothing surprising. I have seen astonishing behavior in young girls towards my technicians whilst I've been shooting films in the *barrios* of Caracas over 30 years. Maroa's teacher, Joaquin, displays irreproachable conduct towards her. He never takes advantage of the distortion of values in a young girl, who more than anything else is looking for a father figure and wants to ensure a home for herself, rather than a lover. He understands this situation and his conduct is that of a teacher, of a guide.

How do you see your films in the context of Venezuelan cinema?

It's something inscribed in the films of my generation. We belong to the generation of 1968, a politicized generation, committed to the conviction that social and economic changes are possible and for that reason we reflect polemical themes in our films, protests and paths that we could follow.

I see that you had to use a Spanish actor — in this case a very good one. But has this distorted your way of representing reality, or rather opened up greater possibilities?

In the Venezuelan National System of Children's and Young People's Orchestras there are many teachers who come from other countries to give classes to children, enthused by the reach of this important project. Many of them work for nothing. *Maroa* is a co-production with Spain. In accordance with the commitments of international co-production we are obliged to include a leading actor from the co-producing country. These are rules that were established many years ago. This was influential in the teacher's nationality being Spanish. *Maroa* pays homage to these teachers, who work every day with difficult children, with kids who lack the most elemental discipline, with monastic patience, and get paid extremely low salaries. These are people with great mystique, who believe in what they do.

Maroa *has been criticized for its very lack of violence: that you are dealing with a social environment but without showing the worst of its consequences. Is this a just commentary?*

In first-world countries, where I have shown the film and I have been present to talk to the public, the shock at the violence that is a part of life in Venezuela has been generalized. We who live in Latin America face the great danger of becoming used to everyday violence, which marks relations between parents and children, between couples, between drivers in traffic and between the forces of law and order and civil society.

Is there a lack of violence in the scene that shows police interrogation of a young girl?

Is there a lack of violence in the treatment of a grandmother's treatment of a child exploited for work?

Is there a lack of violence in an 11-year-old girl selling pornography?

Is there a lack of violence in an 11-year-old girl being illiterate?

Is there a lack of violence in an 11-year-old kid dying from drugs?

If this is not violence and they want scenes with shootouts, let them see some other film...

Analysis

Solveig Hoogesteijn maintains that child sexuality and its exploitation is not a theme of *Maroa*, but should we take this at face value? The sequence in C9 of the DVD acts as a kind of catharsis to the events preceding it, and brings to a head some of the latent emotion that has been causing evident unease to Joaquín. Maroa narrowly escapes from sexual abuse by the police officer Ezequiel in C3. There are also numerous visual inferences to Maroa's precocious sexuality, such as the phallic form of the food she is seen eating. The close-up of her ice cream in C5 is one example: in C8, we observe the shape of the sandwich Maroa is eating when she replies to his fatherly question, "What am I going to do with you?" with "Easy: I'll clean for you, wash and cook, and you screw me."[4] This time Joaquín laughs, albeit nearly choking on his cigarette. But in C9, when she appears in his bedroom dressed and made up to seduce, there is tension created by the camera's dwelling on his face, making the viewer wonder what Joaquín is thinking. He proves to have been wondering about her future and how he can protect her, when he tells her to change and gets off the bed.

We might look at the sequence's initial shot, of Maroa's naked feet, in view of the words of Luis Espinal: "The selection of the cinematic frame does not resemble the selection made by our gaze in real life. The selection of our gaze does not have defined outlines or a precise limit."[5]

So this shot, which pans up the girl's legs to end, disconcertingly, upon the face of a child, imposes its image upon the viewer. This is simultaneously presented as our own viewpoint and that of the other character present — Joaquín, the intended spectator or "audience" for Maroa's performance. Later, when she enters to sleep on the floor, the strategy of filming her feet first is repeated, somewhat ironically since it reduces her from seductress to the far humbler role of child dragging a blanket, seeking a sense of security. The room is in darkness; Joaquín is asleep. Maroa sits momentarily on the edge of the bed before taking her place on the floor.

Linguistic Features

There is an obvious contrast between Maroa's Caracas street slang and the more educated tones used by the Spaniard Joaquín, though this is due more to social background than nationality (for example, he is amused by her erroneous spelling of "*ojos*" as "*ohos*"). In fact, not even the children use slang particularly heavy language, and the script contains less vulgarities and obscenities than everyday vernacular: "*¡qué molleja!*" (what a nerve), "*tombo*" (policeman), and "*epa*" (hi) are a few examples.

For Discussion

1. In what ways do classical and popular music interact in this film?
2. What does the graffiti tell us about the concerns of the local populace?
3. How do European and Latin American conceptions of life emerge from the dialogues between Maroa and Joaquín?
4. In view of Joaquín's responsible treatment of Maroa, is the fact that he accepts her "birthday present" entirely believable?

11. *Paloma de papel*
(Paper Dove)

CREDITS: Peru, 2003; *Produced by:* Luna Llena Films (coproducers: Ibermedia, ICAIC, USAID); *Director:* Fabrizio Aguilar; *Script:* Fabrizio Aguilar, Gianfranco Annichini; *Music:* Irene Vivanco; *Director of Photography:* Micaela Cajuaringa; 35 mm: 88 minutes

CAST: Juan (Antonio Callirgos), Viejo (Eduardo Cesti), Fermín (Aristóteles Picho), Domitila (Liliana Trujillo), Wilmer (Sergio Galliani), Yeni (Melania Urbina), Carmen (Tatiana Astengo)

Synopsis

Paloma de papel tells the story of Juan, a young Andean boy taken from his village by Shining Path guerrillas during the civil war that traumatized Peru, particularly in the 1980s and early '90s. It was filmed in the Callejón de Huaylas, an area of the central Peruvian Andes whose natural beauty nonetheless saw no little violence during the Shining Path years.

About the Film

Development and completion of *Paloma de papel* was made possible by a series of grants from the national film body CONACINE, as well as one from Ibermedia, in 2001. Aguilar's film won the Silver Precolumbian Circle at Bogotá, and the Golden Apple at New York's Latin American Cinema Festival, LaCinemaFe, both in 2004.

About the Film's Creators

Director Fabrizio Aguilar was born in Lima, Peru, in 1973. He studied communication at the Universidad de Lima. He is best known as an actor: he began in soaps (*telenovelas*) and has had roles in feature films such as *Muerto de amor* (Edgardo Guerra, 2000) and *Mercurio no es un planeta* (Alberto Chicho Durant, 2002). His most prominent role to date was as lead in Alberto Durant's *Doble juego* (*Con Game*, 2004) a film that criticizes the hypocrisy and materialism rife in Peru during the presidency of Alberto Fujimori. He also starred in *Both* (Lisset Barcellos, USA, 2005) a film about sexual identity shot in the San Francisco Bay area.

Fabrizio Aguilar on the set of *Paloma de papel* in September 2003. Still photography on theis film was by Loshua Flores Guerra, Adriana Navarro and Fernando Vega.

He has worked as assistant director both to Peruvian Francisco Lombardi (on *No se lo digas a nadie*) and Benito Zambrano (on *Sólas*).

Aguilar's second feature, *Tarata* (2009), also concerns the Shining Path: here, it looks at the profound, varied and long-lasting effects of a bomb attack on a middle-class family in Lima. The film is based on a true event which occurred in Calle Tarata, Miraflores, in 1992.

For Cultural Understanding

SHINING PATH ON FILM

Peru is not one of the more prolific Latin American countries in terms of film production, but the relative prominence of the Sendero Luminoso (Shining Path) theme shows how deeply this episode has affected the nation's psyche. The virtual civil war that developed between this Maoist movement and the state claimed many lives (70,000 according to some estimates) and established an atmosphere of terror that continues to haunt the population. Some of these films approach the subject from a rural perspective, with some anthropological or "folkloric" insights attributable to the filmmakers' local origins, whilst other productions alternate between rural and urban settings.

Sarah Barrow has argued that "Peruvian cinema has never been greatly influenced by the major trends which made their mark elsewhere in Latin America" (2005, 51). It is true, for instance, that the major tendencies of the New Latin American Cinema never quite took hold in this country, reflecting a somewhat different political evolution exemplified by Shining Path's unique marriage of Maoism and Andean culture.

The conflict inevitably affected all social sectors, and consequently the fiction films[1] that deal with it all adopt a definite standpoint — though rarely open sympathy — for the guerrilla movement expressed on film. Many present the viewpoint of indigenous Andean communities ravaged by the conflict. Typically these communities are bled and intimidated as both rebel and military forces treat them as sources of food and logistical support. Both would demand their allegiance and suspect them, often with fatal consequences, of betrayal.

Fabrizio Aguilar's *Paper Dove* clearly belongs to this category. A similar tendency is displayed by Norwegian-born Marianne Eyde; her *Los ronderos* (*The Vigilantes*, 1987) focuses on the armed peasant groups founded in the late 1980s to combat cattle theft and other such abuses, rather than the Self-Defense Committees formed and armed on government initiatives to fight the Shining Path. However, the protagonist of *La vida es una sola* (*You Only Live Once*, 1993), not unlike Aguilar's Juan, is an indigenous girl taken from her community by the insurgents and estranged from her community. This film, as Barrow put it, "dared to show less sympathy for the military than for the rural communities caught up in violence with the Shining Path rebels" (ibid., 52). But not all films on the conflict with rural settings display an interest in indigenous concerns: the title of *Flor de retama* (*Broom Flower*, Martín Landeo, 2004) is that of a song emblematic of Ayacucho. The film supports an individualist viewpoint of those who fight "for their country" (i.e., against Shining Path). The owner of a hacienda, also named Flor de Retama, is in Lima when he receives a message that he must return to reestablish his authority in the Ayacucho area, which has now been "liberated" by the military. The prevailing stance of *Flor de retama* is that of landowners dispossessed by Shining Path, portrayed (through the protagonist Víctor) as benignly overseeing a bucolic world of contented country folk disrupted by the rebels. Resistance to the insurgency is seen through a Manichaean perspective that does nothing to help understand why the rebel movement arose in the first place.

Ni con Dios ni con el diablo (*Neither with God nor the Devil*, Nilo Pereira del Mar, 1990) achieves genuine tension as it follows the dual invasion of the Shining Path and the military into a remote village. Ancestral beliefs contrast with the stark realities as convincing depictions of rebel cruelties and recruitment of young men or boys result in the flight from the village. The film tells the fate of young Jeremías, summed up by Ricardo Bedoya (1995, 295) as "the forced migration to Lima undertaken by a young peasant who is displaced, thrown aside, uprooted from his land as a consequence of the war unleashed by the subversive movement Shining Path in the Peruvian Andes."[2] There are repeated reminders of the historical backdrop, the infamous and never satisfactorily resolved murder of journalists at Uchurracay in 1983. These events are the subject of *Mártires del Periodismo* (*Martyrs of Journalism*, authors and date not provided), presented as a reconstruction of the deaths at Uchurracay and purportedly based on the findings of the Truth and Reconciliation Committee set up in 2001.

An urban slant is provided in *Alias la Gringa* (Alberto Durant, 1986) which portrays a real-life criminal whose exploits gained him a certain popular notoriety. The scenes of his imprisonment in the notorious island jail of El Frontón are made more interesting by the inclusion of Shining Path inmates and their uneasy coexistence with the common prisoners. At issue during the film's exhibition in countries remote from Peru was its image of the rebels, at odds with the somewhat romantic image often cherished by the left. Durant told me: "Abroad they bothered me a lot. At every screening they would get up and argue that my portrayal of [the rebels] was very schematic, a caricature. But in Lima people told me that I had done a very good job, that's just how they were"[3] (personal communication, February 2001). Central to the film is the ironic situation of an unassuming linguistics professor, imprisoned on trumped-up charges of terrorism yet unable to tolerate the slogans and uncritical dogma beloved of his fellow inmates.

Another Durant film, *Coraje* (*Courage*, 1998) is a biopic of María Teresa Moyano (1958–1992), the activist and representative of Lima's shantytown dwellers who came to represent dignity in adversity and non-violence among Peru's poor. Moyano's position resulted in her savage murder by the Shining Path. Rare interest taken in South American political life is shown in *The Dancer Upstairs* (Spain/USA 2002, the directorial debut of John Malkovich), which stars Javier Bardem as the policeman who tracked down the Shining Path leader and ideologue, Abimael Guzmán.

Augusto Tamayo's *Anda, corre, vuela* (*Go, Run, Fly*, 1995) unites two characters from previous films by the Chaski collective, *Gregorio* (1985) and *Juliana* (1988), sadly not repeating their commercial success. Here, their story takes on a political dimension as they are accused of terrorism, but resolve this situation in far too easy a fashion to be credible or dramatically satisfying: Fernando de Cárdenas (1995, 95), for instance, decries the "incredible ease with which both protagonists surmount obstacles."[4]

Some of the filmmakers who had been involved in making films about indigenous culture and reality in the Andes also took on the theme of Shining Path. In Federico García Hurtado's *La lengua de los zorros* (*The Language of Foxes*, 1992), a mountaineer comes to face both the threat of the rebel presence and the locals' suspicion that, as an outsider, he incarnates the *pishtaco*, mythical thief of human eyes and organs.

Gritos de libertad (*Cries of Freedom*, Luis Berrocal, 2003) is an example from Ayacucho of the kind of low-budget, provincial, full-length video cinema becoming ever more common in Latin America. A collaboration between several communities that suffered violence at the hands of both rebels and military, particularly between 1987 and 1991, it curiously uses voiceover commentary from the female leader of the Shining Path unit. The rebel viewpoint is only temporarily expressed, though: a message of recognition appears for the *Rondas Campesinas* and their role in ridding the area of violence. Neither does the film shrink from showing the abuses committed by the military. Particularly affecting is the real-life footage of women speaking in Quechua as they survey the bodies of soldiers killed by Shining Path. Some express pity, others offer a reminder that these people also made them suffer.

Peru's best-known and most successful director, Francisco Lombardi, was also drawn to this theme. His *La boca del lobo* (*In the Mouth of the Wolf*, 1989) uses as its protagonist

Aguilar's film is one of several to examine the effect of the armed struggle on childhood. Still photography on theis film was by Loshua Flores Guerra, Adriana Navarro and Fernando Vega.

a young recruit from Lima sent to the country's most troubled area, the environs of the Andean city of Ayacucho. The film is set during the early 1980s, when, as the film's introductory notes point out, the conflict was entering one of its worst eras — its "Dirty War" phase. Lombardi establishes a sense of total alienation between the villagers and military, with only the most basic contact, even at the linguistic level. This tension is heightened by the rebels' graffiti and other vestiges of a shadowy threat that never becomes a visible presence. The young soldiers are besieged by anxieties: the culture shock they experience in their own country is exacerbated by the unseen enemy. When the new commander arrives as replacement for a lieutenant killed by the Shining Path, he brings with him a macho code that in these circumstances is devastating.

Jim Finn's *La trinchera luminosa del Presidente Gonzalo* (*The Shining Trench of Chairman Gonzalo*, USA, 2007) is set inside Canto Grande, a Peruvian women's jail which has a special block for Shining Path prisoners, in 1989. It is an example of Finn's idiosyncratic and engaging style: combining faux-documentary, dramatic reconstruction and satire to explore the ritual, quasi-religious aspects of Shining Path's dogma and iconography.

The most celebrated film concerning Shining Path's psychological effects is Claudia Llosa's *La teta asustada* (*The Milk of Sorrow*, 2009) which builds upon anthropological findings by the Yale scholar Kimberly Theidon on the prevalence of rape on all sides in the conflict as a war strategy. Llosa's film addresses the stigma attached to children who are products of rape, concentrating on the case of a young woman who, besides, is part of a culturally and physically uprooted community that has moved to Lima to escape the violence.

An Email Conversation with Director Fabrizio Aguilar

The first thing I asked Fabrizio Aguilar about his film had to do with the choice of non-professional actors. Several of the actors in *Paper Dove* are well-known professionals, but were there also amateurs, "*naturales*." Aguilar explained that the amateurs were mostly the kids. The production team made an open call for young actors and looked at more than 500 children in a selection process that lasted over five months. Twelve were chosen to take part in a training workshop, from which emerged Antonio Calligros (Juan, the protagonist) and his three companions. Other natural actors were the film's extras; these were local inhabitants who had never even been near a film set.

There have been a number of other films on the same theme: I asked Aguilar how he saw *Paper Dove* in this context, and what his film brought to the subject that the others lacked. This was answered with a rebuttal — he had never set out to make such a comparison, but rather to tell a crude and violent story through the eyes of a child. This was the most distinctive element in *Paper Dove*. The auteur makes films also to show something of himself, rather than to think in terms of other people's work.

The persistence of the Shining Path theme brings to mind Argentina, where films are still being made about the repression of the 1970s. Aguilar believes and hopes that the same will apply in Peru. Seventeen years of war, during which an entire generation suffered, and there were many thousands of victims killed and disappeared, cannot and should not be forgotten. The marks, scars and wounds remain as testimony to this bloody past. It is Aguilar's hope that such films will continue to be made, and with higher narrative and cinematographic standards than before. In fact, he was working on a new project (*Tarata*) concerning the same era and social conflict, but this time set in the capital.

Another Peruvian, Francisco Lombardi, was criticized for what some saw as sympathy for Shining Path in his *La boca del lobo* (*In the Mouth of the Wolf*, 1989). Aguilar, though, had no such problem. Firstly he had tried to make a film approaching the more human side of the issue: "It's an exaggeration to say that if I show a Shining Path member crying, eating or laughing, then I am *pro-Sendero*; these are beings every bit as human and Peruvian as the rest of us, but with extreme ideological differences. My objective was not to demonize them but even less to glorify them. They started off this violent lunacy, which later spread through the Peruvian army."

Indeed, what the film's audience in Peru saw was the suffering of a populace caught between a rock and a hard place — the army and the rebels. This population, particularly in the Andes, was forced to flee in order to avoid being wiped out.

However, there was a contrasting reaction at the Mar del Plata festival in Argentina, where a large proportion of the press considered the film to be fascist. This was because it allegedly hadn't given sufficient space to military abuses, and what few soldiers there were had been given too human a depiction. Aguilar saw this as curious but understandable: if the Argentines saw *Paper Dove* from this perspective, it is because military violence towards the civilian population is so prominent in Argentine history.

As for the question of sources, *Paper Dove* was based not so much on literary or testimonial works but rather on data from psychological research done on children abducted by Shining Path. This showed what their lives had been like inside the group. In fact, after having written the script, he found the story of a girl that closely resembled that of his protagonist Juan, demonstrating *Paper Dove*'s closeness to reality.

Analysis: Temporal Frequency

We can consider the beginning and end of *Paloma de papel* in the light of David Bordwell and Kristin Thompson's words on temporal frequency; the repetition of the same event during narration is one of "the various ways that a film's plot may manipulate story order, duration, and frequency illustrate how the spectator must actively participate in making sense of the film" (Bordwell and Thompson 1997, 98).

Whilst Aguilar's film is not a complex narrative, it repeats a scene at the beginning and end. Effectively, the narrative is a flashback recounting Juan's childhood memories.

For Bordwell and Thompson (ibid., 99):

> A film does not just start, it *begins*. The opening provides a basis for what is to come and initiates us into the narrative. Typically, the plot will seek to arouse curiosity by bringing us into a series of actions that has already started. This is called opening *in medias res*, a Latin phrase meaning "in the middle of things." The viewer speculates on possible causes of the events presented. Typically, some of the actions that took place before the plot started will be stated or suggested so that we can start to connect up the whole story.

Aguilar's film begins, accordingly, with a slow tracking shot over photographic portraits attached to an adobe wall (these include Juan, his parents and his friend the old blacksmith) as we hear the off-screen sound of a violin. We become aware that this is a commemoration of the dead or disappeared as a woman puts up another photo, followed by shots of villagers kneeling outside a ruined church and lighting candles. The next shot (separated by credits against a black screen) is that of hands making a paper bird, followed by a cut to Juan as a boy being taken from his bunk and led out (more credits). A temporal jump shows adult hands also making a bird, then Juan as a young man, descending alone from the bunk and saying goodbye. As he leaves jail, others in his position are able to tell their stories to the press. He is the only one to receive no attention from the reporters, a fact that begs the question, why he has been in jail? This allows the spectator to begin making sense of what, from this point until almost the end, becomes a linear narrative entering what Bordwell and Thompson describe thus:

> The portion of the plot that sets out story events and character traits important in the opening situation is termed the *exposition*. In general, the opening raises our expectations by setting up a specific range of possible cause for and effects of what we see [ibid., 99].

The beginning is echoed, but not replicated, in the final chapter, which shows Juan as a boy being led to his bunk, followed immediately by a shot of the bus that returns him to his village as a young man. Juan begins his descent to the village with his back to camera: a reverse shot from downhill shows him framed by ruined houses and eventually by the harp. Finally, there is the recognition by his childhood friends and embrace.

These shots of Juan at the beginning and end of his incarceration provide the framework within which to understand the tragedy.

Linguistic Features

One minor criticism of *Paloma de papel* is that not all the characters' accents and use of language are typical of the Andean region. Yeni and the old blacksmith are two supposedly Andean individuals played by actors who betray their Lima origins. The setting is not specified, but the film was shot in the central Peruvian valley known as the Callejón de Huaylas, a region where the indigenous Quechua language is barely spoken. Little Quechua is heard in the film, though in C12 a boy sings a song in that language.

For Discussion

1. What are the advantages of using a child protagonist in presenting this kind of subject matter?
2. In what ways do children and old people interact in this film?
3. How, and to what effect, are the village and its community constructed?
4. The Cuban documentarist Santiago Álvarez (cited in Grupo Rev(b)elando Imágenes 2008, 132) denies the existence of objectivity. "I don't believe there's any cinema in this world that is not subjective and political."[5] Would you agree, given the content and presentation of these films on childhood?

12. Women Protagonists in Latin American Film

The three films closely examined in this section are all by women directors and represent female characters in various types and conditions of marginalization. Beatriz Flores Silva's *En la puta vida* looks at women in a situation of near-slavery; Guita Schyfter's *Novia que te vea* sees young Jewish women in 1930s Mexico escaping oppressive stereotypes; Suzana Amaral's protagonist in *A hora da estrela* is viewed in the context of urban migration, a perennial theme in Brazilian cinema.

This chapter gives as informative an overview as possible of a vast subject, concentrating not so much on the increasing participation of women in Latin American cinema as the representation of female protagonists. In looking at key feminine roles, not only in individual films but in the history of cinema in the region, I take into account work by both female and male filmmakers. If it is true that today there are more central female roles than ever before, it is also the case that these roles have diversified and are less dependent on the representation of heterosexual relationships, or of women in relation to men.

Paul Julian Smith (1989, 177) suggests a parallel between patriarchy's imposition of language upon women and the dominance of European tongues in Latin America. This need to find expression within another's frame of reference recalls the enslaved Caliban in Shakespeare's *The Tempest*, where he uses the "gift" of language from his master Prospero to curse the giver. The Cuban scholar Roberto Fernández Retamar's adoption of Caliban as representative of the Caribbean (in preference to the more sophisticated but obedient Ariel) reflects a will to subvert and adapt the former colonial languages to suit Latin America's own ends. This chapter will look at similar challenges to stereotypes in the case of women and film language, examining a recent diversification of women's acting roles and positions in filmmaking. How far have women's roles developed since the New Latin American Cinema movement began in the late 1960s? Was "old" cinema dictated purely by dualities? To what extent is it true that reality itself, as well as film, is offering greater possibilities for women? Can we necessarily divide films by women from those of male authorship? And does this opening out in thematic terms necessarily mean a true and fair portrayal? In any case, is it valid to measure films against their supposed referent in reality?

If the most important divas of Mexico's 1930s–'50s "Golden Age," such as María Félix and Dolores del Río, were subject to typecasting and manipulation, much the same applied to Latin American women in Hollywood. Helena Solberg Ladd's *Carmen Miranda: Bananas Is My Business* (UK/Brazil, 1995) examines the construction of the screen persona of this Portuguese-born "Brazilian bombshell" and the use of this calculated exoticism for political ends. It is difficult to talk in similar terms of today's counterparts, since the relative lack of studio hype and censorship means lesser public exposure but far greater creative possibilities.

Argentine Ana Katz, for example, is so far one of few Latin American women to write, direct and act in the same film, *Una novia errante* (*A Wandering Bride*, 2007), while Mexican Salma Hayek produced as well as starred in Julie Taymor's *Frida* (USA, 2002). The fine Brazilian actress Fernanda Torres is also known for her activities in writing and production.

An important development has been the possibility of prolonged acting careers for women, who may now work at an advanced age without being constrained to the kind of long-suffering grandmother role epitomized by Sara García (1895–1980) in innumerable Mexican films. As Ana M. López points out (1993, 149) the Argentine one-time tango singer Libertad Lamarque turned actress in Mexico with great success, but was also cornered into portrayals of martyred motherhood. In contrast the Uruguayan China Zorrilla (b. 1922), Brazilian Fernanda Montenegro (b. 1929) and Argentine Norma Leandro (b. 1936) are recent examples of women acting well beyond their more glamorous years and in central roles arguably more complex and interesting than in their youth (though arguably these later roles also entail stereotypes and pitfalls). Zorrilla, in the romantic comedy *Elsa y Fred* (Marcos Carnevale, Argentina/Spain, 2005), plays a geriatric lover whose refusal to grow old gracefully crystallizes in her reenactment of Anita Ekberg's Fontana Trevi scene from Fellini's *La dolce vita*. Zorrilla played a not dissimilar role in Carlos Galettini's *Besos en la frente* (*Kisses on the Forehead*, Argentina, 1996), though here the love is unrequited, for a man some 60 years her junior. Among the lead roles created for a mature Leandro is that of a middle-class woman in *Cama adentro* (*Live-in Maid*, Jorge Gaggero, Argentina, 2004) whose relationship with her home help shifts revealingly against the background of the early 2000s economic crisis. Eduardo Mignogna's *Cleopatra* (2003) presents another unlikely friendship, between Leandro's slightly senile elderly woman and a much younger soap opera star, with whom she embarks on a trip outside Buenos Aires. Montenegro reached an international audience in her 70s with her far-from-grandmotherly role in Walter Salles's *Central do Brasil* (*Central Station*, 1998).

Exoticism and the Erotic

To quote Michael Chanan, "The very idea of the exotic is a creation of imperialism. It expresses the point of view of the metropolis toward its periphery. The concept of exoticism identifies the gulf between the self-proclaimed civilization of the metropolis and ways of life beyond it: primitive societies full of strange and unfamiliar features, the stranger the more interesting" (Chanan 2004, 44). Accordingly, Latin American women in Hollywood were codified in terms of a sexuality that may be tamed, but whose allure lay in the potential danger it presented. Ana M. López (1993, 2000) has looked at the carefully manipulated Hollywood careers of women such as Dolores del Río, Carmen Miranda, and Lupe Vélez, especially during the Good Neighbor era (see also Shaw and Conde 2005). López traces shifts in depictions of Latin America through its personification by Miranda, Del Río, Vélez and others.

Latin America also provided sex symbols for its own consumption — though, as in the example of Argentina's Isabel Sarli, not necessarily exotic figures. Mexican cinema's Golden Age saw imports from other areas of Latin America, as López (1993, op. cit.) shows in her work on Libertad Lamarque and the Cuban Ninón Sevilla. Ethnicity can be a powerful ingredient of sexual projection: Alison Fraunhar (2006, 160–179) argues that the Cuban *mulata* (mix of African and European) can be exotic in her own country, whilst simultaneously serving as national allegory. Fraunhar talks of Cuba's "complex and unstable relations of race and identity" (161) which are clearly visible in Chijona's *Un Paraíso*. Stephanie Dennison (2006, 135–146) investigates mixed ethnicity in a Brazilian film context, where Sônia Braga's *mulata* features have been a factor in her image of sexual availability, prowess and seductiveness. That Braga's racial mix is also a construction (Dennison explores the calculated "Africanization" of her image) is attributed both to White male preference for the *mulata* woman over other ethnic types, and Brazilian national myths of racial democracy.

The vexed issue of the representation of indigenous women's sexuality, particularly in the conquest and colonization of Brazil, is visited in films such as Lúcia Murat's *Brava gente brasileira* (*Brave New Land*, Brazil, 2000) where female seduction of early Portuguese male colonists is a potent political and strategic weapon. The theme is variously treated in previous Brazilian films such as Nelson Pereira dos Santos's *Como Era Gostoso o Meu Francês* (*How Tasty Was My Little Frenchman*, 1971) and Luiz Alberto Pereira's *Hans Staden* (1999).

Another interesting case of filmic combinations of femininity and ethnicity is the work of Peruvian Claudia Llosa, whose largely passive female protagonist in *Madeinusa* (2005) is moved by male counterparts and male-created conditions. Llosa's second feature, *La teta asustada* (*The Milk of Sorrow*, Peru, 2008), nevertheless provides far greater sensitivity and concern for cultural accuracy, as well as a more provocative and complex female protagonist representative of a reality exclusive to Indian female victims of sexual abuse from both army and rebels in Peru's Sendero Luminoso civil conflict. Based on a far-reaching anthropological study[1] of the phenomenon, this portrayal of a traumatized and stigmatized young Andean woman is notable for its radical narrative form, striking imagery and cinematic treatment of feminine sensibility.

Women characters can be used as emblems of adversity; the evicted and abducted Mapuche woman in *Gerónima* (Raúl Tosso, Argentina, 1986), for instance, typifies her people's fate. Luis Ramiro Beltrán, scriptwriter of the pioneering Bolivian fiction-documentary *Vuelve Sebastiana*, told me (personal communication, November 2010) that the notion of using a child protagonist originated with the Chipaya community itself. The anecdote was still being told of a young girl who, some years previously, had wandered off to an Aymara village, causing no little annoyance locally. Director Jorge Ruiz, Beltrán and cinematographer Augusto Roca eventually agreed to use the story, for its allegorical force and humanity. Casting consisted of a visit to the local school where Ruiz chose Sebastiana Kespi, who proved so convincing in the title role.

In the case of *Coraje* (*Courage*, Alberto Durant, Peru, 1998) iconicity stems from a far more active real-life role, that of shantytown dwellers' leader María Elena Moyano in her principled resistance to both Shining Path guerrillas and corrupt state authority.

Undoubtedly, transformations in views of women's positions began to emerge in the so-called New Latin American Cinema movement. If Fraunhar (2005, 160) asserts that female perspectives, especially those of black females, were omitted in Cuban 3rd Cinema, nonetheless one of the most penetrating studies of women's position in Latin American society came from this era. *De cierta manera* (*One Way or Another*, 1977) by the iconic black Cuban woman director Sara Gómez, incorporates questions of gender into a frank examination of a working-class community's revolutionary preparation. As John King puts it (1990, 159) the film "deals quietly and sensitively with workers' responsibilities and with machismo: a very considerable achievement." Tomás Gutiérrez Alea, ever the iconoclastic poser of awkward but constructive questions, probed the limits and sincerity of the liberal mentality among men in the new society. His similarly titled *Hasta cierto punto* (*Up to a*

Point, 1983) takes up the issue of machismo in a context of class difference in a response and homage to Gómez's film. The protagonist, a filmmaker, wants to reasearch machismo among dockworkers but is forced to come to terms with contradictions in his own position when he becomes romantically involved with one of the female workers. As Zuzana Pick argues, this film "emerges simultaneously from the relative stability of production methods and the changing demands made upon creative activity by the Cuban Revolution" (1993, 49). The repeated contrast between the realities of filmmaking and work on the docks runs parallel to this vision of gender relations as part of a social fabric that, according to Gutierrez Alea's version of the revolutionary view, is perpetually to be questioned. Another crucial Cuban film from this period is Humberto Solás's *Lucía* (1969) conceived as three characters having in common not only a name but a role in socially turbulent key historical moments, and each, as Donelan argues, (1993, 3) offering a parallel "between the subordination of women to men and Cuba to colonizing influences."

Some European or US directors show Latin American women in other social and geographical contexts, particularly emigrants: *Princesas* (Fernando León de Aranoa, 2005) deals largely with the fate of Latin American women involved in prostitution in Spain. *Tráfico de mujeres* (*Trade*, Marco Kreuzpaintner, Germany/USA, 2007) concerns kidnapped Mexican girls forced into prostitution in the USA. Fina Torres's comedy *Mecánica celeste* (*Celestial Clockwork*, Spain/Venezuela, 1995) looks at a a runaway would-be opera singer escaping from marriage in Venezuela among a community of Latina women in Paris. *Quinceañera* (Richard Glazer and Wash Westmoreland, USA, 2006) explores a young Latina's options in L.A. as she faces an unwanted pregnancy. Other noteworthy examples of Latina protagonists in the US are Alison Anders's portrayal of Chicana women in *Mi vida loca* (*My Crazy Life*, 1993) and *How the García Girls Spent Their Summer* (Georgina Riedel, 2005).

Latin American Women as Directors

Women directors not profiled in this book who have established a niche in recent years include Mexico's María Novaro and Busi Cortés, Argentines Lucrecia Martel, Lucía Puenzo, Albertina Carri, and Ana Katz, Brazilians Lúcia Murat, Carla Camurati and Tizuka Yamasaki, and the Peruvian Claudia Llosa. To date, however, the Argentine María Luisa Bemberg (1922–1995) is generally acknowledged as the outstanding Latin American woman filmmaker. She made six films as director, beginning when almost 50 when she ceased to be purely a scriptwriter and entered a world described by John King as "almost entirely bereft of women as directors or producers" (King 2000, 16). Significantly, she was spurred into direction by feeling that a male director betrayed her first script.

Bemberg's most famous film, *Camila* (1984), tells the story of Camila O'Gorman, a young woman from a wealthy landowning family who scandalized mid–nineteenth-century Argentina, then under the tyranny of Juan Manuel de Rosas, by eloping with a Catholic priest. The film alludes both to contemporary women's issues, and the repression and stifling conformity under a totalitarianism from which Argentina had just emerged. Its use of melodrama, not often considered a radical aesthetic, was explained by Bemberg as a way to "really hit the audience in the heart and in the pit of their stomach" (Whitaker 1988, p. 117). Bemberg was also interested in the role reversal by which a woman "corrupts" a man (a priest, to boot) through seizing the sexual initiative. (Her *Yo la peor de todas* is discussed in the chapter "Writers as Characters.") The theme of female sexuality as socially intolerable is aired through two biographies of historical "libertine" figures; *Teresa, crucificada por amar* (Tatiana Gaviola, Chile, 2009) and *Felicitas* (Teresa Constantini, Argentina, 2009).

The recent tendency among both female and male filmmakers to present flawed, complex female characters has produced some interesting results, supporting a view that to idealize women or cast them as inevitable victims is counterproductive and delusory. Two films by Argentine Alejandro Chomski are noteworthy here; *Hoy y manana* (*Today and Tomorrow*, 2003) portrays one such self-destructive protagonist, and *A Beautiful Life* (set and made in the US) sees women contributing to their own subjugation, as a mother, intimidated by her husband and fearful of losing him, "gives" him her daughter for sexual gratification. The surprising and entirely convincing protagonist of the remarkable *Anita* (Marcos Carnevale, Argentina, 2009) is a young woman with Down's Syndrome. Ana Katz's films, *El juego de la silla* (*Musical Chairs*, Argentina, 2002) and *Una novia errante* (*A Wandering Bride*, Argentina, 2007) explore the foibles of, respectively, an insufferable mother and a neurotic lover. Another woman writer and director celebrated for such groundbreaking achievements is the Argentine Lucrecia Martel, whose *La mujer sin cabeza* (*The Headless Woman*, Argentina, 2008) looks at the psychological effects on a woman of an incident which she colors according to her own perceptions and preconceptions. In *Las mantenidas sin sueños* (*Kept and Dreamless*, Martín De Salvo and Vera Fogwill, Argentina, 2005), an irresponsible mother is looked after by her resourceful young daughter in a relationship that is presented dispassionately but never seen as other than dysfunctional. Another Argentine portrayal of women relatives in intractable relationships is *Monoblóc* (Luis Ortega, Argentina, 2005). *La Nana* (*The Maid*, Sebastián Silva, Chile, 2009) examines the psychology and social structure of servitude via rivalries in a middle-class household.

The jailed protagonist of Pablo Trapero's *Leonera* (2008) must contend not only with pregnancy in prison, but also with her mother's hostile interpretation of its consequences. Women protagonists are often placed in adverse circumstances which they are challenged to overcome using not just courage and strength but also creativity. This applies to two films by Brazilian (male) director Andrucha Waddington: *Eu, tu, eles* (*Me, You, Them*, 2000) and *Casa de areia* (*House of Sand*, 2005). *María llena eres de gracia* (*Maria Full of Grace*, Joshua Marston, USA/Colombia, 2004) traces a similar situation in the context of drug-trafficking. In *Mujeres insumisas* (*Untamed Women*, Alberto Isaac, Mexico, 1995) a group of wives respond collectively to their husbands' abuse and neglect by simply leaving en masse for new horizons. The comedy *Kada Kien su Karma* (*Each to His Karma*, Leon Serment, Mexico, 2008) sees a jilted wife bent on vengeance against her wayward husband. *Traspatio* (*Backyard*, Carlos Carrera, Mexico, 2009) is a harrowing dramatization of the murder of women in the border city of Ciudad Juárez, linking these to political and economic interests in the area, and offering a reminder that the problem is not limited to northern Mexico, nor indeed to Latin America.

More and more films see female characters appearing (or being thrust into) situations associated stereotypically with masculinity. Among these are participation in violence and life with its consequences. *La negra Angustias* (*Black Angustias*, Matilde Landeta, Mexico, 1950) highlights an outstanding figure in the Mexican Revolution who was not only female but black. These characters are not necessarily heroic: Aluizinho Abranches's *As três Marias* (*The Three Marias*, 2005), set in north-eastern Brazil, adopts a similar revenge theme to that of Walter Salles's *Abril despedaçado* (*Behind the Sun*, Brazil, 1999). Here, though, the feud is sparked and gruesomely maintained by women. *Anahy de las Misiones* (Sérgio Silva, Brazil, 1997) focuses upon the matriarchal head of an itinerant family that makes a picaresque living scavenging nineteenth-century battlefields, and living with the consequences of death until the loss of her son causes Anahy's carefully maintained mask of impassivity to fall.

Films concerning politically active women include *María Cano* (Camila Loboguerrero, Colombia, 1990), a biography of the well-known activist, a film hampered by an aesthetic conservatism that belies its subject matter. Tizuka Yamasaki's *Parahyba mulher macho* (*Parahyba, a Strong Woman*, Brazil, 1983) looks at the relationship between libertine poet-revolutionary Anayde Beiriz and her activist lover in the 1920s and '30s. Jayme Monjardim's *Olga* (Brazil, 2004) is the true story of Jewish socialist and activist Olga Benário, a German-Brazilian socialist whose commitment led her to Europe and anti–Nazi participation in World War II. Her story questions the true place of Jewish women in Latin American nationhood, and suggests collaboration with the Nazis by Brazilian president Getúlio Vargas, who overlooked Benário's pregnancy and extradited her to Germany. *Norma Arrostito, la Gaby* (Luis César D'Angiolillo, Argentina, 2008) is a documentary that uses both actual and fictional footage to create a portrait of one of the military dictatorship's most implacable, controversial and iconic opponents.

Women have also begun to have a stake in traditionally male genres, particularly in buddy/road movies such as *Sin dejar huella* (*Without a Trace*, María Novaro, Mexico, 2000), *Qué tan lejos* (*How Much Further*, Tania Hermida, Ecuador, 2006) and the above-mentioned *Cleopatra*.

Mexican director Jaime Humberto Hermosillo's films specialize in women ingeniously bypassing and dodging patriarchy's inherent contradictions. For example *De noche vienes, Esmeralda* (*Esmeralda, You Come by Night*, 1997) adapts a story by Elena Poniatowska of a cheerfully defiant polygamist who ultimately confounds and seduces the judge intent on her downfall. The protagonist of *Doña Herlinda y su hijo* (*Doña Herlinda and Her Son*, 1985) engineers a solution to the impossibility of her gay son being accepted in his profession.

Female characters as allegories of national or continental realities are seen by Marvin D'Lugo as an "indelible constant" (D'Lugo 280) in his examination of Cuban revolutionary films such as the aforementioned *Lucía*. Other examples include the emblematic Jewish women in *Novia que te vea*. *Sonhos tropicais* (*Tropical Dreams*, André Sturm, Brazil, 2001) opens with the arrival in Rio de Janeiro in 1899 of Esther, a young Jewish woman from Poland typical of many at the time, deceived by the promise that she will meet her betrothed upon arrival, but instead forced into prostitution.

Jorge Bodanzky and Orlando Senna's *Iracema — Uma Transa Amazônica*[2] (Brazil/West Germany/France, 1976) uses its prostituted young protagonist (her name a clear anagram of "America") to allegorize the violation of Amazonia. To some extent Macabéa in *The Hour of the Star* is representative, as Suzana Amaral claims, of her country. Raúl Tosso's *Gerónima* provides a Mapuche female to signify her nation's exploitation in past and present. Juan Carlos Desanzo's *Eva Perón* (Argentina, 1996) is a biography of one of Argentina's most revered political figures, made in response to the perceived insult of Alan Parker's 1996 *Evita*, shot in Buenos Aires but with a cast of outsiders (most controversially, Madonna in the title role).[3] Desanzo instead casts the gaunt, spiky Esther Goris as clearly oppositional to the packaged Madonna. Goris simultaneously portrays Eva's vulnerability and power; despite her terminal cancer she appears standing over gatherings of seated male party members, holding her own in political discussion.

The representation of female indigenous figures can have national as well as ethnic dimensions. Andrea Noble's analysis of Emilio Fernández's *María Candelaria* (2005, 81–

91) argues that the protagonist, undeniably a semiotic embodiment of Mexico, is also inevitably an iconographical complex of pre– and post–Columbian associations including Indian princesses and the Virgin of Guadalupe. Noble argues that "the narrative syncretically encodes María Candelaria simultaneously as indigenous 'idol' and Catholic 'icon' precisely through her association with, and status as, a visual image" (ibid., 84–85). But this also has a gender dimension: "As the film evokes an originary colonial scenario, it also reproduces a time-honoured trope whereby Woman (in this case Indigenous Woman) functions as object-of-the-gaze thereby providing the grounds for an exchange of looks" (ibid., 85). At stake here is not just the confluence and clash of belief systems but also the use of the female face and body as the site for these interactions to take place.

Female characterization that depends neither on sexuality nor the representation of a collective entity is increasingly, if belatedly, visible. Latin American cinema is increasingly presenting feminine characters of interest for their own sake in filmic terms, as complex acting challenges and investigations of individual subjectivities (not without their sociopolitical relevance) rather than simply sexual objects, representations of collective identities, and national allegories.

13. *A hora da estrela*
(The Hour of the Star)

CREDITS: Brazil, 1985; *Produced by:* Raíz Produções; *Director:* Suzana Amaral; *Writing:* Suzana Amaral, Alfredo Oroz; *novel by Clarice Lispector; Music:* Marcus Vinicius; *Director of Photography:* Edgar Moura

CAST: Macabéa (Marcélia Cartaxo), Olímpico (José Dumont), Glória (Tamara Taxman), Madame Carlota (Fernanda Montenegro)

Synopsis

Macabéa is a shabby, unattractive young woman from the impoverished northeast of Brazil who is precariously employed in São Paulo as a typist, despite her minimal education and dire lack of social skills. Her self-definition is "I am a typist and a virgin, and I like Coca-Cola." She meets Olímpico, another outsider, but unlike her streetwise and opportunistic. They begin to spend time together in what is neither an affair nor truly a friendship, until social and personal pressures result in a curious dénouement.

About the Film

That the script for *A hora da estrela* took two years to write was due less to the rigors of what Suzana Amaral called a "transfiguration" of the original than to the fact that she was working at the time to earn the money to build a house. *The Hour of the Star* won the coveted Coral for best film at the Havana Film Festival in 1986 and was nominated as Brazil's Oscar entry for that year. It also won several awards: at the Berlin Film Festival (1985) Marcélia Cartaxo won the best actress award at for her first film role. Awards in Brasilia included recognition for the acting of Marcélia Cartaxo and José Dumont, as well as Suzana Amaral's direction.

About the Film's Creators

Suzana Amaral is a remarkable individual who embarked on a career as a television director at the age of 37, having had nine children. She made *A hora da estrela*, her first feature film, fifteen years later. Her second feature, *Uma vida em segredo* (*A Life in Secret*, 2002) was set in the nineteenth century and is another narrative of a lone woman's transition from rural to urban life. A man's solitary journey through Brazil in Amaral's most recent feature, *Hotel Atlântico* (2009), is a string of diverse encounters and discoveries, welcome or otherwise.

Clarice Lispector (1920–1977), one of Brazil's most celebrated writers, was born in the Ukraine and brought to Brazil when she was one year old to escape the persecution of Jews during the Russian Civil War of 1918–21. Lispector figured prominently in the research of French-Algerian writer and theorist Hélène Cixous, who considered her work a prime illustration of feminine writing.

For Cultural Understanding

Urban migration has surged enormously in Latin America since the middle of the twentieth century, bringing great changes of many kinds: ecological, political, and social as well as cultural. The region's population is now chiefly urban, and cultural identity inevitably changes. São Paulo, with over 11 million inhabitants, is the largest city in the Southern Hemisphere and most of its twentieth-century population increase is due to migration from the poorest areas of Brazil, above all the northeast.

Northeastern Brazil has always provided a source of mythology crucial to the national imaginary. This status was mined by some of the 1960s pioneers of Cinema Novo, the "New Cinema" tendency in Brazil that lasted between the 1950s and 1970s. Cinema Novo was an expression of the need for cultural renovation and social change, which saw numerous phases and relationships to political authority.

Tzvi Tal (2005, 86–90) discusses the use of the arid northeast as a metaphor for Brazil's political turbulence: "the image that reached prime position in Brazilian culture from the mid nineteenth century was the imaginary landscape of the Sertão, a region of the country's interior considered 'empty' of civilization and understood as antinomian to the temperate oceanic coasts"[1] (Tal 2005, 87–88).

The positivist opposition between city and provinces seen in Euclides da Cunha's novel *Os sertão* (*Rebellion in the Backlands*, 1902) evolved into a view of the region as site of Brazilian inequality and injustice. Even before Cinema Novo, the northeastern bandit or *Cangaçeiro* had been celebrated in numerous films (see Chapter 20, Fratricidal Wars and Imperialism). Nelson Pereira dos Santos, the director often considered the pioneer of Cinema Novo, made *Vidas secas* (*Barren Lives*, 1963), an adaptation of the novel by Graciliano Ramos about an indigent family desperately trying to survive in the northeast. Glauber Rocha, the most radical of Cinema Novo's auteurs, mobilized the region's folk tradition to narrate its rebellious history in *Deus e o diabo na terra do sol* (*God and the Devil in the Land of the Sun*, 1964) and *O dragão da maldade contra o santo guerreiro* (Antônio das Mortes, 1969). Ruy Guerra's *Os fuzis* (*The Guns*, 1964) tells a story of popular revolt against starvation. The northeast has not ceased to be a common source of material, as is seen by Rosemberg Cariry's portrayal of the outlaws *Corisco e Dadá* (1996) and Sérgio Rezende's *A guerra dos Canudos* (*The Battle of Canudos*, 1997) which deals with the same rebellion as the Euclides da Cunha novel.

But the issue of urban migration was less of a preoccupation for early Cinema Novo directors, who often couched social issues in metaphorical and poetic terms. Exceptions are Pereira dos Santos's *Rio 40 graus* (*Rio, 40 Degrees*, 1955) and Carlos Diegues's *Cinco vezes favela* (1962). Lúcia Nagib (2003, 158) has written of the "eternal return" in today's Brazilian cinema, repeatedly revisiting and re-exploring the dual themes of rural northeastern Sertão and urban *favela* as "two sides of the same coin."[2]

An Email Conversation with Director Suzana Amaral

Good-natured but notoriously laconic in discussing her work, Ms. Amaral describes herself as "minimalist" in her approach to interviews. I am grateful to her nonetheless for agreeing to offer the following insights. I began by suggesting that Clarice Lispector's *The Hour of the Star* perhaps hadn't been the most obvious book to adapt to the screen, with its ambiguous and introspective discourse. So why had she chosen this work?

She replied simply that she was living in New York, studying at NYU for a master's degree in film, when she "discovered Brazil outside of Brazil." She came across Lispector's book in the university library and, "with these two discoveries" resolved to make the film. When she got back to Brazil, she bought the rights and the film was born.

I somewhat recklessly inquired whether she had set out consciously to reproduce the "feminine writing" that's attributed to Lispector. Her reply seemed to imply that she had achieved the feat; "No, I didn't do it consciously. Maybe it was intuition ... inspiration ... how do I know...."

I was interested in the performance of Marcélia Cartaxo (who also appears in Aïnouz's *Madame Satã*) as practically perfect in the role of Macabéa. Could she tell me something about the process of choosing this actress, at that time almost unknown?

She explained that she had been consciously looking for someone new, looked in the strangest places, and in this way found her Macabéa. Amaral took it upon herself to make Cartaxo into an actress "because I am a good director of actors and I love them a lot. As a director I'm not afraid of them...."

I ventured that there are elements in her film that are almost constants in Brazilian cinema; contrast and complementarity between the northeast and the metropolis is one of these. Another is the alienation felt by provincials in the city. How did she decide to take on these themes in such an unusual way?

Her reply was that Brazilians live with that reality on a day-to-day basis; it was something impossible not to see. She had made a documentary[3] about people from the northeast around that time, so was able to observe their reality and simply reflect that.

Lispector saw Macabéa as a representative of Brazil: does Amaral agree, and did she set out to reproduce this figuration? For her, Macabéa was always a "photo" of Brazil, and of Brazilian people, at least in that era. "She doesn't act; she is acted upon by her surroundings."

Analysis: Transfiguration and Adaptation

However misleading and iniquitous it may be to judge film as some kind of bastard child of literature, in the case of literary adaptations we can often glean insights from the process of transferring ideas from page to screen. Suzana Amaral's decision to film this extraordinary short novel was a brave one, in various senses. Clarice Lispector is one of Brazil's most revered authors, and her book contains very little in the way of storyline, action or visual elements.

Of course, a filmmaker is under no obligation to be "faithful" to a literary source. Indeed, to cite perhaps the most celebrated example of Latin American adaptation, one could argue that it is the cineaste's duty to perform the "betrayal" that, as Cuban novelist Edmundo Desnoes admitted, saw his modest novel *Inconsolable Memories* transformed into one of the great Latin American films, Tomás Gutiérrez Alea's *Memorias del subdesarrollo* (*Memories of Underdevelopment*, Cuba, 1968). In the case of such sublime writing as Lispector's, though, the filmmaker is faced with a certain dilemma as to what to leave out or change. However, a director as confident as Suzana Amaral, even on her first feature, would not be overawed. Her admiration for Lispector was clearly a spur rather than a hindrance.

Nonetheless it is essential to be ruthless with elements deemed essentially literary, and Amaral omitted many of these, such as the book's long and tortuous beginning and life-affirming conclusion, both evidence of Lispector's awareness of the fact that she was dying: "I know well that every day is a day stolen from death," asserts the narrator (30). The film dispenses with the male creator/narrator, Rodrigo S. M., and his agonizing over how to begin. There are other problems in shedding this narrative presence: Maria José Somerlate Barbosa (1989, 237) sees him as "a character whose reflections and inquiries parallel Macabéa's tale, and the fact that he interweaves the narrative with the exposition of his own feelings point to the notion that he is Macabéa's voice." Hélène Cixous argued that only by adopting a male voice could Lispector bring Macabéa into existence, and that the adoption of a male narrator was the transfiguration itself.[4] Darlene J. Sadlier perceptively suggests that "even though the film has no exact equivalent to Rodrigo, it does have a kind of diegetic narrator, in the form of a radio announcer," a cue taken by Amaral from Lispector's own text with its numerous mentions of "Radio Relógio," which does survive into the film version.

Lispector/Rodrigo S. M. offers no less than nine alternative titles to the reader. One of these is "The Blame is Mine," which seemingly refers to the middle-class guilt experienced by someone like Lispector, but which is firmly rejected by Amaral in favor of an affectionately mocking attitude towards her protagonist, Macabéa. This echoes a line in the novel: "Well, it's true that neither do I have pity on my main character, the North-eastern girl: it's a narrative I want to be cold" (27). Another of the titles is "A Tearful Story of *Cordel*" which refers to the moralistic literature sold on strings (hence *cordel*) popular in northeastern Brazil, Macabéa's place of origin.

Amaral also applies humor to the mystical angle exemplified by Lispector's allusion, in the title itself, to metamorphosis in death. The film's ending can be seen as an ironic version of the "star" to which Lispector refers.

Amaral adapts Lispector's vision of the alienation experienced by Macabéa in a city not only indifferent but hostile to her.[5] However, Macabéa's childhood, sketched in the book, is left out of the film. With it go references to Jewish origins; Lispector was Jewish, and the name Macabéa is derived from the Maccabees, a book of the Old Testament. In Amaral's film, though, the name is simply another cause for ridicule, yet another outlandish aspect of this strange young woman who appears to have no cultural affiliation at all. Macabéa shows no awareness of the rich culture of northeastern Brazil, and if it is true, as Foster says, that she is formed by manifestations of popular culture, it should also be pointed out that these (radio, romantic love, a fortune-teller) are of a manufactured and vertically imposed nature, rather than a grassroots and collective form. Macabéa may be nationally representative, but not in the sense of orthodox patriotic glories; rather, she reflects inequality and deprivation — she is unable even to write her country's name correctly.

Perhaps the most significant change from book to film is the setting: Lispector set her novel in Rio, where she lived, making specific references to places in the city. Amaral has instead opted for São Paulo, completely removed from the stereotyped image of tropical *joie-de-vivre*, and conducive to the image of isolation created by Lispector. Solitude as an "American literary motif" as well as its existential companion, silence, are aspects of Lispector's work that have been explored by her main English-language scholar, Earl E. Fitz.[6]

If we look at an early scene from Marcel Camus' *Orfeu negro* (*Black Orpheus*, 1959), the contrast with Macabéa's early scene in São Paulo (some six minutes into the film) is complete. Camus's film has the beautiful Eurídice (like Macabéa, a young woman from the provinces) come off the ferry into Rio de Janeiro and is both fascinated and frightened by a gallery of faces in a riotous and exuberant city in full carnival, as men in the market vie for her attention. Macabéa's unattractiveness, on the other hand, has her fading into the equally drab surroundings of the industrial city.

David William Foster goes as far as to describe her ugliness as the "organizing principle of Amaral's film" (Foster 1999, 71–72). Foster highlights the film's undeniable political dimension, but *A hora da estrela* is far more than a social document; it is illuminated by other elements, such as the paradoxical humanism brought by Amaral from the novel, and above all the humor. The use of music (rhythmic and exuberant in Camus's film, stark and discordant in Amaral's) further conveys the respective positions of the protagonists.

Linguistic Features

Considering the importance of immigration from the northeast in this film, the northeastern accent is not particularly marked and is mixed with that of São Paulo. There are a number of everyday popular expressions such as:

- Puta show de bola: a vulgar way of saying "a great or unforgettable game of football [soccer]."
- Vai encher o saco da sua nega: "go and bother your whore"; in other words, "beat it."
- Fresco, bicha: vulgar, politically incorrect terms for homosexual.
- Macabéa, você é um cabelo na minha sopa, não da vontade de comer: A rather cruel insult — "you're a hair in my soup that takes away my appetite."
- Galega de farmácia (literally "pharmacist Galician woman") means a bottle-blonde.
- Cabeça chata ("square-head") refers to a northeasterner.
- Macumbeira is a person who practices Afro-Brazilian religious rites (macumbe).

For Discussion

1. Discuss issues of individual and cultural identity in both versions of *A hora da estrela*.
2. If *A hora da estrela* is a "distanced self-portrait" by Lispector (Hélène Cixous), how would you define Amaral's relationship to her film of the novel?
3. What is the importance of Lispector's male narrator and its absence from the film?
4. What is gained or lost through the use of São Paulo instead of Rio de Janeiro as setting for *A hora da estrela*?

5. Why does Suzana Amaral prefer the term "transfiguration" to "adaptation" in describing this film?

6. If Macabéa is a photograph of Brazil, as Amaral says, what image of the country is provided by *A hora da estrela*?

7. Fernão Ramos (1987, 450) has written of the "delicate balance between a social perspective and an intimate tone in delineating Macabéa, the northeastern girl."[7] Is this maintained by Amaral?

14. *En la puta vida*
(In This Tricky Life)

CREDITS: Uruguay, 2001; *Produced by:* Hubert Toint, Beatriz Flores Silva, Stefan Schmitz; *Director:* Beatriz Flores Silva; *Script:* Beatriz Flores Silva, János Kovásci; *Music:* Carlos da Silveira; *Cinematography:* Francisco Gozón

CAST: Elisa (María Santángelo), Plácido el Cara (Silvestre), Marcelo (Josep Linuesa), Lulú (Andrea Fantoni), García: (Augusto Mazzarelli)

Synopsis

Elisa is a young single mother of two boys who, at the film's outset, is living with her mother. She dreams of opening a beauty parlor with her friend Lulú, but lacks the funds to do so. She has an affair with her boss García, who has a food stall in the market, stormily quitting the job when it finally becomes clear that Garcia is bluffing about leaving his wife. Elisa follows Lulú into prostitution and begins an affair with the pimp Plácido el Cara, who persuades both women to accompany him to Barcelona. The promise of easy money soon proves to be another falsehood: life in the Catalan capital turns out to be dominated by violence and deceit, and Plácido to be part of a máfia-style operation. Elisa forms yet another relationship, this time with a young Spanish policeman, Marcelo.

About the Film

En la puta vida was financed from Belgium, where the director studied. It was also partly funded through Ibermedia. It won prizes at Bogotá, Havana, Miami, Huelva and Lleida (Spain) between 2001 and 2002.

Elisa's relationship with Plácido el Cara is based on delusion, both romantic and economic. Photograph by Eloy Yorle

104

About the Film's Creators

Beatriz Flores Silva was born in Montevideo in 1956. Her first feature film, *La historia casi verdadera de Pepita la pistolera* (*The Almost True Story of Pepita the Sharpshooter*, 1993), told the story, reported in several Montevideo newspapers in 1988, of an impoverished single mother who takes to robbing banks armed only with an umbrella handle.

Masángeles (Belgium/Uruguay, 2008) follows a girl's life between the ages of seven and fourteen, against both a fraught family background, and the chaos of Uruguay's most politically turbulent years — from 1966 to the end of military rule in 1973.

María Urruzola is a well-known Uruguayan journalist who writes investigative pieces of a social and political nature, challenging some of the nation's cherished and uncritically held beliefs.

For Cultural Understanding

María Urruzola's book *El huevo de la serpiente* (*The Serpent's Egg*) deals with the traffic in women for prostitution between Montevideo and Milan. The European city was changed for Beatriz Flores Silva's film for logistical and financial reasons: the coproduction was with Spain, not Italy. Also, linguistic and cultural heterogeneity would be maintained by using a Spanish city (albeit one where Catalan is spoken).

In his documentary *Aparte* (*On the Margins*, 2002) the renowned Uruguayan filmmaker Mario Handler looks at the precarious lives of Montevideo's poor. The film investigates the political factors behind drug addiction, imprisonment and other social problems. It features a scene in which Handler takes two prostitutes to see *En la puta vida* and registers their reactions. Both the women are visibly moved, clearly identifying with the characters and attesting to the film's accuracy.

Interview with Director Beatriz Flores Silva

KR: The use of humor in a film with this kind of theme means that you have to jump frequently between two emotional registers or poles. Did this present many problems with regard to the script, acting, etc.?

BFS: Of course, the tragicomic style used in the film is something I developed a long time ago, after I finished my studies. Firstly because it's a style that is very honest for me; secondly because it has to do with the reality in which I live. Latin American reality is very much like that: people live in terrible situations but at the same time there is a lot of joy in living, there are many absurd situations. Thirdly because my concern is to reach the spectator, and if one is speaking only of tragic situations, people won't go to the cinema; they're attracted by humor, it's a style that is honest for me, it works well with the public, and whilst they believe in a complex reality, it deserves a reception, which is the only reality of the film, one that people are prepared to receive; things that are happening. People go to the cinema, they laugh, and at the same time they end up accepting what they see because whilst they are laughing there is something that hurts them inside. So as to be able to capture this humor I have looked for absurdities, things that happen all the time in reality. The film also has some surreal aspects; the theme of bureaucracy, the question of norms, how people follow norms and want to escape from them. For me these are sources of humor; the characters basically are very unfortunate people, very desperate, seeking to live their lives within a régime of norms that are not agreeable to them.

In the USA or Europe this theme would be treated with more gravity or solemnity. Were there many problems or criticisms regarding this?

Solemnity is a mistaken option because I've spent time with a lot of prostitutes doing research, and what may appear horrible to you doesn't seem that way to them. To the normal middle classes it seems awful, every time they have to go to bed with a man: how horrible! But not for the prostitutes; they live in a far more fresh, spontaneous way, and the problem we're talking about in the film is how women fall into a network of traffickers controlled by men.

This is a film of two cities, isn't it? On arrival in Europe all the artifices crumble, the lies, the chimera that are presented as what Europe is. It was a coproduction essentially with Belgium, and there was Spanish participation, too, through Ibermedia. What was the influence of its being a coproduction?

In general, none, because the same thing was happening between Uruguay and Europe: the real story happened in Milan, and for us it was very difficult to make the film in two languages, and it occurred to us that the same phenomenon was possible between Uruguay and Spain, and indeed reality proved us right because while we were filming, a network of 200 Uruguayans was exposed, operating in Spain, exactly the same thing. Obviously Latin Americans in Europe move among other Latin Americans, perhaps because they have no access to what the Europeans have, better things. So the story already had the elements of a co-production; we didn't have to invent a Spanish policeman, or invent Brazilians because we had no co-production agreement with Brazil. Initially we had no transvestites, it was a story of war between two groups of Uruguayan pimps, and for the sake of humor we changed the other group from Uruguayans into Brazilian transvestites, but it had nothing to do with problems of co-production.

What co-production does is to make things a lot more expensive; on the one hand it brings in money but on the other it raises costs. But that had nothing to do with the artistic side of the film.

So the love story between Elisa and the policeman wasn't invented?

No, it comes from the real story. Not in the same way in which I told it, certainly in the true story Elisa doesn't denounce the pimp at the trial, and that's where the love story finishes; in my story she goes and denounces him and they help her to go to Uruguay.

On the other hand in the real story, she was helped to return to Uruguay by the Uruguayan journalist who wrote the book, María Urruzola. I felt it wasn't very interesting to open all that out, to add on a character at the end that we hadn't seen before, who only sees all this when it's ending. So I had the policeman do what was done by the journalist. According to the protagonist there was no love story between herself and the pimp. I put that in because I couldn't believe it didn't happen!

In the scene where the Uruguayan and Brazilian "borders" are drawn, and the little bald man points out this is Catalonia, are you talking about some feeling that the latinos are taking over Europe?

No, what I'm saying is that there are people arguing over territories and not over people. And they are definitely treating these people, the prostitutes and the transvestites, as if they were animals and not humans, so the joke rounds off with this comment on what is Catalonia but I'm not saying that Catalonia is being invaded by Latin Americans.

The acting of the two protagonists is very convincing, but there are actors previously little known, at least outside of Uruguay. Where did you find them?

The main actress was a model; she had done acting courses in the USA, but she had no previous experience, and the supporting actor was an Argentine singer who had acted in some soaps quite a few years before, who was quite obscure then. We found him quite by chance in a casting in Argentina. And his physical type corresponded to what I had in mind. When I have to find actors, it's very important for me to do exercises with them, to see if they have some inner thread similar to that of the characters. Because then we work a lot with improvisation.

What market and what kind of public was the film conceived for?

For a general public; prostitution is a universal phenomenon. I think everyone can understand all these things: slavery, exploitation, death, suffering. It's for a general public, anyone over 15. Obviously it tells the story of Uruguayan traffickers. It wasn't conceived with any particular market in mind.

*You're working on another project now [*Masángeles, *released in May 2008]: could you tell me something about that?*

It's a choral film, there are eleven characters. It's the story of a girl who, due to tragic circumstances at the beginning of the story, has to go and live at her father's house, still very much a child, with no idea of what's happening. She spends seven years living with this family; they're all very neurotic, which is a very important source of humor. It's not the story of Cinderella, it's not that they're going to treat her badly or anything like that. These are very special years in the history of this country, from 1966 to the elections of June 1973 and the end of the dictatorship. Although this is not a political film, it has a political background, being set in a very turbulent era here.

Analysis

Much has been made outside Latin America of the use of humor in this film; Beatriz Flores Silva is adamant that this approach is valid given the non-moralistic view of prostitution in her country. Besides, she has used this resource in her two other films, both of which concern far from "comic" subject matter: *Pepita* deals with crime as an escape from abject poverty, *Masángeles* a deprived childhood.

Many of the gags in *En la puta vida* arise from a clash between solemnity and irreverence. The tone is set in the first scene, when Elisa's invocation of the Almighty to look after her father's soul is greeted with a thunderclap and cloudburst. Her confrontation with García in the market pits her reckless vivacity against his wife's dull, clueless conformity.

Beatriz Flores Silva talks above of the absurdity of certain situations in Latin American life, particularly involving officialdom. Humor attracts an audience, and can be used to lower defenses against receiving unpleasant truths, as well as heightening the tragic elements. The director told me that the humor was occasioned more by the sense of tragic inevitability and the grotesque elements stemming from the exploitation: "The protagonist, for example, realizes she's falling into a trap. It's not that I have any a priori moral opposition to prostitution, it's legal in my country, and everyone does what he or she wants, don't they? There's exploitation that brings with it a lot of grotesque elements, it has to do with humor and the film is always on a tightrope between the humorous and the tragic, the realistic and the surrealist, the exaggerated and not exaggerated, and I had to maintain a balance, allow the spectator to feel the emotions and the story and at the same time laugh or cry at different moments."[1]

Flores's use of comedy evokes the crisis management methodology devised by Luis Miguel Díaz (2004) which uses film humor in reaching compromise between even the most entrenched opposing positions. Of course, her film is not intended for conflict resolution but, as Díaz (2004, 13) says, "The cinema is a very effective transmitter of messages, since it constructs realities through scenography and the performances of the leading actors, which exaggerate or simplify our instincts, intuitions and faculties for conflict management."[2] And if cinema is more universal than any verbal language, then its use of humor is even more persuasive: Díaz (2004, 14) maintains that the use of particularly funny scenes "helps the public lower its resistance to change and enjoy itself."[3]

The scene (C5) in which Elisa and her colleagues are raided and taken off to jail culminates in a dialogue between Elisa and a police officer during which she leans upon, and touches, the bust of a glowering dignitary. The man grumbles: *"Si me sigue molestando la voy a meter por desacato a la autoridad"* ("If you keep annoying me I'll put you away for disobedience to authority") which uses language reminiscent of cartoons like the Argentine *Hijitus*, ostensibly for a child audience, in which characters are habitually thrown in jail for being *desacatado* (insubordinate). But the officer follows this with an irritated deadpan delivery of the line *"¡Y no me toquetee el prócer!"* which echoes one of the vulgar phrases used by inhabitants of the River Plate area, and might translate as "don't fiddle with my bigwig!" It raises a laugh because of its ludicrous sexual innuendo, creating bathos between gravitas and ribaldry.

Linguistic Features

Uruguayan Spanish is similar to that spoken in Buenos Aires, but pronounced with a less exaggerated "Italian-style" cadence. Elisa reacts to some of the worst situations in this film with some fierce language — another element of Spanish in the River Plate estuary. The very title uses slang (a common saying) in which the noun *puta* (whore) is employed as an adjective. There is repeated use of slang words like *fiolo* (pimp), *atorranta* (roughly equivalent to tramp), and *gurí* or *botija* (kid).

For Discussion

1. How does the portrayal and fate of Elisa, Lulú and others drawn into prostitution compare with that seen in other films dealt with in this book? Is Subiela's view in *Lado oscuro del corazón* or that of Sergio Cabrera in *Perder es cuestión de método* more accurate or sympathetic?

2. How would you describe the attitude towards authority displayed in *En la puta vida*?

3. What is the "régime of norms" spoken of by the director in the interview, and how do her characters negotiate it?

15. *Novia que te vea*
(Like a Bride)

CREDITS: Mexico, 1993; *Production and Direction:* Guita Schyfter; *Written by:* Hugo Hiriart (script): Rosa Nissan (novel); *Music:* Joaquín Gutiérrez Heras; *Art Direction:* Tere Pecanins; *Director of Photography:* Toni Kuhn; *Sound:* Salvador de la Fuente; *Costume Design:* María Estela Fernández

CAST: Oshi Mataraso (Claudette Maillé), Rifke Groman (Maya Mishalska), Sarica Mataraso (Angélica Aragón), Samuel Mataraso (Miguel Couturier), Abuela Sol (Mercedes Pascual), Eduardo Saavedra (Ernesto Laguardia), Raquel Groman (Verónica Langer), Jaime Groman (Nathan Grinberg), Tío Meyer (Leslie Hoffman)

Synopsis

In 1927, Oshi Mataraso's grandparents arrive in Mexico City after a long journey from Istanbul. The cousin who is to meet them at the train station fails to appear; instead they are fortunate enough to make a chance Jewish acquaintance who invites them to his home. With this man's help they are able to set up a women's wear business and establish themselves in the community. This Sephardic family's peace and stability is challenged, though, when their daughter Oshi begins to question traditional values and befriends another free-thinking young woman, Rifke Groman. Rifke, from a wealthy Ashkenazy family, begins a relationship with a young socialist named Eduardo Saavedra. Meanwhile Oshi has to decide whether to obey her parents' wishes and marry a young doctor, León Levy, in whom she realizes she has no interest. The two women reminisce about decisions made in their youth which have profound consequences for both their lives.

About the Film

Novia que te vea, the first full-length feature film by Guita Schyfter, was made with financial support from IMCINE (Instituto Mexicano de Cinematografía). Unusually, the film's release almost coincided with that of the literary work from which it is adapted; the homonymous novel by Rosa Nissan.

Novia won four prizes at the 1994 Mexican national film awards (Ariel): Guita Schyfter for Best First Work, Angélica Aragón for Best Supporting Actress, Salvador de la Fuente for Sound, and María Estela Fernández for Costume Design.

Paintings provide not only visual information but also context, establishing both the Gromans' relative affluence and sophistication and Oshi's artistic ambition. Photograph by Daniel Daza.

The film has profound implications, not just for Mexico's Jewish community, but for Mexican society and its cultural and ethnic makeup. Consequently, both book and film continue to attract critical and academic attention several years after their release.

Elizabeth Coonrod Martínez (2004, 101) argues that Nissan has also made efforts to salvage and update the Sephardic contribution as she "challenged the official story — both in Sephardic tradition and in the greater Mexican hegemonic system — with her recent stories that collect and portray the cultural memory of a people who are both Mexican and Jewish."

Nayibe Bermúdez (2008, 33–34), meanwhile, views *Novia que te vea* in the light of the "project of incorporation of women's perspectives into a national history and culture that by tradition has ignored and erased this point of view, accompanied by the use and reevaluation of narrative modes catalogued disparagingly as 'feminine.'"[1]

Elissa Rashkin (2001, 142) also sees a problem of exclusion but from the creation of a national essence (*mexicanidad*): "in spite of its deep roots, Mexico's Jewish population has been largely invisible and overwhelmingly excluded from the foundational ideology of Mexico as a mestizo nation, part indigenous and part Spanish."

About the Film's Creators

Guita Schyfter was born into a Costa Rican Ashkenazy family in 1947, but has lived and worked almost half her life in Mexico. She studied psychology at UNAM (Universidad

Nacional Autónoma de México) before taking up film and television production with the BBC in London. Upon her return to Mexico she worked on documentaries for TV and cinema, breaking into feature films with *Novia que te vea* in 1993. She has been married to the scriptwriter and novelist Hugo Hiriart since 1979.

Her documentaries include *Greene, los caminos del poder y la gloria* (*Greene's Roads*, 1987) about English writer Graham Greene's time in Mexico and the genesis of his famous novel, *The Power and the Glory*. *Xochimilco, historia de un paisaje* (Xochimilco, *History of a Landscape*, 1990) concerns an area of Mexico City which conserves some pre–Columbian aspects, including its surviving Aztec canal system. *Tamayo a los 90 años* (1991) is a profile of Rufino Tamayo, one of Mexico's most renowned painters, at age 90.

To date Schyfter has made four full-length films: *Las caras de la luna* (*The Faces of the Moon*, 2002) reflects her interest in the juxtaposition of cultures. It concerns an all-female jury at a Mexico City film festival, and hence the conjunction of women from different nationalities and generations — women united, in fact, by the cinema.

Her two most recent films involve the investigation of individual biographies, or of collective roots. *Sucesos distantes* (*Distant Happenings*, 1996) deals with a Russian wife whose life story becomes an obsession for her Mexican husband. The most recent, *Laberintos de la memoria* (*Labyrinths of Memory*, 2007) is a feature-length documentary which follows the trajectories of two women, both estranged from their family origins. One of these is a girl brought from her troubled homeland of Chiapas in southern Mexico, at an early age, to Cuba. The other is Schyfter herself, who journeys to Lithuania and the Ukraine to seek out her own family origins.

Rosa Nissan, author of the novel *Novia que te vea*, is of Sephardic extraction; of the two main characters in *Novia que te vea*, she is closer in origin to Oshi than Rifke. Her novels explore gender as well as cultural and national issues. *Hisho que te nazca* (*Like a Mother*, 1996) is something of a sequel to *Novia*, while *No sólo para dormir es la noche*[2] is a collection of stories dealing with various aspects of love and sexuality. In *Los viajes de mi cuerpo* Nissan looks at her relationship with her own body, coming to terms with fatness and defying prevailing norms. As Alicia Ramos González (2006, 408) puts it, Nissan "has helped understanding of a more diverse and multicultural Mexico, taking on themes such as immigration, social adaptation, assimilation and adherence to tradition."[3]

For Cultural Understanding

JEWS AND JEWISH CULTURE IN LATIN AMERICAN FILM

The Jewish Diaspora in Latin America is the result of separate waves of population at various historical moments which have brought subcultures from different countries and religious variations. *Novia que te vea* focuses upon the main twofold division between Sephardim and Ashkenazi and the position of both in Mexican society. Previous films highlighted earlier waves of immigration, which faced harsher conditions and more severe expressions of anti–Semitism. Another film featured in this book that refers, obliquely, to Jewish themes is *A hora da estrela*, Suzana Amaral's adaptation of the novel by Ukranian-born Brazilian Jew Clarice Lispector.

A historical perspective is particularly essential in understanding the Jewish presence in Mexico: Arturo Ripstein's *El Santo Oficio* (*The Holy Office*, Mexico, 1974) deals with the fate of a Jewish family whose conversion to Christianity is found to be insincere. They are obliged by the Inquisition to renounce their rituals, but experience difficulty in complying. Another example of Inquisitorial persecution, belonging to very different circumstances, is seen in Tom Job Azulay's *O judeo* (*The Jew*, Brazil, 1996). This biography of the Lisbon-based Jewish Brazilian writer Antônio José da Silva (1705–1739) looks at the difficulties in being both a dissenting voice, and one from an oppressed minority.

Other Latin American films look at the experience of migration. *Los gauchos judíos* (*Jewish Gauchos*, Juan José Jusid, Argentina, 1975) is based on the eponymous collection of short stories by the Russian-born writer Alberto Gerchunoff about the tribulations of the first Jewish populations in Argentina, who fled the Russian pogroms and settled in the province of Santa Fe. *Legado* (*Legacy*, Vivian Imar and Marcelo Trotta, Argentina, 2002) tells a similarly tortuous version of the story, focusing on the first group of Jews to escape persecution in Russia, arriving in Argentina in 1889.

Not all Jewish immigrants to Latin America came in groups, and not all arrived in promising surroundings. In *Sonhos tropicais* (*Tropical Dreams*: André Sturm, Brazil, 2001) a young Polish woman, Esther, arrives in Rio in 1899, having been promised a husband on arrival. The marriage, however, is a sham; Esther has been lured across the Atlantic to be forced into prostitution, a fate that befell many young women on the Atlantic seaboard, Jewish or otherwise.

The persecution of Jews was not a European preserve, as is shown by Herman Szwarcbart's documentary *Buenos Aires pogrom* (Argentina, 2007) on the 1919 wave of anti–Semitic hysteria. Szwarcbart's film uses the memories of his own grandfather, who had arrived from Russia only to be obliged to escape, again, when branded a communist. *Olga* (Jayme Monjardim, Brazil, 2004) is the true story of Jewish communist militant Olga Benári (1908–1942), who was handed over to the Nazis by the then military dictator Getúlio Vargas.

Most of the films directed and written by the Argentine Daniel Burman deal in some way with Jewish family life, in particular the role of the father. Often this patriarchal figure is simply an absence, as in both *Esperando al Mesías* (*Waiting for the Messiah*, 2000) and *Derecho de familia* (*Family Law*, 2006). *El abrazo partido* (*The Lost Embrace*, 2004) replicates the missing father of *Esperando al Mesías* but also accentuates the ethnic and cultural mix of Buenos Aires, with the Jewish presence seen as an element among other ethnic minorities. *El nido vacío* (*Empty Nest*, 2008) also explores absence and longing within a family; this time the father is the one who waits, the missing person being a daughter. Burman was also instrumental in the production *18-J* (2004), a film marking the tenth anniversary of the bombing at AMIA, a Buenos Aires Jewish cultural center in July 1994, in which 86 people died. It consists of ten episodes made by different directors, both Jews and gentiles, presenting a free range of artistic responses to the atrocity.

Palermo Hollywood (Eduardo Pinto, 2004) which styles itself a fable of Buenos Aires, presents Pablo and Mario, two petty thieves from different socio-ethnic backgrounds whose friendship is tested when they are roped into a kidnapping. Mario, also known as "El Ruso" (The Russian, a euphemism for Jew), is in rebellion against his senator father. In one scene he is called a "*judío renegado*" (renegade Jew) as the film alludes to the perception, with its Nazi overtones, that Jews are involved in high-level corruption (the setting of 2002 is a time of the financial collapse widely seen as engineered by vested political interests to rob ordinary people.

Several interesting documentaries deal with Jewish communities in Latin America: Isaac Artenstein's *Tijuana Jews* (USA 2005) explored the perceived incongruity of a Jewish presence in this border city. *Guadalupe* (Santiago Parra, Mexico/Spain, 2006) is a semi-documentary which includes the minor character of Simón (Pedro Armendáriz Jr.) as a Jew who knows a great deal about the famous Virgin. *The Longing: The Forgotten Jews of South America* (Gabriela Bohm, USA, 2007) looks at the dilemma of a people who long since converted to Catholicism and must confront the question of how, and whether, to recuperate their heritage.

Comedy has long been a celebrated Jewish survival strategy, and Latin America several films draw upon Jewish humor, or point out the incongruity of Jewish culture in certain contexts. *Morirse está en hebreo* (*My Mexican Shivah*, Alejandro Springall, Mexico/USA, 2007) tells of Mexican notions of death and the afterlife with the funeral of Moishe, a popular individual in Mexico City's Jewish community. The week-long Shivah ritual serves here to bring characters together, revealing uncomfortable but hilarious family secrets and contradictions. Another Argentine film, Gabriel Lichtmann's 2006 family comedy *Judíos en el espacio* (*o por que es diferente esta noche a las demás noches*) (*Jews in Space (Or Why Is This Night Different from All Other Nights?)*) is also set during a Jewish festivity (Pesaj, a further culinary showcase) again using the comic opportunities of a tense, claustrophobic, traditional family gathering.

Ariel Winograd's *Cara de queso* (*Cheese Head*, Argentina, 2006) is a lighter satire on Jewish mores which also takes on class and generational issues. Its characters are safely ensconced in a condominium, a setting that emphasizes the community's isolation to absurd effect — the subtitle *Mi primer gueto* (*My First Ghetto*) ironically points to the community's affluence, while the film's theme music refers atavistically to Jewish tradition from the outset. Its storyline of adolescent bullying and libidinal angst plays out against a backdrop of petty corruption and violence.

While *Sol de otoño* (*Autumn Sun*, Eduardo Mignogna, Argentina, 1996) is not strictly a comedy, it takes several humorous turns. A mature Jewish lady, faced with the impending visit of an intransigent brother, hires an unknown man to pose as her husband. Problems arise when the chosen applicant turns out to be gentile and must hurriedly learn to assimilate Jewish customs and behavior. The acclaimed *Whisky* (Juan Pablo Rebella and Pablo Stoll, Uruguay, 2004) has a similar plot as well as a unique and brilliantly conceived film language. Its protagonists are two contrasting Jewish brothers, who are both (separately) sock manufacturers. The dour and routine-bound Jacobo, who has remained in Montevideo, feels bound to "hire" a wife to prove his worth to the younger and relatively flamboyant Brazilian-based Herman. *El brindis* (*The Toast*, Shai Agosín, Mexico/Chile, 2007) justifies itself as a Mexican-Chilean coproduction by having its central character, Emilia, fly from Mexico City to Santiago to visit her Jewish father, Isidoro. Emilia is the offspring from his affair with a gentile woman, and so is not readily accepted by the family — despite the effusive welcome she is given. Resentful of her father, and attracted to the handsome local rabbi, she undergoes a process of self-discovery while making decisions about her love life and religious/cultural/national affiliations.

A cinematic demonstration of the strength of the Jewish presence in Argentina can be seen in FICJA, the annual festival of Jewish Cinema in Buenos Aires.

Interview with Director Guita Schyfter

KR: Uncle Meyer expresses a favorable opinion towards diversity, yet your film has had to portray the Jewish community as internally divided. Did this result in any adverse reaction?

GS: Just like Uncle Meyer, I believe that differences are riches and that minorities are the salt of a country. Cultural differences within the Jewish community are what makes that community so interesting and varied: the stories, the food, the music, and its histories. It's difficult to think that these diverse cultural contributions could produce an adverse reaction, and if they did provoke them it would be on the part of people that don't interest me.

Would you say that the anti–Semitism seen in the film has dissipated now, or is it still latent in Mexico?

What is seen in the film still applies. The custom of the Holy Week processions where the Jews murder Christ has not altered. And in Catholic churches the priests still tell the same story, despite the Second Vatican Council having established that the Jews were blameless in the death of Christ. So this anti–Semitism is still latent in Mexico and, no doubt, in all Latin America.

To what extent have things changed for Jewish women in Mexico?

Look, Keith, I'm a storyteller, not a sociologist; nor do I conduct gender research. But I would dare to say that to the same extent as things have changed for women in general, they've changed for Jewish women in Mexico, too.

Recently the Argentine filmmaker Daniel Burman has given a high profile to cinema with a Jewish thematic in Latin America. How do you see this in other countries of the region?

I know of very few films on Jewish themes in Latin America. When *Novia* was made I only knew of one 1970s film from Argentina called *Los gauchos judíos* (*The Jewish Gauchos*) (1975) and [Arturo] Ripstein's film *El Santo Oficio* (*The Holy Office*) (1974). Later in the nineties came the documentaries in Mexico and [Burman's] *El abrazo partido*. I don't know of any others.

You've re-created the era very ably through the use of photos, posters and other resources. Was this aspect of the film a chore, or a pleasure?

Period re-creation was one of the things that I most enjoyed developing in this film. I collected objects from the house of my aunt, Rebeca Arditti, who was Turkish, and from the houses of friends of mine who grew up in Mexico around the same time the film was set. This part was a lot of fun and, of course, one should not forget that my art director was the impeccable Tere Pecanins, a woman with profound experience in national cinema besides the good taste cultivated throughout the years in her family's art gallery.

Several commentators have spoken of the multicultural complexities presented in Rosa Nissan's novel, in which the Sephardim are allied to the Ashkenazim but separated from them by language. Is this something that attracted you to Nissan's work?

Yes, of course. My Ashkenazi characters speak Yiddish and the Sephardim of Turkish origin use Ladino. Besides, one culture's view of another is something that has always interested me and is present in almost all of my work. Languages and accents intrigue me and I very much like hearing them. In *Sucesos distantes* (*Distant Happenings*) my character is a Russian woman who speaks Spanish with a Russian accent (here, too; the actress is Angélica Aragón) and you can even hear a little Russian in the film. In *Las Caras de la luna* (*The Faces of the Moon*) each one of the characters speaks Spanish with accents from different places.

Analysis

Kinestasis is described by Frank Beaver (1994, 204) as a "filmmaking technique in which still photographs rather than moving images are used as the source of visual information." The eye is doubly directed and channeled by this second frame and another mode of representation is introduced. The technique is used repeatedly in *Novia que te vea*: sepia-tinted photographs, apparently an inviolable ontological link to a pre-audiovisual past, combine at the beginning with black-and-white film and voiceover. Later other forms of still, flat images appear which are associated with change and growth rather than immobility and tradition. Painting, for instance, represents Oshi's independence and self-will: at the Gromans' dinner party (C10) she is far more interested in the hosts' art collection than in the conversation. At a pause in the debate over the future of Israel, Oshi simply asks the name of one of the painters. During a university lecture on ancient Mexico, a slide of a pre–Columbian codex is projected onto Saavedra's face when he enters to announce a meeting (C11). This moment is seen by Ellen Rashkin as "no less than the birth of the Mexican nation that is being graphically fused with both radical activism and romantic desire" (Rashkin 2001, 153).

Voiceover (VO) is a narrative resource whose judicious and controlled use can be extremely effective though it is not always considered essentially "cinematic."[4] However, even experimental filmmaker Derek Jarman was capable of *Blue* (1993) which consists purely of VO and a flat blue screen. VO can highlight the protagonist's isolation and the impossibility of real communication, as in *Días de Santiago*. But at the beginning and end of *Novia*, it heightens the opposite — a sense of community and family. Schyfter uses it in conjunction with the kinestasia discussed above — neither element being seen as quintessentially cinematic. The opening passage of *Novia* (C2) features the unusual device of an expository dialogue, rather than a monologue, in VO. Oshi's off-screen voice explains her family history to Rifke, contextualizing her grandparents' arrival at Buenavista Station which coincides, as we see from the array of posters and other material, with Lindbergh's visit to Mexico. As the group moves out of the station, the young man in the party (Oshi's father) pauses and almost freezes for an improbably long time, presaging the interaction that is to follow between fixed and moving images. As the grandfather and Señor Calderón pose for the camera and their printed image appears, the narrative enters another stylized mode, that of still photography. The group photograph taken in front of the church comes to life in color, and we move from the oral introduction into the film narrative proper. However the VO does not yet disappear, and the stasis-movement dialectic continues with the two-dimensional tailor's dummies in the market — flat images, rather than the characters who are speaking.

Several commentators have mentioned the use of photographs to frame the narrative: these include Elissa Rashkin, who has spoken of the paradoxical Jewish horror of representation violated in this opening: a step toward assimilation into Mexican reality. Jorge Ayala Blanco, (2001, 351) sees these dual reminiscences as "interchangeable and fixed, as fixed as the yellowing ancestral photos"[5] — apparently paradoxical qualities, but a reminder of the odd alliance here between orality's license and photography's permanence.

Flat, static images are used throughout the film to provide historical and iconic context to the live action. Beaver (op. cit.) tells us that "kinestatic interludes suggest the changing social, cultural, and political climate brought by the passage of time."

This is reversed towards the end of the sequence, when Oshi's 1951 childhood picture outside a church returns to live action and the VO dialogue ends. The church setting is used to bring in the theme of religion, the thorniest issue confronting Jews in a conservative Catholic society.

Family pictures are present in various household scenes, in which they seem to support the Mataraso family's conservatism and reverence for tradition. They reappear at the very

From the outset the narrative combines still photography and live action. Photograph by Daniel Daza.

end, with a repetition of Oshi's reminiscences. But these images also connote change, as in Oshi's choice of a career in painting over marriage, a crucial defiance of convention. As Ron Burnett argues (1995, 149–150) "if projections are not pictures precisely because viewers are always recontextualizing the act of seeing, then the film may simply provide the background upon which an activity of interpretation is being created." In his chapter *Camera/Text/Frame* (86–90) Burnett looks at the inherent elusiveness of the cinematic image, which has already moved on by the time we come to analyze it. What Burnett calls "the stability of the pictorial" is achieved, he asserts, by projecting film one frame at a time, but the perceptibility of such images within a film is uncertain. "A filmic image is never simply just out there on a screen awaiting a description. It has already passed by, been projected, and as a result the discourse constructed around it is faced with the urgency of understanding memory, of exploring memory and experience" (88). Schyfter's use of this imagery is conceived precisely to explore these elements: in her film the static image, paradoxically, is more evocative of movement than stasis.

Linguistic Features

Novia que te vea features a number of languages, as befits its narrative of migration. The Sephardic immigrants speak Ladino (otherwise known as Judeo-Spanish), which became a language in its own right after the expulsion of the Jews from Spain in 1492. Ladino preserves many features of Spanish as it was in the late fifteenth century since the Sephardic

Rifke's fascination with ancient Mexico is also rendered through static imagery, both three- and two-dimensional. Photograph by Daniel Daza.

people settled in Turkey, remote from the broader subsequent developments in the language. As is pointed out in the film, Ladino speakers had little difficulty in communicating with Spanish-speaking Mexicans. This was not the case with the Yiddish-speaking Ashkenazi community, whose language is far closer to German. Some of the divergences between Ladino and standard Spanish are "*pedrón*" for "*perdón*" (pardon) or "*me acodro*" for "*me acuerdo*" (I remember). Other words are borrowed from Turkish or Arabic: "*Mashalá*" is used in all three languages as a form of congratulation (C6 of DVD). On the other hand, Rifke is learning the indigenous tongue Nahuatl, spoken since Aztec days, an indication both of her solidarity with marginalized elements in Mexican society and of her interest in the country's pre–Columbian history.

See Alfassa (1999) for a brief explanation of Ladino (Judeo-Spanish).

For Discussion

1. At the beginning and end of *Novia*, Oshi tells how, as a child, she thought the family photos were Bible illustrations. How does this affect the way we perceive the images, and digest the story they presage?

2. According to Elissa Rashkin, the film questions not the institution of marriage but the lack of choice. Is this a fair assessment?

3. How does Schyfter's film see the future of Mexico, and the way the country should be configured culturally and ethnically?

4. Does *Novia* present the diverse and complex identity of Mexican Jewry as ultimately more important than individual problems?

5. What is the brought to this film by the alternation of black and white and color?

6. Is *Novia* ultimately a conservative film?

16. A Spectrum of Criminality: Gangsters, Politicians and the Military

Any discussion of non–U.S. crime films almost inevitably invites comparison with Hollywood, traditionally the genre's chief exponent. But Latin American film criminals offer a divergence, most strikingly through their humanity and believability; their crimes are less likely to succeed, go undetected, or be perpetrated without some degree of soul searching, and are committed by rather more than just an anti-hero with a get-rich-quick motive in a film that caters for the public's taste for violence, luxurious surroundings, and aggressive posturing. A Latin American playboy or gentleman thief *à la* Thomas Crown is unusual. Often there is some critical or ironic distance between the positions of filmmaker and protagonist, allowing for some explanation of the latter's actions and social position. And finally, crime films often allow room for social commentary, whether through state involvement or police implication in the crimes depicted, displaying a cross-section or interaction between rich and poor and often a direct encounter between social classes.

This is not a definitive distinction, of course: Mexican *Cholo* films, for example, usually glorify machismo, buying into the thrill of violence and the criminal ethos. Argentina also has a long history of *policiales* (essentially, films that deal with crime and its detection): Pazos and Clemente's dictionary (2004) lists over 300 films associated with the crime genre between 1937 and 2001. They include films of covert institutional violence such as Marco Bechis's devastating "Dirty War" drama *Garaje Olimpo* (1999) and Juan José Jusid's *Bajo bandera* (*Under the Flag*, 1997) concerning the investigation of conscript deaths through army abuse.

One of the first Latin American crime films was *El automóvil gris* (*The Grey Automobile*, Enrique Rosas, Mexico, 1919) which told the true story of the hunting down and capture of a notorious Mexico City gang who, taking advantage of the revolutionary turmoil of 1915, passed themselves off as army officers in order to rob the houses of rich families. One of the most successful films of Mexico's silent era, *El automóvil gris*, benefitted, as Federico Serrano and Antonio Noyola have put it, from "a combination of the documentary nature of early Mexican cinema, the melodramatic elements of Italian film, and the technical discoveries of North American movies."[1] (Cineteca Nacional 1981, 16). The documentary *La banda del automovil gris* (Alejandra Islas and Alejandro Quesnel, 2004) features a theatrical re-creation with voiceover performance from actors and piano accompaniment.[2]

The Picaresque tradition has been associated with Hispanic fiction since the Golden Age: it is widely thought that the genre proper begins with the 1554 Spanish novel *Lazarillo de Tormes* with its survival tale of a streetwise urchin. In Latin American film the picaresque is best represented in the comedies of Mario Moreno "Cantínflas": however, the Mexican comic's humor worked through an irreverent attitude towards authority and a subversion of the Spanish language rather than criminality. The best example of the picaresque in recent Latin American crime films is Fabián Bielinsky's magnificent "sting" *Nueve Reinas* (*Nine Queens*, Argentina, 2000). The posturing protagonist's downfall is used to comic ends in *Mala leche* (*Bad Blood*, León Errázuriz, Chile, 2004) as well as Bruno Stagnaro and Israel Adrián Caetano's excellent *Pizza, birra, faso* (*Pizza, Beer, Smokes*, Argentina, 1998), a film that uses humor to heighten its characters' pathos and hopelessness rather than counteracting the general tone. Sequences like the aborted raid on a restaurant, after which the gang has to pay off a crooked policeman and ends up out of pocket, amuse without counteracting the pervasive bleakness. Even as scabrous an antihero as the John Travolta–obsessed Raúl in *Tony Manero* (Pablo Larraín, Chile, 2008) has to be seen in the context, albeit far from mitigating, of the desolate inhumanity of Pinochet's late–1970s Chile where political delinquency, common criminality and slavish cultural imitation are complementary elements.

A recurring theme in Latin American cinema is the role in crime, often intrusive and at best unhelpful, of the media. A clear loss of public faith in the reliability of news media is visible in films such as Gustavo Graef Marino's *Johnny Cien Pesos* (Chile, 1993) in which four students bungle an attempt at robbing an undercover black market currency business. Their leader, the eponymous Johnny, lacks any Hollywood criminal qualities, apart from good looks. He is green, and not only as a criminal; he loses his virginity during the long police siege which becomes a media-feeding frenzy, and ironically the front for the heist-targeted currency racket is a video store. There are multiple implications here of media complicity in criminal activity and creation of criminal role models. In two other Chilean comedies, media attention hypocritically undermines its own declared anti-crime stance. The farcical hijack of a taxi driver in *Taxi para tres* (*A Cab for Three*, Orlando Lubbert, Chile, 2001) is largely prolonged by parasitic media attention. And the absurd but effective masked vigilante in *Mirageman* (Ernesto Díaz Espinoza, Chile, 2007) is hampered by a seductive TV reporter out to improve ratings by revealing his identity. Sebastián Cordero's *Crónicas* (*Chronicles*, Ecuador, 2004) has John Leguizamo as a cynical TV reporter whose desire (under pressure) to tie up his story of a child murderer has dire consequences for the correct prosecution of justice. *Géminis* (Albertina Carri, Argentina, 2002), a film which delves into the taboo subject of incest, carries an echo of this in the *telenovela* watched by the family's maid in which the lovers' horrified discovery that they are brother and sister contrasts with the furtive, guilt-ridden siblings of the main story.

Youth and Gang Culture

Two of the most successful Latin American films of recent times have investigated marginality and crime among urban youth: *Cidade de Deus* (*City of God*, Fernando Meirelles and Kátia Lund, Brazil, 2002) traces the history of a Rio de Janeiro *favela* from its optimistic, God-fearing foundation through its decline into a gang-infested hellhole. The film is stylistically innovative in its use of editing techniques and digital camera effects, but to this observer the film is ultimately sterile, unrelentingly pessimistic and locked into a hermetic aesthetic of violence as impenetrable as the *favela* itself (the spectator walks away thinking less about solutions than of ways of avoiding the place). The film has provoked considerable controversy and debate, and not just in critical circles: the volume *City of God in Several Voices: Brazilian Social Cinema as Action* (edited by Else R.P. Vieira) includes contributions by the filmmakers themselves, critics such as Ismael Xavier, and even the then Brazilian president Luiz Inácio (Lula) da Silva. Another eminent critic, Lúcia Nagib, has also analyzed innovative techniques such as the film's percussive use of language in the chapter on *City of God* in her book *The New Brazilian Cinema*. This film also provoked a spin-off television series later made into another accomplished film, *Cidade dos homens* (*City of Men*, Paulo Morelli, Brazil, 2007).

Despite the undeniable quality of its photography, and its anthropological scrutiny of underworld codes and credos, Carlos Moreno's *Perro come perro* (*Dog Eat Dog*, Colombia, 2008) errs, like many such films, in falling under the spell of the very machismo and brutality it purports to examine. There are several less ostentatious and more edifying films than *Perro come perro* and *Cidade de Deus* about gang life in marginal surroundings. Víctor Gaviria's *Rodrigo D no futuro* (*Rodrigo D. No Future*, Colombia, 1990) is at once distanced and involved with its subject, whilst refusing to offer a vapid "positive message." *Caluga o menta* (*Candy or Mint*, Gonzalo Justiniano, Chile, 1990), and *Hasta morir* ('*Til Death*, Fernando Sariñana, Mexico, 1994) examine the cult of loyalty and ultimately self-defeating codes of honor of the Mexican capital's street gangs.

The phenomenon of Alejandro González Iñárritu's *Amores Perros* (*Love's a Bitch*, Mexico, 2000) both as a cinematic portrayal of Mexico City and as a remarkable critical and commercial success, offers a number of insights into questions of cultural globalization, the spatial and temporal dimensions of Latin American postmodernity and the continuing redefinition of national cinemas in the region. The film has won prizes for best film at no fewer than 13 international festivals across the Americas and Europe (including the critics' special prize at Cannes) — not the first film from Mexico to achieve international fame, but surely the first success of this kind for a relatively unknown debut director. *Amores perros* is particularly striking for its exploration of violence as a form of social currency through which all kinds of emotional and personal relationships are shaped and molded to the forces of power and money.

Social and Political Elements

Adolfo Aristarain, one of Argentine film culture's outstanding elder statesmen, showed how the crime film (*policial*) can work against the most implacable dictatorships under the noses of their censors. Two films he made during the "Dirty War" make resounding social statements: in his debut film, *La parte del león* (*The Lion's Share*, Argentina, 1978), an initially innocent bystander becomes involved in crime through happening upon the considerable spoils of a robbery (Brenner 1993, 17–18), whilst in *Tiempo de revancha* (*Time for Revenge*, Argentina, 1981), a mining engineer devises a way of avenging a colleague's death through corporate neglect. *Nissa Torrents* (King & Torrents et al., 1987, 104), noting that at that time "no overt political themes could be addressed," saw this film as "a brilliant parable about collective exploitation, repression, and the possibility of individual response, though at heavy personal cost."

The connection between the leisured classes and the criminal underclass is dealt with ably in *Ratas, ratones, rateros*, and is even more central a theme in *Secuestro Express* (Jonathan Jakubovicz, Venezuela, 2006), about kidnapping, probably the criminal activity most feared among the wealthier classes (this is the "fast track" version). Kidnap films offer the dramatic opportunity of juxtaposing characters from very different social backgrounds or countries.

The latter applies to Alberto Lecchi's *Operación Fangio* (Argentina/Cuba, 2000), based on a true story: the abduction of Argentine race-driving legend Juan Fangio by Cuban revolutionaries in 1958. *Palermo Hollywood* (Eduardo Pinto, Argentina, 2004) permits a view across social class boundaries in a screenplay that also brings in politics and ethnicity. One of the two antiheroes is Jewish, his politician father is under investigation, and he is fatally attracted to a world of drugs and petty crime. Consumerism and crime are graphically juxtaposed in a scene from Alejandro Agresti's *Buenos Aires viceversa* (Argentina, 1996) where a street child is shot by a security guard in a shopping mall for trying to steal a video camera, while the young woman who befriended him is blissfully unaware, listening to classical music on headphones.

Cangaçeiros

Not all crime films have urban or contemporary settings: the Brazilian *cangaçeiro* genre took its cue from the Western in creating a body of national myth from the nineteenth to early twentieth century in the northeastern *sertões*, an era of lawlessness in Brazil's greatest wilderness. The best example is probably still *O cangaçeiro* (*The Bandit*, Lima Barreto, Brazil, 1953), which shows characteristic ambivalence towards the *cangaçeiro*—a figure traditionally driven to banditry by hardship and social inequality. Other examples are *Lampião, o rei do cangaço* (*Lampião, King of the Badlands*, Carlos Coimbra, 1964), a portrait of the most famous and celebrated of the bandits. A previous, homonymous version was made in 1950 by Fouad Anderaos. Other examples of the genre are *Maria Bonita, rainha do cangaço* (*Queen of the Outlaws*, Miguel Borges, 1968) and another film by Carlos Coimbra entitled *Cangaçeiros de Lampião* (1967). Far later, *Corisco e Dada* (Rosemborg Cariry, 1996) a fanciful Bonnie-and-Clyde characterization of a real-life couple, avoids none of the ambiguity surrounding either the nature of their liaison or their relationship with the populace.

Prison Films

Prison films have long been adopted as a vehicle for social issues. An example is Felipe Cazals's brooding, at times almost surreal *El Apando* (Mexico, 1975), adapting José Revueltas's novel of gross mistreatment in the notorious Lecumberri jail, emblematic of the pre-revolutionary Porfirio Díaz era but used, in this case, by the PRI government against students convicted after the 1968 disturbances. The film was powerful enough to contribute to the prison's closure, though not before the release of *Lecumberri* (Mexico, 1977), a feature-length documentary by Arturo Ripstein about the jail's conditions, social organization and famous escapes. Héctor Babenco's *Carandiru* (Brazil, 2003) dramatizes the events leading up to the world's worst-ever prison massacre, in 1992. This São Paulo prison was also demolished, in 2002.

Nelson Pereira dos Santos's *Memorias do carcere* (*Memoirs of Prison*, Brazil, 1984) was another adaptation (of the homonymous novel by Graciliano Ramos) in which, according to Teresa Toledo (1990, 298) the prison is a metaphor of Brazilian society: "Within the confined space of the prison, everyone's dynamic is clearer: the middle-class intellectual, the military man, the worker, young and old, men and women, people from the northeast and the south of Brazil."[3] *Quase dois irmãos* (*Almost Brothers*, Lúcia Murat, Brazil, 2004) presents another cross-section, concentrating here on the uneasy and at times downright hostile coexistence between political and common prisoners. The treatment of political prisoners is also explored in two Peruvian films dealing with the impact of the Shining Path on Lima (see chapter on *Paloma de papel*): Alberto Durant's *Alias "La Gringa"* (1991) and Danny Gavidia's *Reportaje a la muerte* (*Report on Death*, 1993).

Several films by Francisco Lombardi have demonstrated an interest in corrupt police procedure and the abuse of authority. His thriller *Bajo la piel* (*Under the Skin*, Peru, 1996) applies a Hitchcockian viewpoint to its tale of the perversion of pre–Columbian sacrificial practice to occlude modern-day serial killing (ably analyzed by Ricardo Bedoya 1997, 141–150). *Sin compasión* (*No Mercy*, 1994) adapts Dostoyevsky's *Crime and Punishment* to the background of constant threat and unease in Lima during the acute social and economic problems of the 1990s.

Breaching Genre Limits

Numerous films have creatively infringed genre boundaries seen as unnecessary confines. *La fuga* (*The Escape*, Eduardo Mignogna, Argentina, 2002) is ostensibly a prison film which nonetheless takes its theme as simply a starting point from which to explore the varied backgrounds and perceived wrongdoings of the fugitives: the escape is a force at once centripetal and centrifugal. The film also satirizes the inauguration of the Obelisco, a monument described by one dignitary as "the soul of Buenos Aires," with graffiti dedicating it to the escapees.

An unusual triple collaboration on adolescent criminality and violence involves two Mexican filmmakers, José Buil and Maryse Sistach. All three films, *Perfume de violetas: nadie te oye* (*Violet Perfume: Nobody Hears You*, 2000); *Manos libres: nadie te habla* (*Hands Free: Nobody Talks to You*, 2004) and *La niña en la piedra: nadie te ve* (*The Girl on the Stone: Nobody Sees You*, 2006) explore their themes with a refreshing lack of either didacticism or prurience.

Depictions of crime as a social condition are varied, at times ridiculing the authorities' inadequate response. *La zona* (Rodrigo Plá, Mexico, 2007) examines the perception of crime among the rich, with the surveillance camera, poised on the walls of the condominium that is about to be raided, almost mocking security measures rather than supporting them.

The Chilean mock-superhero film *Mirageman* is, on the one hand, a satirical look at the country's flawed entry into the modern ambit (see also Ricardo Larraín's 2008 comedy *Chile puede*): the Stan Lee–inspired vigilante has no superpowers and is an object of derision until he finally devises a plausible "look." Latin America has no credible superheroes, which in the U.S. originally embody some unchallenged belief in rightness of cause. Cop films are scarce; those that do emerge rarely have a policeman as hero or even sympathetic figure.

Corruption

Corruption is the focus of *Perder es cuestión de método*, and is touched upon in numerous other crime films, but there is no space here to fully extend a definition of crime to official and corporate corruption and state crime against the populace. All were being vigorously denounced during the 1960s and '70s by filmmakers of the New Latin American Cinema movement. Such elements have always been present in the films of the Argentine Fernando "Pino" Solanas: even the musical content in *Tangos, el exilio de Gardel* (*Tangos, the Exile of Gardel*, 1985), and *Sur* (*South*, 1988) carries a political charge, and Solanas has since become if anything even more militant with documentaries like *Memorias del saqueo* (*Social Genocide*, 2004) and *La dignidad de los nadies* (*The Dignity of the Nobodies*, 2005). The radical nature of Bolivian Jorge Sanjinés is typified by his *Yawar Mallku* (*Blood of the Condor*, Bolivia, 1968) which exposed alleged Peace Corps moves, supported by the then Bolivian government, to sterilize Indian women. Patricio Guzmán denounced an elected government's brutal removal in his three-part *Batalla de Chile* (*Battle of Chile*, 1975–1979).

Silvio Caiozzi is not a filmmaker normally associated with radical New Cinema, but his *Cachimba* (Chile, 2004), an ingenious adaptation of the novel by José Donoso,[4] decries political opportunism in the rush to partake in the "discovery" of a great surrealist painter. Earlier Caiozzi films, *Julio comienza en Julio* (*Julio Begins in July*, 1977) and another Donoso adaptation in *Coronación* (*Coronation*, 2000) had also looked at corruption and decadence in the Chilean oligarchy.

Film Noir Pastiche or Homage

Some films make overt reference or homage to the film noir subgenre. *La señal* (*The Signal*, Ricardo Darín and Martín Hodara, Argentina, 2007) does so through a lovingly recreated 1950s setting (the death of Eva Perón as background), murky plot and femme fatale. *El atraco* (*The Hold-Up*, Paolo Agazzi, Bolivia, 2004), based on the true story of a lucrative but messily executed robbery of a mine payroll in the 1960s, also contains several noir elements. Agazzi told me:

> *El Atraco* does indeed make reference to film noir, of which I'm a great fan. Various aspects of my film use noir clichés, like the blonde femme fatale (cabaret singer) who falls for the good cop, even though she's still involved with the baddies; the corrupt policeman; the honest (but not entirely) policeman; the use of jazz-inspired music, even though jazz isn't exactly a very common genre in Bolivian cinema; the lighting, and the use of somewhat "dirty" photography in the brothel and cabaret scenes.[5]

Otario (Diego Arsuaga, Uruguay, 1997) ably handles both the plastic quality and the spirit of *noir* in rendering such unsavory elements as pedophilia and corruption. *La historia del baúl rosado* (*The Story of the Pink Trunk*, Libia Stella Gómez, Colombia, 2005) works well enough as an era recreation and even homage to the film noir aesthetic, but blows itself up in a smug finale that gives itself away with too knowing an acknowledgment of the artifice and anachronisms.

Crime and Street Kids

For the purposes of this study, films about street kids are being treated as a different subgenre, through there is inevitable overlap. Here I include Gilberto Gazcón's *Perro callejero* and its sequel (*Street Dog* 1 and 2, 1980 and 1981) because they follow a protagonist into adulthood. Gazcón's work is a curious mix of documentary aspirations (the first film opens by stating that it was based on a sociological study) and patchy acting and direction. Nevertheless, the overall package convinces, if only due to its raw feel. The first film follows a boy from the year 1959 in Mexico City using apparently real street scenes featuring less than convincing staged action scenes. The film follows Perro, as he comes to be known, from the violent death of his father, through his "adoption" by an old vagrant and theft from a blind, geriatric street musician (both moments reminiscent of Buñuel's *Los olvidados*) and onwards. Perro survives several jail terms on his wits, making and losing friends and lovers. Gazcón, keen to root his narrative in its time, includes newspaper headlines referring to such events as the Kennedy assassination, and footage of the Tlatelolco massacre that preceded the 1968 Mexico Olympics. The hopeful note which ends the series appears somewhat out of tune with the rest of the content, but this is nonetheless a worthwhile saga on several levels.

En este pueblo no hay ladrones (*In This Town There Are No Thieves*, Alberto Isaac, 1964), based on a Gabriel García Márquez story of small-scale theft that escalates into violence, is a curiosity that features an array of Latin American artists as actors — including the author.

Drug Crime

Drug crime films adopt varying attitudes to the often Pablo Escobar–style figures they portray. Some of these delve into the background, social and personal relations of their protagonists. *El Rey* (José Antonio Dorado, Colombia, 2004) is based on the real-life Cali drug baron Pedro Rey, 1970s precursor of Escobar. An unusual approach is taken in *Sicario* (José Ramón Novoa, Venezuela, 1994) which cleverly interweaves the story of a cocaine mafia hit man with the progress of Colombia in the 1990 World Cup, establishing a link between the young man's coerced entrance into the business and the mistake by goalkeeper René Higuita that may have cost Colombia the championship. Another film directed by Novoa, *El don* (Venezuela, 2006), traces the trajectory of a drug lord from poverty to extraordinary wealth, a journey through which he does not sever ties, particularly affective ones, with his origins. Víctor Gaviria's pause from filming Medellín street life, *Sumas y restas* (*Addictions and Subtractions*, Colombia, 2004) tells the chilling story of a middle-class professional's dabbling in cocaine, first as recreation and then as investment.

The increase in crime in Latin America makes it unlikely that this genre will diminish in importance in the region. As well as a means of understanding and pondering the less sympathetic areas of the human psyche, the crime film remains relevant to a social atmosphere that is all too unhealthy. Some self-examination is needed from filmmakers accused of pseudo-anthropology and faux documentary. Moreover, macho posturing and a fascination for violence is seen as central to marketability in certain areas of crime film. Nevertheless, the genre's overall aesthetic and social value is undeniable.

17. *Ratas, ratones, rateros*
(Rodents)

CREDITS: Ecuador, 1999; *Produced by:* Cabeza Hueca Producciones Independientes; *Director:* Sebastián Cordero; *Script:* Sebastián Cordero; *Music:* Sergio Sacoto-Arias; *Director of Photography:* Matthew Jensen; 35 mm: 107 minutes

CAST: Ángel (Carlos Valencia), Salvador (Marco Bustos), Mayra (Cristina Dávila), Marlon (Fabricio Lalama), Carolina (Irina López), J. C. (Simón Brauer)

Synopsis

Salvador is a youth who lives in his native Quito and whose horizons are extremely limited. He indulges in drugs and petty crime, but this is nothing compared to the effects on his life, and those of everyone associated with him, when his ex-convict cousin Ángel comes to town.

About the Film

The title renders a progressive diminution of criminal status. *Rata* (rat) is bigger than *ratón* (mouse) but the smallest of the three is *ratero* (petty crook).

Ratas, ratones, rateros, an entirely Ecuadorean production, achieved the then highest box-office revenue for any national film. More details are given in the interview with Sebastián Cordero below.

About the Film's Creators

Director **Sebastián Cordero** was born in Quito, Ecuador, in 1972. He lived in France between the ages of 9 and 15, before going to Los Angeles to study film in 1990. *Rodents* was his first feature film. It was followed in 2004 by *Crónicas*, which starred the Mexican actor Damián Alcázar as a child murderer, and Colombian-American John Leguizamo as an unscrupulous journalist. Cordero was due to make *Manhunt*, a project about the murder of Lincoln, but this project was shelved. His third feature, the brilliant *Rabia* (*Rage*, Colombia/Spain/Mexico, 2009), maintains Cordero's favored criminal-marginal thematic with its story of a murderer in hiding.

126

For Cultural Understanding

Since the oil boom of the 1970s, Ecuador's rapid infrastructural and social change has rarely accompanied an equitable distribution of wealth. The country's cinema was slow to emerge, develop and keep pace with this change: today it is a far greater priority than ever before. Credit for this is due largely to Camilo Luzuriaga, an individual seen as the founding father of Ecuadorian cinema and certainly the most celebrated of the nation's filmmakers. He has made four features: *La tigra* (*The Tigress*, 1990), *Entre Marx y una mujer desnuda* (*Between Marx and a Naked Woman*, 1995), *Cara o cruz* (*Heads or Tails*, 2003) and *1809–1810: Mientras llega el día* (*When the Day Comes*, 2004). Luzuriaga also appears as an actor in Sebastián Cordero's second feature, *Crónicas* (2004).

With the addition of Cordero, the country's cinema has reached a level inconceivable before the 1990s and bolstered by more recently established directors like Tania Hermida, who became the country's first woman director of a full-length feature in 2006 with *Qué tan lejos* (*How Much Further*). The editor of *Ratas*, Mateo Herrera, has won prizes and acclaim with four features of which the most recent, *Impulso* (*Impulse*, 2005) won the grand prize at the prestigious Toulouse Latin American Film Festival in 2009.

Interview with Director Sebastián Cordero

KR: In both Rodents *and* Chronicles *there is an opening scene which unequivocally "establishes" the nature and identity of the protagonist or antihero. What would you say is brought to a film by this strategy of putting your cards on the table in such a forceful and immediate way?*

SC: I've always thought it's important to begin a story in a way that has great impact. Every image that goes into a film has to deserve its place (just like every dialogue and every action), and to me, a memorable introduction that unequivocally establishes a protagonist seems essential. I want to capture the spectator's attention immediately so that he/she will feel a great curiosity about what will come later. I always remember the first moments of *The Good, the Bad and the Ugly*, or of *Mean Streets*, because they manage to tell us a lot about the characters whose stories we're about to be told during the film: they're all "baddies," but fascinating at the same time!

I'm very much interested in having my films generate questions in the viewer. To achieve this, you need to capture their interest, make them feel they're seeing something unique and very dynamic; once they're hooked, I want them to ask themselves why they are fascinated by such questionable events and characters.

Film narration is always manipulative but never mendacious, and the opening scenes of both *Rodents* and *Chronicles* try to get the audience to identify with antiheroes who are real pigs. When people run away because their life is in danger, or they're the victim of an extremely violent act like a lynching, it's inevitable that we'll put ourselves in their shoes, want that character to be saved. I've never believed in moralistic films, and I think the viewer identifies with a character through the conflicts s/he goes through as the plot unfolds, and not because that character is "good" or "bad." I'm a great admirer of North American cinema of the '70s because it's a cinema of antiheroes (*Five Easy Pieces, Dog Day Afternoon, All That Jazz, The Godfather* ... there are so many examples!), but we get involved with all these characters and their nature just as we find them questionable. That's human nature.

Rodents appears to present crime as a leveler that involves all social classes. Is this also a reflection of the effects of economic crisis?

 Rodents presents many interconnected realities that coexist within a world in crisis. That is, an economic and moral crisis, as well as one of identity. In Ecuador many rivalries exist, not only between social classes but also between regions. Ángel (Carlos Valencia) comes from the coast and Salvador (Marco Bustos) from the mountains, two regions that have been in mutual confrontation for a long time (politically, economically, in sport...). I love films that show the complexity of a situation through the conflict of interests between multiple characters united by a common plot (John Sayles's *City of Hope* was a great influence to me when I wrote this script). Obviously a story like that can only develop in a world where values are in crisis, which is what breeds crime, and that's the context of the film. All the same, people aren't happier because they have money: their everyday problems are simply different, and I wanted to portray how we can all touch rock bottom, independently of our economic situation. A character like J.C. (Simón Brauer) becomes just as questionable and harmful as Ángel himself.

None of your films to date has painted a very flattering picture of Ecuadorian society. What reception have they had in your own country?

 Nobody is bothered if Coppola or Scorsese display a New York full of crime in their great Mafia films, because that city has been portrayed over and over again, with many different perspectives. In Ecuador there's not much cinema, unfortunately, and people sometimes expect films to help "sell" a positive image of the country. However, my way of thinking is that my cinema is not a postcard. I'm not the Minister of Tourism, and I don't want to accept responsibility for portraying the things I see in a distorted way so that people feel better. When *Rodents* was premiered in Venice, some girls from Guayaquil came up after the showing to complain that I had presented such a violent and "ugly" Ecuador: they had taken their Italian boyfriends to the cinema to show them how "pretty" our country is, and they all left terrified. I was a little scared by this initial reaction, but fortunately the Ecuadorian public was more intelligent, and wasn't at all angry at what I'd put on the screen. In fact the film was a landmark in Ecuador, and ran for almost six months, becoming a symbol of the fact that, "yes, we can" achieve a quality product despite all the crises in which we find ourselves.

Ángel's arrival means a new level of criminality and excess. Still photography on this film was by Paco Caizapanta, Lorena Cordero, Isabel Dávalos, and Pablo Iturralde.

 With *Chronicles*, the critical reception in Ecuador was very positive, but we only did half as well with spectators as with *Rodents*. While *Rodents* became a national icon (and a film that

Ecuadorians consider very amusing), *Chronicles* deals with a very tough subject (the story of a man who rapes and murders children), which I think did frighten off a lot of people. All the same, it's very difficult to say whether a film is going to be commercial whilst you're producing it.

Also, I think one of the great strengths of contemporary Latin American cinema is that at last it has taken up the challenge of entertaining and hooking its public, while at the same time choosing to show the world around us, with all its problems. We have a great heritage regarding social cinema, and our stories often require us to show worlds that are far from pretty. When I saw *Los Olvidados*, it revealed to me the kind of cinema I wanted to make. I saw it in Los Angeles, when I was studying film, and for me it was incredible to discover that you could tell stories with so much social conflict and characters, within an environment that wasn't my own, but that was certainly familiar to me. When I began to write the script of *Rodents*, my starting-point was to take a couple of characters to extreme situations, because I thought their stories would be more interesting that way. I wasn't about to write an adventure story or a script about secret agents, because that didn't seem to be appropriate for a debut film, but I did want action and a lot of dynamism, and that could easily come from the world of the streets. Apart from Buñuel's film (with its great character, Jaibo), I was also inspired by North American independent cinema of that time (which in turn is rooted in the cinema of the '70s). The first film by Nick Gómez, *Laws of Gravity*, had a great impact on me, and it was made with very little money. I thought that if such a great film could have been made in New York, I could do likewise and make a similar film in the streets of Quito and Guayaquil.

You use Camilo Luzuriaga as an actor in Chronicles: *you are the two major figures of Ecuadorian cinema. Does this solidarity exist throughout your national cinema community?*

Absolutely. We Ecuadorian filmmakers are very supportive of one another. Camilo has always given me great backing, and a lot of the people who worked with me on my films are now directing their own. Just to name a few, Tania Hermida (director of *Qué Tan Lejos*, the most successful Ecuadorian film to date at the box office) was assistant director on *Chronicles*; and Mateo Herrera, editor on *Rodents*, is now working on his fourth feature film as director. The local cinematographic community is growing gradually, but in a very diverse manner, and I'd say we're pretty united.

Some Latin American filmmakers (Alfonso Cuarón, Alejandro González Iñárritu) are making a career for themselves in the USA. It seems that you're following their example with Manhunt, *about the search for Lincoln's assassin.*[1] *Do you think you'll continue to make films in Ecuador?*

The example of Cuarón or Iñárritu working in Mexico and internationally seems excellent to me, and very inspirational. Things Latino are in vogue internationally and this is the moment to take advantage of it. I'm very much interested in working internationally, but the stories to be found in Ecuador are unique, and I'll want to keep telling them for the rest of my life.

All the same, my case isn't very typical. I was born in Ecuador, but I spent my adolescence in Paris, and after that I went to university in Los Angeles. This mix of diverse roots and influences has been very important in defining who I am. Today's world is getting smaller all the time, and I feel that I can be reached emotionally as much by an Iranian film as by a Korean or a Brazilian one. The same goes for music and literature. Art can function in a universal way, without necessarily losing its local flavor. In fact, my favorite films tell stories that could happen in very distinct places, but the strength given to them by the local context is extremely important. And in the end cinema is a mixture between macro and micro: the details are what make a film grow, but ultimately the conflicts faced by the human being around the world are essentially the same.

When I finished studying film in Los Angeles, I thought it was going to be impossible to go back to Ecuador and make films there. At that time, we were producing on average one feature film every three or four years, and making films in my country seemed to me an absurd and impossible challenge. Nonetheless, things somehow worked out, and after one project that didn't work out in the United States, I decided to go back to Ecuador with the idea of making films there. I began to write the script for *Rodents* taking into account all the limitations that could arise in Ecuador, incorporating them into the film's visual language. Fortunately, the project went ahead, and the fact of having made it in a country with such little activity helped me a lot in that people took notice of the film. When we were accepted at the Venice festival in 1999, *Rodents* was the first Ecuadorian film in the history of the festival! And with *Chronicles*, ours was the first Ecuadorian film in the history of Cannes. In fact now I think that making films in Ecuador was much better for me in "internationalizing myself" than what would have happened if I'd stayed in Los Angeles.

At the moment I'm developing one project in Spain about immigrants, another in the United States (to be filmed in several Latin American countries), and a third in Ecuador.... Time will tell if my career takes me abroad, or leads me towards my own country's stories. The reality is that it's very difficult to get finance in Ecuador for local films, and the possible co-productions oblige you to think towards the exterior. However, Ecuador is currently going through an important period in the development of its cinema: not long ago the first film law was approved, accompanied by the formation of a National Film Council, and they announced a competition for projects. I think that in two or three years we will begin to see the results of this historical process.

Analysis

Ricardo Bedoya and Isaac León Frías (2003, 69) explain camera movements in their admirable *Ojos bien abiertos* as follows: "Unlike other figurative or representative arts, in the cinema the frame can be mobile. Not only because the elements of the visual field have the capacity of movement — in which case we perceive an internal movement in the frame, even when the camera remains static — but also because the camera is an apparatus that, when placed upon a support, can vary its physical position with respect to the filmed objects, producing in the spectator the impression that the limits of the screen are not fixed and that the visual perspectives change with extraordinary fluidity."[2]

This is illustrated in a complex sequence (C3 of *Ratas*) with only one cut, filmed outside Quito's bus station where Salvador and Marlon, walking up a ramp on their way to meet Ángel, happen to spot a car with one hubcap missing. They successfully execute the scam of removing a second hubcap and selling it back to the driver, who remarks approvingly that it's "*igualito al que tenía*" ("just like the one I had before").

This is an important transitional scene, preceded by juvenile games with a revolver, stolen in one of the group's opportunistic robberies. Once Ángel appears, the play and the opportunism vanish, to be replaced by deadly earnest and premeditation.

Gabriela Alemán (2007) sees this as a turning point in the film: "The scene is almost a *sketch*, a carnavalesque wink at the spectator; a lightness that will be lost as Ángel turns

Salvador amuses himself with the group's new acquisition. Still photography on this film was by Paco Caizapanta, Lorena Cordero, Isabel Dávalos, and Pablo Iturralde.

into the central character of *Rodents*. As the hierarchy of the rat is imposed upon that of the mice. But up to this point in the film the youths' small crimes appear more as a utopian essay of subversion of powers, present in the language itself."[3]

The scene orchestrates an optical illusion combined with a confidence trick reflected in the fact that we don't see things from the viewpoint of the driver, who is objectified throughout. Marlon, who doesn't immediately look like a crook, establishes contact and wins the man's confidence, whereupon he signals to Salvador. There is a change from page 15 of Cordero's original script, in which Salvador enters the bus station (the director probably preferred the perspective offered by the ramp): instead Salvador walks further up the ramp, out of the driver's field of vision, and reverses his jacket. Then comes a cut to the back of the car: Marlon is still talking to the driver, and the camera picks up Salvador coming into shot to our left and crouching to remove the hubcap. Salvador stands and reverses the jacket back; the camera moves towards the front of the car as the three men are together for the first time — allowing a neutral medium shot. The camera again follows Salvador, who now goes to the opposite corner of the car and replaces the missing hubcap with the one freshly stolen.

The dialogue begins in the previous scene as a sound bridge; then the two approach (long shot) until seen from the waist upwards (medium shot). Marlon notices the car across the street, and the camera pans to follow his gaze, remaining on the car as Marlon walks towards it (again a long shot). The camera again follows Marlon's lead as it pans back to Salvador (MS). A tracking shot (subjective) follows Salvador up the ramp, while Marlon's conversation with the driver continues (off). The cut presents a stylistic break with the rest of the sequence, perhaps made for logistic reasons due to the difficulty of crossing a lane of traffic. But cutting here also allows an ellipse: whilst the conversation off-screen continues, Salvador appears behind the car more quickly than we might expect, yet the feeling of "real time" is not spoiled. Salvador's kick to fix it in place neatly ends the sequence and marks a cut.

Linguistic Features

Much of the speech heard in this film is reminiscent of the "aesthetic of the vulgar" and Rabelaisian *jocose grammar* posited by Claudia Alemán. There are examples of the picaresque (*viveza criolla*) in speech that matches the characters' actions. To be *vivo* is "alive" in the sense of street-smart: this is associated with the Creole population (those of Spanish descent born in the Americas) who are traditionally used to living on their wits. In the Andean countries, *sapo* (literally "toad") is crafty or cunning: accordingly, *una sapada* is a streetwise action. *Onda* (literally "wave") is closer to the hippie "vibe." "Man" (also used in Colombian slang) is an alternative to "hombre," but as street jargon, not as a biological category. The slang term *bacán* (great) is also used in Peru.

For Discussion

An approving review of *Ratas* by Óscar Contreras says: "Here the criminal world is viewed realistically. There is not the slightest opportunity for symbolism or lecturing discourses; everything is registered so that defeat and self-destruction compete with the slang and picturesque detail."[4]

1. Why are these considered positive features? Is Contreras's evaluation an accurate one?
2. What are the differences between *Rodents* and a comparable U.S. feature dealing with similar material?
3. How would Scorsese or Tarantino have treated the subject?

18. *Perder es cuestión de método*
(The Art of Losing)

CREDITS: Colombia/Spain, 2004; *Produced by:* Gerardo Herrero, Tomás Darío Zapata and Marianella Cabrera; *Director:* Sergio Cabrera; *Script:* Santiago Gamboa, Jorge Goldenberg; *Music:* Xavier Capellas: Aterciopelados; *Director of Photography:* Hans Burmann (ASC)

CAST: Víctor Silanpa (Daniel Giménez Cacho), Quica (Martina García), Vargas Vicuña (Jairo Camargo), Estupiñán (César Mora), Esquilache (Víctor Mallarino), Tiflis (Humberto Dorado), Susan (Mimí Lazo), Guzmán (Gustavo Angarita)

Synopsis

The crime journalist Víctor Silanpa receives a phone call from Colonel Moya of the Bogotá police, instructing him to investigate a bizarre murder. Silanpa is drawn into an intrigue involving corrupt property deals, and has to negotiate a world of *esperpento*[1] which begins with the discovery of an impaled body — the first of a series of grotesque images, and the catalyst that thrusts the journalist-turned-detective into an investigation that turns into a labyrinthine journey of unpleasant discovery. Silanpa is assisted in his quest by Estupiñán, who is searching for a lost brother, and by Quica, a young prostitute with whom he becomes romantically involved.

Absurdo Fea Ridicula

About the Film

Sergio Cabrera talks of *Perder es cuestión de método* as a film in which he sets out to "reject the conformity, the indolence, the passivity and the fatalism that we have become accustomed to."[2] It follows the eponymous novel by Santiago Gamboa in delving into the links between high-level political corruption and the underworld of Bogotá, displaying in the process a prurient interest in various personal foibles and idiosyncrasies.

Gamboa follows the offbeat detective norm established in the USA during the 1950s: his reluctant detective has to negotiate a marginal world peopled by lepers, prostitutes, and nudists. There are also oddballs such as Guzmán, an ex-journalist in an asylum, and the overweight police chief Moya who employs Silanpa to transcribe and give literary form to his dietary journal, as well as distorting the facts of the case. In this ambit, even the ostensibly sympathetic characters are narcissistic and egotistical, hardly an improvement on the underworld that feeds on their scraps.

133

About the Film's Creators

Sergio Cabrera is one of the most innovative and controversial filmmakers to have come out of Colombia. He was born in Medellín in 1950 of Spanish parents, both actors, who had fled the Franco dictatorship. The family moved to China ten years later, and Sergio was to become a member of the Red Guards. He returned to Colombia, and between the

ages of 19 and 23 was active in the Popular Liberation Army (EPL). A fascination with cinema brought him to study at the London Film School in 1975. However, Cabrera did not entirely leave politics; he became a parliamentary representative and served from 1998 to 2002, after which death threats from the extreme right forced him to leave for Spain.

His first feature film was *Técnicas de duelo* (*Details of a Duel*, 1989), a satire on machismo with the clash of two oversized egos, erstwhile friends in a small town. But Cabrera really made his name

Sergio Cabrera. Photograph by Juan Antonio Monsalves.

with *La estrategia del caracol* (*The Snail's Strategy*, 1994), a great success with its blend of political consciousness, fantasy and humor. *Águilas no cazan moscas* (*Eagles Don't Hunt Flies*, 1995) is largely a return to the theme and setting of *Técnicas de duelo*. *Ilona llega con la lluvia* (Ilona Arrives with the Rain, 1996) is an adaptation of the Colombian "tropical gothic novel" (Cabrera's term) by Álvaro Mutis. *Golpe de estadio* (*Time Out*, 1998) is a satire based on a recurrent theme in Colombia: the critical role in national life of association football (soccer). This film uses as background the unending civil strife between the army and left-wing guerrillas, a conflict suspended (fictionally) so that both parties can watch a (real) World Cup qualifying match played in Buenos Aires.[3] The full-length documentary *Ciudadano Escobar* (*Citizen Escobar*, 2000) sets out to present a Colombian viewpoint, much needed according to the director, using hard-won testimonies from people who knew the Medellín cocaine baron. Cabrera, who has lived in Madrid since the year 2000, has also worked extensively for television.

The novelist **Santiago Gamboa** (Bogotá, 1965), a writer associated with the McOndo[4] group, has studied in Madrid and Paris and now resides in Rome. He has also worked as a journalist. He published the novel *Perder es cuestión de método* in 1997. His other fiction includes *Páginas de vuelta* (1995), *Vida feliz de un joven llamado Esteban* (2000), and *Los impostores* (2002). The protagonist of his latest novel *Hotel Pekín* (2008) is another Colombian expatriate and investigator.

The Argentine scriptwriter **Jorge Goldenberg** has collaborated on numerous projects with Sergio Cabrera and other acclaimed Latin American directors such as María Luisa Bemberg, Carlos Sorín and Ricardo Larraín.

Aterciopelados, the Bogotá rock duo that provides four songs for this film, has been successful since the early 1990s and won a Latin Grammy award in 2006 with the album *Oye*. The opening song "*Untados*" ("Smeared") carries the apt refrain, "*Todos estamos untados—Todos estamos involucrados*" ("we're all smeared, we're all involved").

For Cultural Understanding

Sergio Cabrera, like many Colombian artists and other public figures, has had a difficult relationship with his own country; since 2002 he has lived in Spain because of threats on his life. Despite the country's undeniable attractions, its level of violence and corruption has been particularly intense since the mid–twentieth century. The Colombian-born writer and sometime filmmaker Fernando Vallejo, a nationalized Mexican, can be seen in Luis Ospina's film profile *La desazón suprema* (*The Supreme Uneasiness*, 2003) declaring to the children of Colombia: "you have had the misfortune to be born, and to do so in the craziest country on the planet. Don't pay attention to it, don't let yourselves be dragged along by its insanity...."[5] Others among Colombia's most famous artists live elsewhere for various reasons. The writer Gabriel García Márquez has divided his time between different countries since the 1970s, whilst painter and sculptor Fernando Botero has lived in Italy for some 30 years. Gamboa's character Barragán also yearns to live in London or Paris, far from the perceived dangers and discomforts of Bogotá.

Close (2008) sees this as part of what he terms the "Post-Boom autopsy" in Colombian fiction (an element shared with García Márquez in *Chronicle of a Death Foretold* and Fernando Vallejo in *Our Lady of the Assassins*). The autopsies presented in these novels can be read as denunciations of the Colombian state; far from reflecting "faith in science, rational subjectivity and state justice" (Close 2008, 121), a procedure that results in "no certain or useful knowledge, enables no legal justice and thus no vindication of individual dignity. Procedures are executed and reports filed, but autopsy is represented as a futile perpetuation of violence rather than a rational instrument of knowledge and justice" (Close 2008, 125).

Interview with Director Sergio Cabrera[6]

ESB: In several of your films you've set out to make social commentary through humor. But The Art of Losing *delves into a grotesque world that goes beyond the comic. What led you to choose Santiago Gamboa's novel?*

SC: Well, I chose Santiago Gamboa's novel because it coincided with a period of my life when I had retired from the cinema in order to participate in politics. I had stood for Congress and been elected. It was a period when I brushed against corruption on numerous occasions without being able to avoid it. And I saw the difficulty in unmasking corruption and avoiding it and struggling against it. And well, in that novel I found an illustration of what I had lived through during that time and I was interested in the way the corruption theme works through the novel. I like to make a kind of film that generates reflection, as a way of continuing politics. What I originally wanted was to change the world, that's why I was active in politics. In cinema I found a very agreeable way of expounding my points of view and of trying to do political work. Michel Foucault said the role of intellectuals on the left was that of social cartographers. As filmmakers we cannot put society right or change society, but we can make a plan, a map of what society is, then the specialists will come along, or the politicians and scientists, to modify it. I believe this very strongly. I think that, for example, in a film like *The Art of Losing* it was very interesting to make an X-ray of corruption using an everyday case. I was interested in working on this theme because it had ingredients that I liked: the black humor, the fact that it was a thriller, the possibility of making a kind of tropical thriller, to give it some kind of name. And well, basically that's why, ha, ha, ha.

Whilst we're on the subject, Oswaldo Osorio, in Kinetoscopio, *has criticized your film precisely for not fulfilling the requisites of a thriller. This seems unfair to me, criticizing the film for not managing something it doesn't even attempt. How did you conceive your film in terms of genre?*

Well, I have always avoided doing genre cinema. I respect genres a lot when I do television or when I do work to order. But for my own projects, I give myself the freedom to think independently. For that very reason I don't belong to pure commercial cinema. I try to make cinema the way it pleases me, without commercial or technical ties. To make a film that respects genre, I don't think it implies great difficulties, but I wanted to make a film in my own way, without respecting the traditional codes which of course I know; it isn't that making such a film is that complex.

Santiago Gamboa's novel flirts with the black novel genre without attempting to be one. Neither does the novel respect genre in itself, rather it takes several liberties. In fact, one of the difficulties in adapting the novel was that the plot of the novel wasn't sufficiently "detective fiction" to put together a crime story. I was much more interested in the characters, the situations. No, it wasn't my intention to make a traditional thriller.

What do you mean by making a "tropical thriller"?

To make a thriller that wasn't ruled by traditional canons. I refer a little to the case of Álvaro Mutis who wrote a tropical gothic novel (*Ilona Arrives with the Rain*) that was also other things.... The thriller has two very traditional, precise variations. There is the kind of thriller where everything happens in a house, like in Agatha Christie, where the house stands in for the city in some way. And then there is the urban thriller where everything happens in the city. I chose to make a thriller that was set in a city that is Bogotá....

Daniel Giménez Cacho specializes in strange and eccentric roles, and Silanpa seems perfect for him. How was the process of integrating him into the rest of the cast, Colombian actors you've used repeatedly?

No, really it was very simple because Daniel is a very fine actor, who has vast experience as an actor. I chose Daniel because I liked him, rather than for any reasons to do with coproduction. I could have chosen anybody. I liked the figure, I liked the way in which Daniel constructs his characters. The reason I thought of Daniel is that at one point we were thinking of the possibility of making a Mexican version of the film. Originally the producer, Gerardo Herrero, wanted to make a film set in Spain, with Silanpa as a Madrid journalist investigating a crime in Galicia. I read the script and didn't like it. Then we thought of the possibility of the story unfolding in Mexico. Since there was a possibility of coproducing in Mexico, there was Mexican money to make the film and it was when I was studying this possibility that I thought of Daniel. Then I finally got money in Colombia and was no longer obliged to use Daniel, I could choose any actor, but I'd already visualized, I'd already spoken to Daniel and I was enthusiastic about the idea of working with him. And I decided to stick with him even though he wasn't Colombian. But this is another of those absurd taboos: in Colombia there are many Mexicans, and there are many Colombians in Mexico. There's no problem with a Mexican journalist who works in a Bogotá newspaper, nothing to explain to anybody. But we are so stuck in certain ways, and they've blocked the freedom to imagine what might sometimes seem strange — that there should be a Mexican in Colombia — but it's the most natural thing in the world.

It seems that politics has always been present in your life as much as in your cinema, but how do you see your link with the militant cinema of the '60s and '70s?

Mine is an almost nonexistent link because ... I have great respect for the Latin American masters of militant cinema of the '60s and '70s, and I've watched it with admiration, you understand. But I don't like militant, political cinema. I like cinema that speaks of politics, but not cinema that takes sides. I was a militant, but not in the cultural area... For me it's important that cinema speak of reality, directors should have a political position with regard to reality, the country and society. But I don't think that their level of militancy should necessarily be reflected in their work. I'm not against it. I mean, it's fine to me; directors who have made militant cinema are very important but I think times have changed. There's a need to make a cinema that responds to public needs in some way. The militant cinema of those years was a cinema that wasn't seen, it didn't have an outlet. In a way it was a cinema that responded to its times... It was very important and helped us arrive at today's cinema. But today it's very difficult to make the kind of films that were being made in the seventies.

Over recent years Colombian cinema has shown great activity and variety, with an impressive volume of production. How do you see this, in terms of quality and continuity with previous generations?

Well, unfortunately I haven't followed it... I mean, I've followed the process and I'm aware that there is an important level of production, but I've seen few Colombian films. They don't get shown here. I'm afraid of being unjust, mentioning only what I've seen by chance. But for example, lately I saw *Satanás* (*Satan*, Andrés Baiz, 2007) which I liked. I saw *Paraíso Travel* (Simon Brand, 2007) which I liked. I saw another that I liked a lot, called *La primera noche* (*The First Night*, Luis Alberto Restrepo, 2003).

Would you prefer to be considered a Latin American filmmaker, a Colombian filmmaker, or simply an auteur?

Well, yes, a Latin American filmmaker, of course, right? Ha, ha. I don't believe very much in national cinemas... I mean, there's cinema made in Colombia, Peru, Ecuador. But in order to globalize it, it needs to be more Latin American. There is a way of making cinema that is very much our own. I am a Colombian filmmaker, of course. My notion is that we should make Latin American auteur cinema. What seems dangerous to me, and what I sometimes observe as something that happens and is happening in many countries, including Colombia, is that the tendency to copy Hollywood is very great. It's relatively easy to copy models, and that's a danger. Latin American cinema, Colombian cinema, any kind that isn't commercial Hollywood cinema will only be interesting in so far as it's authentic and different from Hollywood; it should be auteur cinema. By which I don't mean boring films, or French auteur cinema, no? It has to be a Colombian auteur cinema. That implies having charm and humor and pleasing the Colombian public. The idea of auteur cinema isn't hostile to that of box-office success. Far from it, but the idea of auteur cinema is contrary to that of making commercial, industrial cinema, of a hamburger factory, do you see? That's what I understand by it and that's where the difference should lie. I think Latin American cinema is an auteur cinema in general. That's one of its characteristics and one of its virtues. And it's a virtue that we have to take good care of, because the danger of starting to copy Hollywood, of becoming *maquiladoras*[7] for Hollywood films, is very great. The studios are hunting talent, looking for opportunities to make money so that we make in our countries the cinema that they consider conducive to their own commercial benefit. It looks dangerous to me.

Analysis: Crime Novel Adaptation

Sergio Cabrera's political convictions have made him an enemy of the corruption that he sees as endemic to a Colombia that has by now become accustomed and inured to it. He saw in Santiago Gamboa's novel "a portrait of the vicious and repugnant world of the speculators and the corrupt, of the mafias who organize themselves in the shelter of the tiny spaces the State leaves free for them so that they can enrich themselves as they wish. It was then that I saw a film in the novel, the kind of film I like to see and to make...."[8]

Clearly, the two artists share a certain interest in laying bare Colombian social hypocrisy. But does the process of adaptation for the screen need to be concerned with fidelity to the original? María Lourdes Cortés (1999, 24–30) considers that, in the "alchemy" of adaptation, "the problem of fidelity is a false problem. How is it possible to be faithful in a transfer of codes, of subjects, of disciplines that, in any case, handle different modes of production and reception? Besides, how can one be faithful to a text when the only way to approach it is through reading; all reading is interpretation and, consequently, the taking of sides?"[9]

Sergio Cabrera's film supports Cortés's view: an autonomous entity which does not owe any debt of fidelity, it both echoes and departs from the original. The two works do not differ greatly in terms of what Cortés calls "effect"—their aesthetic and discursive impact on reader and spectator. The film uses visual composition and perceptual succession to create its bizarre impression of Silanpa and his world.

An element partly retained in the film is the tailor's dummy (or doll, from *la muñeca*) that Silanpa oddly keeps in his living room for company. In the scene that introduces Silanpa (C1) the *muñeca* is what is seen first: she comes immediately after the impaled man (a strange visual echo) preceding the journalist himself as a form of alter ego. Silanpa's voice is heard off screen; then the journalist himself appears, reading aloud what he has just written and turning to the doll for approval.

Gamboa, however, has the doll as Silanpa's mute interlocutor and mirror for his emotional states. In the novel, Silanpa takes the doll with him into taxis and hotel rooms, asking her opinion on diverse subjects and apparently worrying about his relationships with Quica and with his ex, Mónica (all but absent from the film). Cabrera elects not to complicate his narrative and clutter his visual composition with such details and escapades, which are far more easily and suggestively conveyed in print and which would turn his film into a grotesque charade.

C5 sees another scene in Silanpa's house, this time with Quica present. The first shot is of the doll in close-up but out of focus, to the left; Quica comes into frame and examines it quizzically. Cut to a reverse shot, again with Quica in central foreground and the doll to

Silanpa under the vigilant eye of the *muñeca*. Photograph by Juan Antonio Monsalves.

left. When Quica moves (the doll is temporarily out of shot) Quica encounters other human vestiges that inhabit Silanpa's life. She picks up the recorder and switches it on, smiling as Moya's voice is heard. Silanpa comes into frame; when Quica asks about the voice, then the doll, he explains simply that the latter is a gift from his maestro, someone to talk to when lonely. The composition places Silanpa equidistant from the doll (left) and Quica (right) in a straight line. A reverse shot then gives a triangle, this time with Quica in the middle as she picks up yet another vestige, the photo of his ex, Mónica. Who's this? Silanpa's reply, "Ya no es" ("She is no longer") is only a partial explanation. A further shot presents, from left, the doll, Silanpa, a photo and Quica; all the females in his life in effigy, photo and flesh-and-blood respectively. Even when Silanpa and Quica kiss, the doll is in the background or in its habitual left of frame.

The last scene in Silanpa's apartment (C10) begins with a shot of the recorder being switched on: as Moya's voice is heard we see a close-up of a beaten Silanpa, who lowers his head in fatigue and disgust at what he hears. A reverse shot shows him surrounded by fragments of the doll, now broken and bald. Silanpa answers Quica's knock on the door, and a series of close-ups — reverse shots follow their conversation until a two-shot, with the take maintained as Silanpa is left alone. This scene, which does not appear in the novel, reveals Silanpa's inability to form a relationship, eloquently expressed by Quica's retort "Stay with your doll!" (*¡Quédese con su muñeca!*). The effigy, even in its shattered state, gives him a certain security; it cannot leave or disappoint him.

Linguistic Features

Colombian Spanish, in particular the Bogotá region, is distinctive for its singsong quality. It prefers the *usted* form of address, even in informal speech, to the usual *tú*. Another peculiarity is the use of the diminutive "*-ico*" instead of the usual "*-ito*." Some slang terms are used, such as *vaina* (thing: Guzmán) and *chévere* (great: Quica).

The actor Daniel Giménez Cacho gives Silanpa a slight Mexican accent, but not particularly notable or intrusive.

For Discussion

1. How does the film support the content of the story with its use of visual and verbal language?
2. Are this film's "romantics" (as Cabrera sees fit to call them) adequately rewarded?
3. Cabrera sees *The Art of Losing* as his return to filming in an urban setting: what does this imply, in the light of a comparison with, say, *Golpe de estadio* (*Time Out*)?

19. *Días de Santiago*
(Days of Santiago)

CREDITS: Peru, 2004; *Produced by:* Enid Campos, Chulluchaki Producciones (Peru); *Direction and Script:* Josué Méndez; *Music:* M. J. Laroche; *Sound:* Francisco Adrianzén; *Cinematography:* Juan Durán

CAST: Santiago Román (Pietro Sibille), Andrea (Milagros Vidal), Mamá (Lili Urbina), Papá (Ricardo Mejía), Coco (Erick García), Inés (Ivy La Noire)

Synopsis

Twenty-four-year-old Santiago has recently returned from six years' national service in the army (either against the Shining Path guerrillas or at the disputed northern jungle frontier with Ecuador; this is not specified). It is clear that Santiago has become used to a military lifestyle, relying on his wits and solidarity with his comrades. His earnest attempts at reinsertion into civilian life are frustrated by the changes that have taken place in his native Lima. People are neither aware, nor particularly concerned about, the sacrifices he has made: former pals from army days attempt other ways out of their difficulties. Santiago tries to control the emotional cocktail of residual rage from his experience of combat, and nostalgia for the order and existential simplicity of military life. This situation complicates his relationship with his partner and does nothing to help him face painful realities in his family.

About the Film

Días de Santiago was entirely Peruvian-financed. It won prizes at festivals in Lima, Fribourg, Bratislava, Cluj (the Transylvania festival in Romania), and Valladolid, all in 2004.

About the Film's Creators

Director **Josué Méndez** (Lima, 1976) studied film and Latin American culture at Yale, graduating in 1998. His short film *Parelisa* won him the best young director prize at the Huesca (Spain) Latin American film festival in 1999. He trained in film editing and worked in television and theatre before making *Dias de Santiago*, his first feature. Méndez spent a year with the English director Stephen Frears under the Rolex Mentor and Protégé Arts Initiative. During this period he shot his second feature, *Dioses* (*Gods*, 2008), a satirical examination of the pampered and insular youth of Lima's upper classes. It won the prize for best young director at the Biarritz Latin American film festival, 2008.

For Cultural Understanding

The Peruvian military is infamous for its indifference to the rights of the young men it recruits (and at times even press-gangs) as manpower with which to deal with national crises, whether real or invented. During the 1990s it was occupied on three fronts, by no means mutually exclusive: the long-standing border dispute with Ecuador, the conflict with the Shining Path Maoist guerrillas and the struggle against cocaine trafficking. This turmoil had terrible consequences for the civilian population, particularly in the Andes. Many people migrated from troubled areas like Ayacucho to the relative safety of Lima to escape the appalling violence being wreaked by both Shining Path and the army, both of whom distrusted the peasantry's loyalties. Coca-growing areas, previously occupied with satisfying demand for traditional ritual and medicinal purposes, have had to contend with conflict (and often collusion) between the military and the drug barons as cultivation spreads and is met by U.S.–led crop-spraying campaigns, with dire ecological consequences. The border dispute with Ecuador is currently dormant, but is prone to be reactivated whenever demagogic governments such as that of Alberto Fujimori require a convenient political smokescreen with which to distract their respective populations. It is in this context that the generation represented by Santiago Román grew up and was used as cannon fodder.

An excellent article by Ricardo Bedoya (Russo 2008, 151–168) looks at modes of portrayal of this phenomenon in Peruvian cinema, particularly as regards the city of Lima. He particularly explores the context of Peru in the crisis-ridden 1990s, when Sendero's presence was manifested by car bombs and other random violence, used by Alberto Fujimori as a pretext for autocratic rule, and weakened by the capture of the movement's leader, Abimael Guzmán. Filmic responses, not only to the conflict but the atmosphere it created, include Lombardi's *Bajo la piel*, Augusto Tamayo's *El bien esquivo*, Claudia Llosa's *La teta asustada* and, of course, *Días de Santiago*.

Interview with Writer-Director Josué Méndez

KR: Your presentation of the group of former combatants is very convincing—their way of speaking and body language, etc. Was this observation born of your own personal experience?

JM: No. It comes from the research that I did for the film and the support I had from Santiago, a real-life soldier, who told me all about training and his own experiences, and gave me anecdotes about military life. He also helped us a lot in rehearsals, helping actors to learn how to greet each other, speak and generally behave like true veterans.

The jumps from black and white to color are intriguing, particularly in the early shots of the city with Santiago as a passerby. It's something that recalls the radical aesthetics of the 1960–70s. Did you conceive this as a reference or tribute to these tendencies?

That's probably true. But unconsciously. Yes, I think it is a kind of homage, probably also nostalgia. I don't know. Intuitively it seemed to me interesting to mix formats because the character's subjectivity was so chaotic that I thought it would work.

The image given by the film of Peru, and in particular Lima, is far from flattering: violence, machismo and social injustice. What was its reception in your country? '

It is definitely a tough image of Lima, but I believe that for us natives of the city it was more like a documentary than anything else. I believe there was more resistance among Peruvians living abroad than Peruvians in Peru. For us it was natural, but for Peruvians based abroad it was more of a shock.

The script takes an unexpected turn: I, at any rate, was bracing myself for a bloodbath. Why does Santiago not take out his resentment and frustration on his brother or his father?

Because I simply didn't believe it was true to life. After getting to know ex-combatants quite closely, I learned that they are people with a lot of self-control, who would never shoot somebody from their own family or innocent people, however much they might disagree with them. The idea of a bloodbath seemed to belong more to an action film, it did not seem realistic to me for the character Santiago, because someone like him simply would not kill anybody in the civilian world.

The use of music is striking, especially the central Jewish Klezmer theme often used in quite incongruous scenes like the discotheque. Was it chosen for its surprise value in a Peruvian context?

It was the result of a search with the editor of the film. We felt that it reflected very well the emotional state of the character. It is sad without being very dramatic. It also provides a feeling of ritual, and a particular kind of nostalgia. And in the case of the discotheque we thought it was more important to reflect the emotional state of the character through music than the objective reality of the situation, which is what the mere use of disco music would have meant.

You make repeated use of extradiegetic voiceover and to great effect, although many consider this not a particularly cinematic resource. Do you not consider that the images and dialogues explain themselves sufficiently?

I believe this is an answer that the viewer would have to give. There are probably those who would consider the voiceover effective, and others who would not consider it effective. As for me, I felt the voiceover necessary to add dimensions and meaning to the character. The intention is not to explain, the film never explains anything, it simply portrays, and we chose to express the contradictions of the character through voiceover.

Your next project is a commentary on another, very different aspect of Lima society. Could you tell us something about it?

The next project is *Dioses* (*Gods*), a kind of chronicle about an upper-class family in Lima. The intention is to portray their way of life, their values and the lack of dialogue between the different strands of Lima society.

Analysis: Character Construction

A chapter on character construction in Peruvian director Augusto Tamayo's book on scriptwriting (2003) tells us that "in creating a character for a fiction script, we are necessarily creating those actions that allow him/her to be defined as a human being — imaginary but true to life — immersed in the imagined story"[1] (2003, 48).

One of the key points in the construction of Santiago as a character is his first visit to

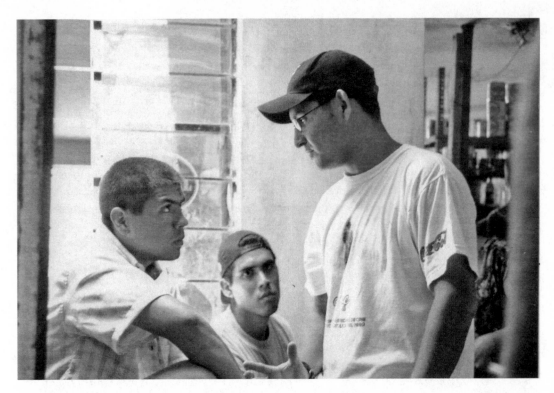

Josué Méndez directs Pietro Sibille on the set of *Días de Santiago*. Still photography by Melanie Hammond and Santiago Barco. Copyright © Chulluchaki Producciones.

the discotheque (C8). By the time this scene appears we have already learned certain bare facts, or have suspected unpleasant traits, about the protagonist. As the film progresses we are told by his voiceover commentary that he is jobless. His aspect and conduct display a social awareness: his first monologue (C2) talks of social responsibility, and he helpfully informs a young woman that her skirt is undone rather than just stare, as do the antisocial individuals for whom he has no patience. He is aware of the need for self-control, and is aware that indulging in violence is an abuse of his military training (despite his fantasies about this, and the hint in the very first shot of domestic violence). His adeptness at hand-to-hand fighting, and his talk of being no longer "there," confirm he is an ex-combatant. Now back inside society, however, he must adapt his need for order, a strategy, a "line." His body language is that of a military man, ready for combat if necessary and re-living army life in solitude. He had longed to return to the city, but is now unable to adapt, shorn of status and caught in an undisciplined and conflictive family environment. No relationship here is adequate; the problems with his wife, Mari, are compounded by the unconvincing camaraderie expressed by his father, tension with his violent and irresponsible brother Coco, and discomfort with sister-in-law Elisa's flirting. His mother's advice to make the most of married life and have children comes directly before the visit to the disco.

This scene, then, reveals frustration and deprivation; a desire to compensate for years without normal social or personal contact. We hear this in his comment about having been away six years, while other kids have been partying as if nothing had happened. It appears in his repeated preening and rehearsal of his moves, and his refusal, at least at first, to dance with the four girls he had met as a taxi driver. His uncertainty is manifested when, after protracted imagining and mental rehearsal of his approach to the single girl in the discotheque, he finally allows the four to take him onto the dance floor.

The character's obsessive military bearing inhibits his simple desire for fun. Apparent are not only Santiago's shyness and emotional need, but also his compulsive assessment of his "objective"; even in his imagination he gauges the girl's attitude when she dances with him, observing her hands, feet and hips to measure and follow her rhythm. He is sincere and anxious to demonstrate his lack of macho aggression.

Bedoya (Russo 2008, 160) asserts that *Días de Santiago* "works within the codes of the realist tradition, but dispenses with the conventional effects of recognition, mimesis and verisimilitude. The details and signs of urban culture are there, including the most strident, but they are dissolved in a mechanism of obsessions, reiterations, fixed ideas, diverse audio-visual treatments, transfigurations that force the logic of normal perception."[2]

This is visible in various aspects of this scene, in which Santiago's "advice" to himself is at times stilted and contradictory. The lack of verisimilitude in his picking out the girl points to a need to shape reality into something it clearly is not. The imagined repetitions of his approach betray an inability to make real decisions despite having been drilled for decisive action in another sphere.

Linguistic Features

The slang used in this film belongs to several categories: some of it is everyday Peruvian or Latin American vernacular such as *chela* (beer), *pulirte* (to become tame, in order to restore goodwill with wife or partner), *chamba* (work), *jato* (home), *vaina* (literally sheath, or pod, but also slang for issue or problem).

Other uses of language are specifically military, or refer to aspects of jungle life and combat: *promoción* is a term for military colleagues from the same year or unit. *Hombre punta* (literally "point man") refers to the unit member everyone looks to for initiative. *Pequepeque* is an onomatopoeic term for a jungle canoe, and *rancho* is a soldier's food ration. *Monos* (monkeys) is slang for Peru's long-term border rivals and perceived adversaries, the Ecuadoreans. The other enemy faced by Santiago, the Shining Path guerrillas, are *tucos* (an abbreviation of *terrucos*, slang for "terrorists").

For Discussion

1. Méndez's film has been compared with Scorsese's *Taxi Driver*, but what justifies this, beyond the obvious superficial consideration that both Travis Bickle and Santiago Román drive taxis?

2. Méndez answered the question about the use of voiceover by saying it's a question that the spectator should answer. What do you feel? Which other means could he have used to convey the subjectivity of the main character?

3. Hand-held camera is used almost exclusively in this film, and is rarely stable. What is the reason for this, if any? What does it contribute to the overall effect?

4. Ricardo Bedoya (2008, 161) has stated that the story "unfolds in a permanent tension

between contradictory forces of destruction and integration, of irrationality and chaos."[3] What are the technical resources used to create this feeling?

5. Augusto Tamayo (2003, 65) states that "a character's progress towards a new state of consciousness is one of the ways in which the plot provokes expectation and intrigue."[4] How do we see the character of Santiago develop and change after the first disco scene (C8)?

20. Fratricidal Wars and Imperialism

This chapter will examine types of conflict and their treatment on screen. Chronologically the first of these, the Conquest itself, is dealt with in the chapter on indigenous peoples: film treatments of the Falklands-Malvinas conflict (1982) are explored in the chapter on *Iluminados por el fuego*, and those of the Shining Path in Peru are in the chapter on *Paloma de papel.*

The stereotyped image of Latin America may be that of a troubled region, but very few full-scale wars have taken place here. Adolfo Colombres,[1] among others, argues that it had the world's "least demented" twentieth-century history, with the fewest wars and the highest degree of rationality. The Argentine writer's observation is to be seen as part of a thesis (Colombres 2007) that posits the emergence of a new era of civilization in the Americas. Other types of armed conflict are far more common than wars between neighbors: guerrilla warfare, manifestations of foreign intervention (direct military action, "proxy" warfare or sabotage), and state terrorism. Some conflicts have decided the formation and delineation of states, and there are still occasional border disputes. Nonetheless, it is misleading to regard the region as lagging in terms of basic humanity behind Europe and North America, which have provoked and sponsored conflict in Latin America and elsewhere. The consolidation of power bases and imposition of political and economic models obedient to the West have rarely been achieved without bloodshed. Such confrontations are largely responsible for Latin America's geopolitical and cultural configuration, as well as its cultural and psychological imaginary.

If we are to identify an almost constant difference between the Latin American war film and its Hollywood counterpart, it would be the lack of an escapist, "entertainment" element. Conversely, neither does the pious "anti-war" film often appear. Rarely do Latin American films, explicitly or otherwise, express the inherent correctness of a national cause or God-given right to make war.

Conflicts taken as cinematographic themes include most of the types listed above. Some armed confrontations are too recent or politically sensitive to film, or otherwise publicize. War films sometimes appear when conservative social and political interests require that an event should be within the public domain, fixing boundaries in the national or collective imaginary. The creation of "enemies within," such as Indian populations, or rebellious outlying communities, aids their stigmatization as undesirable obstacles to progress. Political and social change can be bolstered and justified by airing such historical events, and film is a persuasive means of doing so. In contrast, many films within the New Latin American Cinema's response to dictatorial conditions in the 1960s and '70s took an oppositional view of warfare. The same, of course, applies to certain films made before this movement, but more notable is the examination of these dictatorships in subsequent decades, particularly in Argentina.

Independence

One of the earliest Latin American films with a war theme was *La Batalla de Maipú* (Argentina, 1912), Argentina-based Italian Mario Gallo's reconstruction of the 1818 defeat of royalist forces in the campaign for the independence of Chile. The film marked a foundational moment not only at a national but also regional level.

In Cuba the Spanish presence ended far later through the 1898 Spanish-American War. Film was in its infancy, but could purport to be an eyewitness presence. Michael Chanan's seminal *Cuban Cinema* (2004, 43) looks at cinematic versions of this conflict, by filmmakers unable to obtain footage of the event improvised naval encounters with models, passing them off as authentic. The prime example is Albert Smith and Jim Blackton's *The Battle of Santiago Bay* (1898). García Mesa, Douglas and González (García Mesa 147) corroborate that "brief and dubious takes were filmed in Cuba of ambushes, skirmishes, the famous Taking of the Loma de San Juan, a panorama of the Castillo del Morro in Havana, and a naval combat in Santiago de Cuba ... which was actually filmed in New York using models."[2] The documentary *Viva la república* (*Long Live the Republic*, Pastor Vega, 1972) re-contextualized original footage from this era in a conscious use of anachronism described by Michael Chanan (2004, 38) as a "historical compilation juxtaposing a variety of old newsreels, photographs, political cartoons, and similar visual material." Its newsreel footage includes the landing of Roosevelt's Rough Riders and shots of the Spanish-American War itself, part of a U.S. media and political stance towards Cuba that, the film implies, has not significantly changed since the Revolution.

La primera carga al machete (*The First Charge of the Machete*, Manuel Octavio Gómez, 1969) sets out to imitate early newsreels, despite taking as its subject the previous (1868, pre–cinematic) anti–Spanish struggle, shot with pseudo-documentary elements and filmed "interviews" with soldiers.

Manuel Herrera's full-length documentary *Girón* (*Bay of Pigs*, 1974) also juxtaposes oral history, as participants tell their stories, with reconstruction of the described U.S.–backed invasion. There are overt references to misleading film versions of war: for example, a man tells of almost breaking his teeth trying to pull a pin from a grenade. John Mraz (1993) explains this aesthetic in opposition to the war film as entertainment: "*Girón* attempts to cut against the grain of this tradition through juxtaposing documentary material and filmed reenactments in order to draw attention to the cinematic discourse by heightening the difference between documentary and re-creation through alienation techniques."

The Cuban-Spanish conflict spawned a children's revolutionary figurehead, Juan Padrón's *mambí*[3] colonel Elpidio Valdés, in the first animation films produced in the Caribbean region.[4] In 1998, the centenary of Cuba's independence, the Teodoro and Santiago Ríos film *Mambí* (1998) analyzed the various factors contributing to a conflict that was ultimately to Washington's advantage, creating a nominally sovereign state but one very much within the U.S. sphere. Far from being a triumphalist reconstruction, *Mambí* adopts the viewpoint of soldiers from the Canary Islands whose scant respect for their declining "motherland" leads them to change sides.

In Argentina, *Guerra Gaucha* (*The Gaucho War*, Lucas Demare, 1942) reveals a little-considered aspect of the war of independence, namely that it was largely fought on behalf of the elite by downtrodden Gauchos and other marginal elements highly unlikely to benefit from the outcome.

The **Texas War** (1835–36) and **Mexican-American War** (1846–48), evidently episodes both sides have preferred to forget, have had little representation in film. Productions acceptable to both sides are even rarer: the two patriotic U.S. versions of *The Alamo* (John Wayne, 1960, and John Lee Hancock, 2004) have reveled in events bitterly resented on the Mexican side. Mexican viewpoints of the war are rarely presented; an exception is *El cementerio de las águilas* (*The Eagles' Cemetery*, Luis Lezama, Mexico, 1939), which deals with the battles of Churubusco and the role of the young soldiers known as "Niños Héroes" who resisted U.S. entry into Mexico City. *One Man's Hero* (Lance Hool, USA, 1999) presents a very different perspective, that of an Irish battalion that reacted to prejudice against them north of the border by changing sides, crossing to join the Mexican forces.

Curiously little cinematographic attention has been given to the 1860s **Mexican-French War** in which French forces invaded Mexico and imposed the Austrian "emperor" Maximilian, who was subsequently defeated and executed by President Benito Juárez. Some of the film versions that do exist, such as William Dieterle's *Juárez* (USA, 1939) and Steve Sekely's *Furia roja* (*Stronghold*, Mexico/USA, 1950), were at least partly made from a North American perspective — the latter with versions in both English and Spanish, reflecting shared interest at the time in demagogic reminders of resistance to European invasion. Of the purely Mexican productions, *Cuatro contra el imperio* (*Four against the Empire*, Jaime Salvador, 1957) was an adaptation of Dumas' *Three Musketeers* transposed to this new context. *Juárez y Maximiliano* (Miguel Contreras Torres and Raphael J. Sevilla, 1934), according to Emilio García Riera, dwells on the relationship between Maximilian and his wife Carlota to the extent that the film's historical content and implications are almost buried. The patriotic *Mexicanos Al Grito de Guerra*, also known as *Historia del Himno Nacional* (*Story of the National Anthem*), directed by Álvaro Gálvez y Fuentes and Ismael Rodríguez in 1943, was one of national icon Pedro Infante's earliest films. It traces the composition of the anthem, played by a young Mexican soldier (who has ironically fallen in love with the French ambassador's niece) to inspire his countrymen against the invaders. Felipe Cazals' 1978 biopic *La Güera Rodríguez* (*The Fair Rodríguez*) stars Fanny Cano as a rich and eloquent early–nineteenth-century lady whose relationships with powerful men scandalized society at the time, but here provides the background for the French invasion and presents her as an advocate of independence.

Internal Repression

The formation of the Latin American republics involved considerable coercion and bloodshed, both in conquest and in the repression of dissenting political and religious views. As in North America, "Indian wars" saw indigenous populations decimated and even eliminated. *El ultimo malón* (*The Last Indian Attack*, Alcides Greca, Argentina, 1917) is a silent showing a formative event (the final defeat of indigenous rebellion in the northern Chaco region) whose evident sympathies are not exclusively with the victors.

Federico García Hurtado's *Tupac Amaru* (Peru, 1984) rather theatrically dramatizes the great Andean Indian rebellion of 1780, whose far-reaching cultural ramifications and political consequences continue into the present day.

Leopoldo Torre Nilsson's *Martín Fierro* (Argentina, 1968) is based on a narrative poem that is emblematic of the country's painful entry into modernity. Its protagonist, a national (albeit fictional) hero, is a gaucho forced to fight in the so-called Conquest of the Desert (1879-80) which fixed Argentina's western frontiers and finally quashed Indian resistance to White settlement.

A curious blend of political and religious differences with the state brought provincial resistance in the Canudos conflict in 1890s Brazil, in which a remote northeastern community defied the recently established republic, its moves to impose taxes and exert other forms of central control. The epic *A guerra de Canudos* (*The Battle of Canudos*, Sérgio Rezende, Brazil, 1997), well-acted and shot, uses a female protagonist to explore the religious and mythical dimensions of this tragic war as well as its political and economic causes. The same is true of Sérgio Silva's *Anahy de las misiones*, whose emblematic heroine dates from the Cisplatine War (1825–28) but was filmically transferred to the Farroupilha Revolution (1835–45) perhaps due to the latter's greater historical impact.

Patagonia rebelde (*Rebellion in Patagonia*, Argentina, 1974), telling of a rural workers' rebellion over pay and conditions in 1920s southern Argentina, is one of several films made by Héctor Olivera that re-examine the repeated use of violence, throughout his country's history, as a form of maintaining social inequality. His *No habrá más penas ni olvido* (*A Funny Dirty Little War*, 1983) looks at another flashpoint, adapting a bitterly satirical novel by Osvaldo Soriano on the Peronist movement's degeneration into brutal factionalism. It takes as a microcosm a provincial town's nightmarish descent from a facade of everyday bonhomie into a murderous rampage. The process is accompanied by a disquieting fluctuation in the film's tone between humor and horror. Yet another harrowing Olivera film, *La noche de los lápices* (*Night of the Pencils*, 1986), tells the true story of the torture and "disappearance" of student activists in 1975, the outset of the Dirty War. The sheer volume of films that have explored this savage repression is an indication of the psychological effects of the military's reign of terror (see also Chapter 8 on the children's perspective).

Political violence in Brazil is portrayed in two further films by Sérgio Rezende; *Lamarca* (1994) is the true story of an officer in the Brazilian army who changed sides to fight for leftist guerrillas. Another real-life narration, *Zuzu Angel* (2006), sees a successful fashion designer delve into her own past, braving the memories of abuse suffered under the dictatorship to reconcile herself with the murdered son she was unable to bury. Bruno Barreto's *O que é isso, companheiro?* (*4 Days in September*, 1997) recounts a true story of the revolutionary MR-8 group's kidnap of the U.S. ambassador in 1969.

Territorial Disputes

In **The War of the Pacific** (1879–83) Chile defeated the combined forces of Peru and Bolivia, depriving the latter of its entire Pacific coastline. *Caliche sangriento* (*Bloody Nitrate*, Helvio Soto, Chile, 1969) advances an unusual Chilean perspective — that of the (albeit partial) loser. It follows a handful of soldiers, lost in the desert, as they attempt to rejoin their nation's forces. Their misadventures heighten the absurdity of the situation, as do discussions of the war between the jingoistic captain and his skeptical lieutenant, who argues that the Chilean government and army are being manipulated by foreign capital. *Amargo mar* (*Bitter Sea*, Antonio Eguino, Bolivia, 1984) advances the thesis that Bolivia's catastrophic defeat resulted from connivance between Chilean authorities and Bolivian private interests. This departs from the usual nationalistic demagoguery that presents Bolivia as purely a victim of Chilean expansion, backed up British diplomacy. The TV series *Epopeya: la guerra del Pacífico* (2007) provides another Chilean viewpoint, though here opening up a debate with both Peruvian and Bolivian historians, a welcome approach in view of the current political climate and talk of Latin American integration.

The Chaco War (1932–35) between Bolivia and Paraguay is generally viewed as one of the most tragic and senseless of all Latin American conflicts (see the chapter on *Hamaca paraguaya*). *Hijo de hombre* (*Son of Man*, Lucas Demare, Argentina, 1961) was based on a section of the eponymous novel by the great Paraguayan writer Augusto Roa Bastos. Argentine Demare's film relates the Paraguayan viewpoint, avoiding any notable chauvinism other than the Manichean shots of Bolivian pilots grinning in satisfaction as they destroy water trucks attempting to relieve Paraguayan soldiers. The film is also known as *La sed* (*The Thirst*); dehydration was identified by Roa Bastos as the main killer in "a fratricidal war whose causes have now been clarified: instigated by powerful oil companies, whose interests were pinned on black gold deposits in the bowels of the immense northern Chaco territory"[5] (Roa Bastos 1993, 179). Roque Funes's documentary *En el infierno del Chaco* (*In the Chaco Hell*, 1932) offers valuable images of the war from both sides.[6] Alfonso Gumucio Dagron's discussion of Bolivian film treatments of the war includes an account of the making and suppression of the film *Alerta* (*Alert*, Mario Camacho, Bolivia, 1932), confiscated by the Bolivian army because of its less-than-favorable view of the higher ranks. Gumucio goes on to speculate about other such possible cases: "When we come to think of the films that, through confiscation and other means, came into the army's hands, we dream of the Bolivian film collection that it would have been possible to establish. But it is most likely that ignorance has by now caused the disappearance of the originals of all these films. The cans must have been used as ashtrays in some barracks' canteen"[7] (1982, 144–145).

Another absurd conflict (for its one-sidedness alone) was the **War of the Triple Alliance** (1864–1870), in which Paraguay took on the combined might of Uruguay, Brazil and Argentina. The war left the Paraguayans economically crippled for decades, with a severely depleted male population. The final battle at Cerro Corá confirmed their reputations as indefatigable warriors but is generally described as a symbolic effort by hopelessly outnumbered and pitifully ill-equipped survivors. Guillermo Vera's *Cerro Corá* (Paraguay, 1978), made under the dictatorship of General Alfredo Stroessner, was conceived as a patriotic rallying cry, haranguing spectators with the heroism of this doomed last stand. A more recent documentary on a soldier who painted scenes from this war, *Cándido López, los campos de batalla* (*Cándido López, the Battlefields*, José Luis García, Argentina, 2005) presents a human rather than demagogic image of the Paraguayan debacle.

Guerrillas

Film versions of guerrilla warfare in Latin America are comparatively infrequent, mostly depicting victorious Cuban revolutionaries or state campaigns against insurrection in Colombia and Peru. Cinema remains fascinated by Ernesto "Che" Guevara, the most attractive of Latin American revolutionaries for reasons including the political polarization he still provokes, the romance and mystery surrounding his death, and his physical attributes. U.S. versions range from the reportedly most risible (Richard Fleischer's *Che!*, USA, 1969) to the most credible (Steven Soderbergh's *The Argentine and Guerrilla*, both 2008, two of the best North American films on Latin America yet made). The best Latin American fiction films on Guevara's life do not deal directly with warfare. *Diarios de motocicleta* (*The Motorcycle Diaries*, Walter Salles, 2004) looks at an episode that pre-dates any fighting. The aftereffects of Che's campaign in Bolivia (1968) are dealt with fictionally in the intriguing *Di buen día a papá* (*Say Good Morning to Dad*, Fernando Vargas, Bolivia, 2004).

Other guerrilla films have taken a perhaps surprisingly comic tone, such as Sergio Cabrera's *Golpe de estadio* (*Time Out*, Colombia, 1998) in which rebels and military agree to a truce to watch a World Cup qualifying match (real footage is used of Colombia's celebrated 5–0 win in Buenos Aires in 1993). *Los actores del conflicto* (*Actors in the Conflict*, Lisandro Duque Naranjo, Colombia/Venezuela, 2008) follows a mime troupe's semi-accidental involvement in drug-running and armed rebellion. *Punto y raya* (*A Dot and a Line*, Elia Schneider, Venezuela/Spain/Chile/Uruguay, 2004) tells of a farcical but fateful encounter between members of opposing sides in the confused, multi-faceted Venezuelan-Colombian border situation. The strange but true story of *Soñar no cuesta nada* (*A Ton of Luck*, Rodrigo Triana, Colombia, 2006) concerns the dilemma faced by Colombian soldiers after their discovery of a fortune hidden by guerrillas.

In contrast, *Oedipo alcalde* (*Oedipus Mayor*, Jorge Ali Triana, Colombia/Spain/Mexico/Cuba, 1996) is Gabriel García Márquez's adaptation of Sophoclean tragedy to the Colombian situation. The feature-length documentary *La guerrillera* (*Guerrilla Girl*, Frank Piasechi Poulsen, Denmark, 2005) looks at a serious aspect of Colombian FARC rebels' reality — the dedication of their numerous female members.

Revolutions

The **Mexican Revolution** is the most screened of Latin American conflicts, whether in newsreel, fiction, or, as often happened, a combination of the two. Films first appeared whilst the struggle still continued; these were usually newsreels filmed at the cameraman's own risk and often shown before the government could remove them from exhibition (González Casanova, 245). Apart from hazards of filming on battlefields, there was the danger of favoring the losing side: as García Riera explains, the prolific Alva brothers (Salvador, Guillermo, Eduardo and Carlos) carefully avoided such indiscretions with *Revolucion orozquista* (1912) and openly took the official line against Zapata with *Sangre hermana* (1914). Raymundo Gleyzer's documentary *México, la revolución congelada* (*Mexico: The Frozen Revolution*, Argentina/U.S., 1973) uses clips from the era to illustrate its thesis of frustrated political change. The revolution had a long wait before becoming a fictional theme; the most famous early example was Fernando de Fuentes's 1930s trilogy; *El prisionero 13* (*Prisoner 13*, 1933), *El compadre Mendoza* (*Godfather Mendoza*, 1934) and *Vámonos con Pancho Villa!* (*Let's Join Pancho Villa*, 1936). The treatment of the Mexican Revolution in film is discussed at length by Zuzana Pick.[8]

The fighting offered up ready-made heroes in Pancho Villa and Emiliano Zapata, both of whom have been copiously portrayed on screen. Villa famously even had a film career, on both sides of the border, explored in the TV movie *And Starring Pancho Villa as Himself* (Bruce Beresford, USA, 2003). The images of both men have inevitably suffered distortions as attitudes and perspectives change. Zapata received fairly sympathetic and accurate treatment in *Emiliano Zapata* (Felipe Cazals, 1970). In the U.S., Elia Kazan's *Viva Zapata!* (1952) brought the Revolution to a far wider audience but failed to elicit one of Marlon Brando's more convincing performances. The most recent screen version of the leader is Alfonso Arau's trivialization *Zapata — El sueño del héroe* (2004) in which a whitened Zapata (played by the singer Alejandro Fernández) is seen first and foremost as a dashing ladies' man, guided by pseudo-ethnographic rites through a series of romantic encounters and, occasionally, battles. In another personification of the struggle, *La negra Angustias* (*Black Angustias*, Matilde Landeta, Mexico, 1950), highlights the important role played by women in the conflict (see Feminine Protagonists). *Reed: México insurgente* (*Reed: Insurgent México:* Paul Leduc, Mexico 1973), based on the memoirs of the U.S. journalist John Reed, is widely considered the best film of the Mexican Revolution. Filmed in sepia tones to evoke period documentary, it typifies director Leduc's minimization of the spoken word and concentration on visual narration.

The film most associated with the **Cuban Revolution**, apart from biographies of Ché Guevara, is Tomás Gutiérrez Alea's *Historias de la revolución* (*Stories of the Revolution,* 1960), the first feature film made in Cuba after the defeat of Batista. As Michael Chanan points out, Gutiérrez Alea's presentation of three separate moments in the revolutionary struggle against Batista served to consolidate feelings of audience identification and involvement with the process represented on the screen (Chanan, 144–145).

Numerous filmmakers from Europe and the Americas became interested in Central American unrest during the 1970s and '80s, particularly the civil wars in Nicaragua and El Salvador. *Carla's Song* (Ken Loach, UK/Spain/Germany, 1996) tells of a Nicaraguan woman, exiled in Glasgow in the 1980s. Her relationship with a local man, who accompanies her when she returns home, provides the framework for an examination of the legacy of prolonged warfare her Central American homeland. Loach, as ever, implacably but subtly opposes neo-colonialism, whoever its perpetrator.

Miguel Littín's *Alsino y el cóndor* (*Alsino and the Condor,* Nicaragua/Cuba/Mexico/Costa Rica, 1982) treats the issue of Nicaraguan independence and self-determination allegorically, using fantasy in a gritty rather than whimsical manner. The U.S. military presence is personified by actor Dean Stockwell's army officer, increasingly sympathetic to the Sandinista rebels. Renowned Chilean exile Littín, then based in Nicaragua, also made the biopic *Sandino* (1990), a disappointment given the iconic status of its protagonist and the film's being the most expensive yet made in Central America. Two U.S. productions from the 1980s took on the theme of the U.S. role in Central American conflict. *Salvador* (Oliver Stone, USA, 1987) and *Under Fire* (Roger Spottiswoode, USA, 1983) both adopt an exclusively North American viewpoint, with avowed concern for their troubled settings but little evident attempt to understand local subjectivities. *Walker* (Alex Cox, USA/Mexico/Spain, 1997) is a fanciful and extravagant biography of William Walker, the U.S. millionaire and filibuster who took a private army into Nicaragua (1855–57) on one of the last of several disastrous and vainglorious adventures in Latin America. Cox, the English maverick whose other work in Latin America includes *El patrullero* (*Highway Patrolman,* USA/Mexico, 1991) courted ridicule with his flamboyance but *Walker* has undeniable cult appeal and the substantial presence of Ed Harris in the title role, a prototype for reckless invasion.

Héroes de otra patria (*Heroes from Another Land,* Iván Dariel Ortiz, Puerto Rico 1998) addresses a theme since repeated in Iraq: the participation of Latino soldiers in a war waged by the USA (in this case, with Vietnam) and the effects of the experience upon the lives of two young Puerto Ricans. A similar theme, but with yet more disastrous consequences, is explored to great effect in Andrés Baíz's *Satanás* (*Satan,* Colombia, 2007) based on the homonymous novel by Mario Mendoza, the true story of a traumatized Colombian Vietnam vet who killed 30 people in a single night in 1986.

The war film in Latin America has served revisionist views of history across the ideological spectrum, whether relatively recent or dating back to national foundations. It also helps to define relationships with foreign powers, both in the Americas and Europe. As such it appears to be a genre dependent on political contingency whose future development, given the current international climate, is difficult to gauge.

21. *Iluminados por el fuego*
(Blessed by Fire)

CREDITS: Argentina, 2005; *Produced by:* Ana de Skalon: Morocha Films; *Director:* Tristán Bauer; *Script:* Tristán Bauer, Miguel Bonasso; *Sound:* Martín Grignaschi; *Songs:* León Gieco; *Director of Photography:* Javier Julia; *Montage:* Alejandro Brodersohn, Martín Subirá; 35 mm: 100 minutes

CAST: Esteban Leguizamón (Gastón Pauls), Alberto Vargas (Pablo Riva), Marta/María Vargas (Virginia Innocenti), Juan Chamorro (César Albarracín), Pizarro (Víctor Hugo Carrizo)

Synopsis

Journalist Esteban Leguizamón receives a late phone call in his office from the wife of a friend, Alberto Vargas, who has been rushed to hospital. Vargas, whom Esteban has known since his time as a combatant in the Falklands-Malvinas war, still has not recovered mentally from the experience. Esteban begins to recall his time as a young conscript, and the film alternates between his time on the islands and present-day Buenos Aires.

About the Film

Blessed by Fire is the English title preferred at festivals, but *illuminated* or *enlightened* might be a more accurate translation. The film deals with a theme whose importance to the Argentine national consciousness cannot be exaggerated. This is reflected in its reception — 46,000 spectators in the first four days made it the most viewed national production in Argentine history.

In an interview[1] the leading actor Gastón Pauls asserts that this film was made as a necessity — every prize it wins serves to honor the truth and the memory of those who died. He reminds readers, as does Tristán Bauer (see below) that the military warned survivors of dire consequences if they did not keep quiet about the war.

An UNSAM (Universidad de San Martín) production with coproduction by Morocha Films and economic support from INCAA, Film Law of the Province of San Luis, the Province of San Luis and Fomicruz. The project was completed with funds from the prize "Cine en Construcción" from the festivals of Toulouse and San Sebastián.

The film has received numerous awards, including the Special Jury Prize at the 2005 San Sebastián Festival, Gran Coral (Havana 2005), Goya prize for best non–Mexican

Spanish-language film (2005) and award for best narrative at the Tribeca Film Festival (2006).

About the Film's Creators

Tristán Bauer (born in Mar del Plata, 1959) is one of Argentina's most respected filmmakers. His first feature film, *Después de la tormenta* (*After the Storm*, 1990), looks at the consequences of Argentina's dire unemployment problem. He has made films on two of his country's most famous writers: Julio Cortázar (*Cortázar*, 1994) and Jorge Luis Borges with *Los libros y la noche* (*The Books and the Night*, 1999). *Evita, la tumba sin paz* (*Evita, the Unquiet Grave*, 1997) deals with another national icon — Eva Perón — and the bizarre and repulsive treatment given her corpse by a military resentful of her leftwing sympathies and intolerant of opposition. Bauer's acclaimed documentary about Ernesto "Ché" Guevara, *Che: Un hombre nuevo* (*Che: A New Man*) was released in 2010.

Edgardo Esteban (Buenos Aires, 1962) is a journalist who has worked for both press and television. The first edition of his war memoirs, entitled *Iluminados por el fuego: Confesiones de un soldado que combatió en Malvinas*, ("confessions of a soldier who fought in the Malvinas") appeared in 1993. The second edition, co-written with Gustavo Romero Borri and published in 1999, is *Malvinas, diario del regreso* — the "diary of the return"' so longed for by the characters in Bauer's film in order to banish their demons.

The celebrated journalist and writer **Miguel Bonasso** (Buenos Aires, 1940) collaborated on the script for this film, having also done the research for Bauer's *Evita, la tumba sin paz*. His work has persistently uncovered truths about the abuse of political authority in Argentina. This resulted in his persecution by the military dictatorships of the 1970s, when he lived in hiding before going into exile. He has published numerous works of history, political commentary and testimony.

The Argentine singer-songwriter **León Gieco**, who wrote and performed the songs for this film, is a voice long associated with opposition to dictatorship. Significantly, a version of his most famous song, *Sólo le pido a Dios*, is also heard at the end of the Chilean film *Mi mejor enemigo*.

For Cultural Understanding: The Malvinas/ Falklands War on Film

This unseemly brawl over one of the last British colonies was the final gesture of the Argentine military dictatorship. The invasion of the islands ordered by Leopoldo Galtieri was a cynical appeal to nationalism calculated to touch a raw nerve among the populace. Victory for the British forces spelled the end of the Argentine military dictatorship.

The radical filmmaker Raymundo Gleyzer became the first Argentine to film on the disputed territory in 1966, with the 30-minute film *Nuestras Islas Malvinas* (*Our Malvinas Islands*). Gleyzer was given official permission and welcomed into several homes by hosts who seemed blissfully unaware of his less than pro–British stance.

Most Argentine films of the war, whether individual stories, documentaries or more philosophical and poetic works, oppose the military's doomed adventure. Any patriotic angle is generally limited to sympathy for the young men who died. One of the most informative documentaries is Matías Gueilburt's *Malvinas: La retirada* (*The Retreat*, 2008) which exposes the craven opportunism in the military junta's exploitation of nationalist feelings. The invasion of the islands was a perfect illustration of the famous dictum attributed to Samuel Johnson.[2]

The documentary also addresses what journalist Jorge Lanata calls the "collective amnesia" of those who uncritically supported the recuperation of the islands by an autocrat such as Leopoldo Galtieri. Miguel Bonasso describes his country as one with considerable political energy but scant political culture, unable to reflect on the subtleties of a situation such as this. In Britain, the invasion was eagerly grasped by a then deeply unpopular Thatcher government as a heaven-sent opportunity to improve poll ratings. A hastily assembled and pitifully ill-equipped force of young Argentine recruits was sent to wait, in sub-zero temperatures, for their highly trained and well-equipped adversary. Washington dropped its original diplomatic support for the Argentine junta and instead backed the British. Galtieri's regime made a disastrous miscalculation: even with hindsight, its myopia as to the international situation and the likely British reaction seems incredible. Their incompetence was not limited to diplomacy: officers with experience only of victimizing defenseless civilians were found seriously exposed when it came to true combat. Those who paid the ultimate price were the Argentine recruits, over half aged 18 to 19 and with only the most basic military training. This is the context in which Bauer's film unfolds.

Other documentaries concur with the general line taken by Gueilburt. The second part of Miguel Pérez's historical documentary series *La república perdida* (*The Lost Republic*, 1986) addresses the war as part of its examination of military dictatorship in Argentina. Federico Urioste's *Hundan al Belgrano* (*Sink the Belgrano*, 1996) takes another documentary view, this time of the war's most significant incident — the psychological blow landed by the Thatcher government, costing 323 lives. Jorge Denti's *Malvinas, historia de traiciones* (*A Story of Betrayals*, 1984) is another documentary concerning the military's duplicity in the conduct and presentation of the war. The full-length documentary *Operación Algeciras* (Jesús Mora, 2004) tells an extraordinary story of covert action by Argentine agents thwarted in their attempt to blow up British ships at the Gibraltar naval base during the early weeks of the war. The conflict had far less impact on the British national psyche, but several features and documentaries were made, perhaps the best of which is *An Ungentlemanly Act*, written and directed by Stuart Urban in 1992. Its opening shots of penguins "marching" to a military band sets the overall tone, mockingly spurious and outdated colonial hubris. The film shows bravery, on both sides, from men betrayed by opportunistic and treacherous governments. It recalls the words of the most famous Anglo-Argentine, writer Jorge Luis Borges, who likened the war to "two bald men fighting over a comb."

Some films examine the incompetence with which the war was handled and the vicious contempt with which recruits were treated. Bebe Kamin's film *Los chicos de la guerra* (*The Boys of War*, 1984) was the first film about the war: it exposes the boundless cynicism of the military, who went so far as to steal supplies naively collected by the public for the recruits. The filmmaker Miguel Pereira is from the impoverished province of Jujuy, northwest Argentina, an area remote from Buenos Aires which was exploited by the military as a source of young recruits. His film *La deuda interna* (*The Debt*, 1988) is also known as *Verónico Cruz* after the boy befriended by a trainee schoolteacher posted at a remote Andean village.

Verónico, who has never seen the sea, becomes one of those killed on the ill-fated Belgrano. *Pozo de zorro* (*Foxhole*, Miguel Mirra, 1999) tells of a group of soldiers stranded after a lost battle, waiting and hoping for redemption. A similar idea is used to satirical effect in Bruno Stagnaro's short *Guarisove* (a mangled rendering of *War Is Over*) made as part of the compilation *Historias breves IV* (1995). Here an Argentine platoon, reminiscent of certain Japanese units at the end of World War II, roams the islands unaware that hostilities have ceased.

Other films have concentrated on the consequences, social and individual, of the conflict. *El visitante* (*The Visitor*, Javier Oliveira, 1999) focuses upon a Malvinas veteran still suffering the traumatic effects of combat. *Locos de la bandera* (*The Insane of the Flag*, Julio Cardoso, 2005) tells of bereaved family members unable to visit their sons' graves either because these were on the islands or because the bodies were unidentified.

Among more offbeat treatments are *Vamos ganando* (Ramiro Longo, 2001), whose title sarcastically uses the slogan ("We're winning") employed by propagandists during the conflict, while the film presents repugnant images of insanity and suffering. A documentary by the same director, *No tan nuestras* (*Not Really Ours*, Ramiro Longo, 2004), offers a psychology, not only of the war's prosecution and effects, but of the islands' place in the national consciousness.

The conflict threw up some oddities: José Luis Marqués' *Fuckland* (Argentina, 2000) takes as a dubious premise the alternative to military action of "reclaiming" the islands by having Argentines impregnating Falklands women. *Argie* (Jorge Blanco, 1983), filmed in the UK where Blanco was living at the time of the conflict, takes as its title the contemptuous nickname for Argentines invented by the British sensationalist press. Blanco, who plays himself in the film, declares war unilaterally on the UK. *Palabra por palabra* (*Word for Word*, Edgardo Cabeza, 2008) tells of two Argentine soldiers, one of them wounded, taking refuge with a local woman and her daughter — a situation made farcical by the lack of a common language.

The islands and the conflict still provide a compelling theme for filmmakers: Rodrigo Fernández's *Cartas a Malvinas* (2009) looks at the daily experience of conscripts through their reliance on letters — whether from the mainland, or elsewhere.

A Conversation with Director Tristán Bauer

I met Tristán Bauer when he was in La Paz in September 2006 looking for materials, at the Cinemateca Boliviana and elsewhere, to include in his documentary on Ernesto Che Guevara, *Che: Un hombre nuevo* (*Che: A New Man*, Argentina/Cuba/Spain, 2010). He told me that when they were in Havana the previous December with his partner and collaborator Carolina Scaglione to prepare *Iluminados por el fuego*, they had been approached by Guevara's widow, Aleida March, and began to talk about the possibility of making the documentary.[3]

I asked about their numerous film biographies (Bauer often uses the first person plural). He sees this aspect of the work as not entirely voluntary, a genre that in some way has pursued them. The biographies have dealt mainly with writers: Julio Cortázar, José Luis Borges and San Juan de la Cruz, as well as aspects of Eva Perón (see below).

He agreed that there are two main currents in his work: the personal concerns have a social element running through them. A good example of this intersection, he accepted, is the 1994 film *Cortázar*, which is also partly a cross between documentary and fiction. "In documentaries there's always a touch of fiction, and my fictions always have a touch of doc-umentary, too. I'm always working with these lines that cross."

I suggested that was also the case with *Después de la tormenta* (*After the Storm*, 1994). Bauer had made several documentaries, including work as a cameraman for Miguel Littín and Estela Bravo. His first feature, *Después de la tormenta* deals with what he calls the "terrible social scourge" that is unemployment. A fiction film, it was nonetheless shot in real settings, with also a mix of professional and non-professional actors. This is the film he considers the origin of this blend of genres.

Moving on to *Iluminados por el fuego* it seemed to me that, unlike the much-pho-tographed Che Guevara, here one could even talk of a scarcity of images. He told me that the idea for the film came from having met the Malvinas veteran, Edgardo Esteban, and being deeply moved: until that point, like any Argentine, he had read journalism and a few books offering a geo-military or political analysis. But Esteban's book was a moving depiction of the war through the eyes of a young man of 18. Like many young men taken off to the islands, he was not a professional soldier but a conscript doing obligatory military service, who was suddenly expected to face the professional might of the British army. This was an unexpected encounter for Bauer, who had just finished his documentary about Eva Perón. Esteban, who is now foreign correspondent for a North American chain, had just interviewed him and handed him a copy of the book saying, "Take this, it will be your next film." Bauer read the book and phoned Esteban to tell him, "You're right, it looks like this will be my next film." This isn't a linear adaptation, it later involved a lot of research, almost enough for a documentary, with several veterans. From this the story of three friends was invented, and what Bauer terms the "terrible theme of the suicides — a subject that hadn't been touched upon in Argentina," which were the materials out of which the story was built. But to Bauer the film is, essentially, an evaluation of this viewpoint of a very young man taken off to fight.

I mentioned the constant coming and going between today's Buenos Aires and the islands at that time. He agreed that there is also a play between present and past, something that appears through wanting to talk about the period after the war, and what these postwar suicides meant. Now, there were more deaths from suicide than from combat in the islands, a terrible drama for Argentines. "As you were saying, the subject is one that was absolutely hidden, nobody wanted to talk about it, when the war ended these young men received orders from the higher echelons not to talk about the islands, almost a prohibition, a pact of silence." This applied not only during the military dictatorship but also when Alfonsín[4] assumed power in the first constitutional government after the dictatorship, when this policy of "de–Malvinization" continued. Bauer considers that, in this sense, what happened with his film was something that occurs occasionally, and what makes cinema so marvelous; sud-denly a film provoked a whole debate — it had people in Argentina talking about Malvinas, a subject that was hidden, covered up, which society did not want to take responsibility for.

We talked about some of the other films about the war such as Bebe Kamin's *Los chicos de la guerra* (*The Boys of War*, 1984) which also had quite an impact in Latin America. Bauer sees his own film as the first that genuinely set out to reconstruct the battles and other events in the territory of the islands. "In that sense, this is the first film to immerse itself in that hell."

I mentioned that there had been certain British features and documentaries dealing with the war and its consequences. Of course, these are inevitable from the winner's perspective, if it was true that there was a winner. I semi-joked that Argentina at least got rid of its dictatorship whilst the British were stuck with another eight years of the demagogue Thatcher....

Bauer laughed: it was true that this was a great triumph for Thatcher. It was absolutely true that for the Argentines, the war provided a turning point, ending the tragic dictatorship which began in 1976 and crumbled after the Malvinas conflict.

Not having been in Britain when the film appeared, I wondered how it was received when presented at several British festivals and in itinerant exhibition. Bauer was unable to travel because of other commitments, but Edgardo Esteban did accompany the film and returned moved, feeling that the film had a strong impact there, too. There were some very emotive showings given for British ex-combatants army, which was marked more by emotion than by reflection, and the film was bought by a UK distributor.

As for the film's reception on the islands themselves, Bauer talked about a proposal, along with the British Embassy, to premiere it on the Malvinas/Falklands; finally the governor of the islands decided against the premiere. However, according to Esteban's wife it was seen by almost all the inhabitants (there aren't that many, around 1,800) and from commentaries Bauer received from contacts on the islands it was also a very respectful viewing. He stressed that when they traveled there (part of the film was shot in the islands) they received very respectful treatment.

I had been particularly struck by the scene when the protagonist goes back to the islands and breaks down when he finds personal items from the war.

Bauer said that it was something that made a big impression on the filmmakers, too, because it didn't come from the imagination of any of them. When they went to the Malvinas, they were surprised that, more than twenty years later, it was still possible to find soldiers' footwear; on getting close to the trenches they found forks, spoons, glasses, various items that in some way functioned as fragments of the memory that is still raw on the islands. For them it was very striking, and for that reason they included it in the film and used it as a dramatic element.

Responding to my question about recent Argentine cinema, Bauer described it as very dynamic at the moment, a very vital cinema. On the one hand there are established and celebrated filmmakers like Fernando "Pino" Solanas, Luis Puenzo, and Adolfo Aristarain, as well as the legacy of María Luisa Bemberg, who died in 1995. At the other extreme, younger people are pushing very strongly from below and working with new technologies; there are some 16 thousand film students, more than in the entire European Community put together, 16 thousand who are making short films, documentaries, and debut features. An important factor is the national law that protects cinematography, meaning that there are resources for production. All this, moreover, occurs within a framework of great diversity, because Argentine cinema is not limited to one single line or school, as Bauer considers to have been the case with Italian Neorealism, or the French Nouvelle Vague. It is a very diverse cinema that embraces genres such as comedy and drama, war films such as *Iluminados*, and documentary. He perceives in this diversity a very rich movement, dynamic and participative, and a presence not only on a national level but also internationally. There are many films made in co-production, particularly with Spain, and plenty of films that manage to reach an international market, especially the television market so important for Latin Americans. However, the reason this is a strong, vibrant cinema is not only co-production, but also the internal strength of Argentine cinema. It is a national cinema that depends relatively little on factors abroad.

For Bauer the national film law has been fundamental. For every spectator in Argentina who goes to see a film, whether it be North American, French, Bolivian, Argentine, ten per cent of the entrance fee goes to the institute's funds; the same applies to video or DVD rental ten percent of which goes toward cinematographic production. There is also a fund taken from the broadcasting of feature films on television, which benefits the National Institute of Cinematography. This means that Argentine cinema is genuinely financed by cinematographic exhibition in its distinct formats — of great value, according to Bauer, to the national treasury and a support for all Argentine cinematographic activity.

I wanted to return to the subject of his film *Evita, la tumba sin paz* (*Evita, the Unquiet Grave*, 1997). Bauer explained that this was an entirely British production. Channel Four hired him as director after Miguel Bonasso (see above) wrote a script based on his own journalistic research, and Bauer was called by the producer, Ana Scanlon. For the director this really turned out be an enthralling and fascinating story, focusing on what happens to the corpse of Eva Perón (1919–1952), a figure of immense popular affection who had two and a half million people clamoring for her to be made vice president of Argentina. Bizarrely, the body of this very same woman-symbol was "disappeared" three years later and interred under a false name in a cemetery in Italy. He sees this as symptomatic of the tremendous contradictions in his country; in some way Evita became the first *desaparecida* in the history of Argentina, as her cadaver was stolen by the army and vanished for 20 years. Eventually it was returned (in 1975) but in a beaten and violated condition. For Bauer this was a really tragic, revolting story. But it was very interesting to make, because several elements appeared such as photographs of the body and data from the army's intelligence service on those responsible for the abduction. It achieved the highest ratings of any television documentary in Argentina, (even more than the biggest football matches) it was seen alongside the televised version of the 1996 Alan Parker film *Evita* (starring Madonna), and also had important global distribution.

Analysis: Narrative Transition, Sound and Temporality

Luis Espinal's *Narrativa cinematográfica* (1976, 29–30) tells us that

> **Transitions** between one sequence and another are a further component of cinematic temporality. They are transitions; for example, the dissolve, the cut, the wipe, the iris.... Transitions are like **punctuation marks** (comma, period...) in writing. But they have a clear temporal sense.
>
> For example the **lap dissolve** or **cross dissolve** (dissolves one image whilst another emerges on the screen) is a way of telling us that time has been suppressed. On the other hand, the **fade to black** puts a full stop to a scene and has the value of a change of chapter; as such it denotes a temporal jump. On the other hand, the **wipe** accentuates temporal continuity within a spatial change. These forms of transition can also convey a sense of **causality**. For example, a long lap dissolve, or a figure that emerges from out of focus, can be the movement from reality to reverie[5] [author's emphasis].

The temporal and causal elements are clear in Bauer's film. At the end of C4, Marta, trying to prevent Vargas's death, repeats, "*Volvé*" ("come back"). Meanwhile Esteban is seen lost in reverie; a dissolve reveals him standing on a clifftop on the islands. Afterwards (C6) we see an example of creative, expressive transition when the three soldiers have finished eating and complaining about the food. As they walk away, Esteban pauses (the other two

Esteban, Chamorro and Vargas suffer the cold along with the food and drink. Still photography by Gabriel Costa and Alfredo Rodríguez.

are heard talking off screen) and looks suddenly sad, as if anticipating what is to come. A faint whining noise is heard, accompanied by a superimposed image — what appears to be a travelling aerial shot of the sea. In fact it is a molded glass panel, next to which the older Esteban (seen from the same angle) is standing. The noise proves to be the life-support machine, and we are again in the hospital where Vargas is under intensive care. Esteban appeared to be remembering, looking from right to left. The camera moves in the opposite direction, as if reversing through time; is it taking us forwards chronologically, or backwards perceptually?

Then Marta's line "*No tenía suerte, pobre*" ("he was unlucky, poor guy") acts as a sound bridge that moves us into the next scene — a café, with Marta and Esteban in M-shot, followed by an orthodox shot — reverse shot dialogue during which the two exchange family information. The camera lingers on Marta's pained expression as she tells of her relationship with Vargas. She is on the subject of their decline (*caer y caer*) when there is a cut to a tracking shot of booted feet moving along rocks; this leads to the bathetic humor of an attack, not on enemy soldiers, but on a flock of sheep. This at least temporarily resolves the food theme, as well as providing some comic relief.

With regard to the two sound bridges (the machine and Marta's voice) Espinal (op. cit., 30) explains that "**sound** has become one of the most important components of cinematographic temporality. This non-plastic element accentuates the time that passes. We should think, above all, of **noise** as temporal value: a siren, the monotonous and repetitive noise of a machine.... Sound can create a polifacetic and multiple temporality, not only through the content of a conversation, but through **asynchrony**, juxtaposing an image with a sound that does not correspond to that image."[6]

Esteban looking back from the clifftop. Still photography by Gabriel Costa and Alfredo Rodríguez.

Linguistic Features

Argentines are known for their use of some robust language at the best of times, let alone in a situation such as the Malvinas war. It is not surprising, then to find such phrases liberally used (probably, if anything, kept to a minimum). An example is the scene in which Esteban, on guard duty, tries to identify a figure approaching in the mist (a severe visibility problem mentioned by Malvinas veterans), who turns out to be Corrientes. Leguizamón almost kills his mate in fright, then treats him to a stream of obscenities.

More printable Argentine slang, used by Marta as she shows Esteban the apartment where she used to live with Vargas, includes *laburo* (work), *cana* (police), *guita* (money). This is an argot accepted and used by most classes in Argentine society.

For Discussion

1. The British are barely seen in *Iluminados*; how are they portrayed in their absence?
2. In what ways does sound play an important part in telling the story and creating atmosphere?
3. How does the Argentine-British relationship appear, upon viewing *Iluminados por el fuego* and reading the interview with Tristán Bauer?
4. A number of veterans have voiced opposition to perceived inaccuracies (betrayal of the cause, displays of cowardice) in the version of events presented by Esteban and Bauer. Does this necessarily detract away from the film's persuasive power? (Their objections can be seen at: *ILUMINADOS POR EL FUEGO* [online]. You Tube. Available from: http://www.youtube.com/watch?v=aeraHA15U_c [Accessed 13 December 2009].)
5. How does the sheep-stealing scene in *Iluminados* (and its effects or consequences) differ from, or converge with, the similar sequence in *Mi mejor enemigo*?

22. *Mi mejor enemigo*
(My Best Enemy)

CREDITS: Chile, 2005; *Production: Mi mejor enemigo* was a Chilean/Argentine/Spanish co-production involving Chilean government organizations CORFO & FONDART as well as the Argentine film institute INCAA. It was part-financed by a grant from the Spanish-based Ibermedia and aided by Spanish production companies Alce, Matanza and Wanda. Alex Bowen and the noted Argentine director Pablo Trapero also did production work on this film; *Director:* Alex Bowen; *Script:* Julio Rojas and Paula del Fierro; *Music:* José Miguel Tobar and José Miguel Miranda; *Director of Photography:* José María Hermo

CAST: Chilean Soldiers, Rojas (Nicolás Saavedra), Sargento Ferrer (Erto Pantoja), Mancilla (Juan Pablo Miranda), Orozco (Víctor Montero), Almonacid (Chilote) (Andrés Olea), Salazar (Pablo Valledor).

Synopsis

Rojas is one of many young men aged around twenty who are called upon to defend disputed territory in the south of Chile, a landscape and climate far removed from their native regions. His patrol of five conscripts and a sergeant becomes lost on the *pampa* and receives help from two highly unexpected sources. Meanwhile the undeclared war is subverted by a series of farcical situations that reveal as absurd the whole question of hostility between these two nations.

About the Film

Mi mejor enemigo has won prizes at festivals in Chile (Valdivia, 2006), Peru (Lima, 2005), Belgium (Brussels, 2005), the USA (Los Angeles, 2005), Colombia (Cartagena, 2006), France (Marseilles, 2006), Spain (Lleida, 2006) and Israel (Isoltel Eilat, 2006).

About the Film's Creators

Director **Alex Bowen** was born in Talca, south-central Chile, in 1977. His first film, the thriller *Campo minado* (*Minefield*, 2000), is also set among near-hostility between Chile and Argentina; a prospector's find is located in the middle of a minefield laid against invasion.

163

He must also handle growing tensions and threats within his group of assistants. Bowen's next feature is *Los mil colmillos* (*The Thousand Fangs*), which again examines human interaction in a war setting: here, erstwhile Chilean political foes are forced into collaboration as mercenaries in Iraq.

José Miguel Tobar and José Miguel Miranda, a Chilean musical duo, have worked on numerous films, particularly for the acclaimed director Andrés Wood.

For Cultural Understanding: Historical Context

The territorial dispute between Chile and Argentina over areas of southern Patagonia dates almost from their beginnings as republics. The problem, almost inevitably, has imperialist roots: Chile has long been Britain's foremost ally in South America, and London supported Chilean claims to the islands south of the Beagle Channel. Patagonian borders were ratified by the signing of a treaty in 1881; nonetheless, subsequent Argentine maps showed the islands as their possessions. This remained a bone of contention for most of the twentieth century and, in 1970, both countries agreed that Queen Elizabeth II should oversee a British tribunal to decide the fate of the territory. Despite this process, which eventually granted sea lanes to both countries in 1977, the Argentines were dissatisfied. The British position was clearly pro–Chilean — a fact that led to Chile, alone in the region, supporting the British position on the Malvinas/Falklands war in 1982. The respective governments, despite ideological links as right-wing military dictatorships, were both averse to being perceived as weak or acquiescent to their long-standing geopolitical rival. When tension again mounted in 1978, with the possibility of Argentine aggression (see *Operativo Soberanía*), war was only averted at the last minute thanks largely to mediation by Pope John Paul II.

For Cultural Understanding: Displacement and Internal Exile in Chilean Film

For several years, Chilean film was effectively a national cinema in exile. Filmmakers like Miguel Littín, Patricio Guzmán and Raúl Ruiz fled the country after the Pinochet coup in 1973. Some have since returned, but the experience of forced expatriation has left a mark on film just as other activities. Some films made outside the country are conditioned by that experience: the writer Antonio Skármeta, for example, directed a film version of his novel *Ardiente paciencia* (*Burning Patience*, 1983) in Portugal, using that country's coast for the setting of Pablo Neruda's home on Isla Negra, Chile. The later remake, *Il postino*, was an international success. Another curiosity was *Acta general de Chile* (*General Statement on Chile*, 1986), filmed bravely and clandestinely by Littín and the crews he coordinated in defiance of the ban on his return.[1]

Some Chilean films dealing with the Pinochet era concentrate on the use of internal exile as the dictatorship's alternative to murdering or "disappearing" its political opponents during the coup and its aftermath. Ricardo Larraín's *La frontera* (*The Frontier*, 1991) is an occasionally comic drama concerning a teacher banished to the remote south of the country. The all-male dance scene in Alex Bowen's film is based on a similar scene in Larraín's film (occasioned in both cases by a lack of women). A similar approach to political repression, but treated with a heightened sense of the absurd and grotesque, appears in Gonzalo Justiniano's *Amnesia* (1994), in which the survivors of a prison camp in the northern deserts fortuitously meet up some years later with their erstwhile captors. *Mi mejor enemigo* does not quite tread the same thematic ground, but the sense of dislocation among northern Chileans sent to the far south is palpable. As for the political context, it must be remembered that the narrowly avoided conflict in Patagonia was in keeping with the interests of the dictatorships on both sides: to maintain a war footing and an anxious populace. Alex Bowen's film opens with a monologue in voiceover describing the atmosphere of the times, when the word "exile" is on everyone's lips, whilst the spectator contemplates the emptiness of the *pampa*.

Interview with Director Alex Bowen

KR: I see you mention La frontera *in your DVD commentary, because of a similarity between all-male dance scenes in the two films. You also mention* Machuca, *and your film reminds me of Gonzalo Justiniano's* Amnesia *with its absurd humor. Do you also see these as influential? What other films do you see in this way?*

AB: Your mention of those three films moves me, since they are among the best of our cinema, and to be placed beside them is reason for great pride. I don't know whether you know this but I had the opportunity of working with Ricardo Larraín in the first stages of *La Frontera* and unfortunately due to human envy I was left out of the shooting, but that didn't stop me admiring that film and Ricardo's work — especially the dance scene between men. I think that in *MME* the women's presence works precisely on the basis of their absence and consequently the idea of solitude is emphasized; the dance in my film seeks to recount and reinforce that. In Ricardo's film, too, though it deals rather more with customs, with something that actually occurs in my country. I think the difference between the two is humorous tone. Both achieve the same effect, that of moving the viewer.

I like *Machuca*, I think Andrés Wood's work was very good; he achieved a great film for Chile and the world.

I don't feel that *Amnesia* was an influence on my work, perhaps it is, but the moment at which I saw it was so dramatic for my country, so strong, that it was never a reference — except maybe in a negative sense...

One film that was indeed a reference, and a strong one, was Sergio Cabrera's *Time Out*. I remember that when I saw it, I had two very strong sensations: the first was of anguish, because I felt he had "beaten me to it"; this was the film I wanted to make but now it had already been made and, in my view, with very good results. The other sensation was that of happiness on finding the solution to my problem ... concentrating on something more dramatic and with darker humor, not as obvious as in Cabrera's film.

I must say, besides, that I am absolutely "gringo" in my way of taking on my projects, and in that sense I really have to cite U.S. films as influences — Westerns, crime and war films and so on. Their way of setting out a conflict, of resolving it, is an influence that is lodged in my memory, despite myself, and I have recourse to these films unconsciously, because they are the films that most often reached Chile with the dictatorship and the free market system that was installed in my society. I think it's due to that, and due to the struggle not to be so "gringo," that *MME* has its humor, its own character.

With the music you avoid the obviously Chilean, you even use an Argentine song ("Sólo le pido a Dios," by León Gieco). It reminds me of the inclusion of a poem by the Peruvian César Vallejo in Entre Marx ... by the Ecuadorian Camilo Luzuriaga; a fraternal gesture (between two countries that are supposedly enemies). Was that your intention?

Maybe because of what I cited above ... this weight, of the cinema that I saw in my adolescence, is what partly obliged me not to use typically Chilean music in the film. To be frank I was tempted to do that, strongly tempted, but I decided to look for music that would serve the film and elevate it to its maximum expression, be that what it may. That's why I sought out Tobar and Miranda (*Machuca*), as the ideal people to do the music and as director I restricted myself to setting out what I was looking for in each scene and then observing their work and approving, if it was what I wanted. I've carried León Gieco's theme in my soul since the eighties and I knew, from the moment I first thought of the film, that it would go in somewhere. A fraternal gesture? No, sadly not, it was more of an egoistic gesture, including this song, that had moved me many times during my youth, in the film I was directing. There was a lot of resistance from my crew to the inclusion of this song, which I had to overcome. Apart from that, I think the film as a whole is much more fraternal than just putting song in the film, which is why the egoistic gesture fitted perfectly.

This isn't a film question but, given the current political climate, do you see the possibility of doing away once and for all with fratricidal wars in Latin America?

I believe that if there isn't a water shortage in the near future, we won't see fratricidal wars in Latin America. I hope I'm not mistaken...

Did your idea of filming a game of football on the pampa have a lot to do with the famous encounter between German and British soldiers between the trenches during the First World War?

Again, I return to my influences ... and of course, it has to do with that event... Nevertheless it had to be transferred to our story and that's what we did (scriptwriters Julio Rojas, Paula del Fierro and I). The match has to do with the fact that I'm not a particularly big football fan, so when I was at school I had to suffer some solitude, but those lonely reflections made me realize that football is politically correct war: nobody dies, there are clear rules, plenty of witnesses and at the end of an agreed period of time there is a clear winner or loser or else a draw, but there are no half measures... In war there are no clear rules, the victor is never such a clear winner, there are a lot of deaths without testimony ... so then my decision was to use football as a representation of what in reality our countries wanted to do in those years ... and putting it in an absurd ambience like the pampa gave us a memorable scene because of its absurdity and humor.

How difficult did it turn out filming in a place like the pampa *without visual points of reference?*

It wasn't so difficult because in cinema one works with the frame, and in truth the place in which we filmed had many visual points that we constantly had to avoid, but maybe the most complex thing was to achieve something that was visually always interesting without being an image that was exhausting. And we managed that due to the art direction, to the photography of José María Hermo and to the marvelous light of the *pampa*.

Two of the most interesting elements seem to me to be Chilote (the fat kid always to be seen in school films) and the dog. What did you have in mind when you included them in the script?

We've all been close to, or have known about, somebody who was denied respect due to beliefs or ways of thinking and who as a result was isolated by a group, or else reviled, thus constantly managing to carry out a self-fulfilling prophecy. This is the fat kid. In our society, historically, fat people do not represent canons of universal beauty; some manage to lift this sentence and others don't, but I liked the idea of the fat boy because then it was very easy to portray a character who could be destroyed by the others because of a certain physical incapacity. On the other hand, the fat boy allowed me to put together that kind of Latin American version of *Stripes*, so different from the one the gringos sell us.

The canine element is an irony: the most human figure in the story is a bitch ... paradoxical, no? Besides, it was an instrument used by the patrols as a way of communicating and avoiding the need for direct contact, in this way making things more complex and giving more edges to the conflict's development. We humans could do everything more easily but why should we, if we can complicate things?

How much of a difference did winning the Ibermedia prize make for the project?

In terms of money, Ibermedia meant $120,000. In prestige it had a much higher value than that. When we won the Ibermedia prize we knew we wouldn't just get the money but also the support of the Chilean government to get the film made and the will of the other member countries to back the initiative. But the most interesting thing is in the preparatory work that has to be developed in order to win the Ibermedia prize. You have to work rigorously and very professionally; doing that work permitted us to be very solid when it came to developing and carrying out the shooting. Many questions that were unanswered before we presented the project to Ibermedia were things we absolutely had to answer, by ourselves, in order to win the prize; all of this translated into clarity for the project and its objectives, bringing the prize as a consequence.

Analysis: Circularity as Dramatic and Cinematic Device

Circularity, a motif in *Cabeza de Vaca*, derived from indigenous shamanism, describes the hopelessness of attempted escape. In *MME* the camera is situated at the center of the circle in two important scenes in which the soldiers gather to eat. In the first of these (DVD, C1) they introduce themselves by name and geographical origin — information easily processed by a Chilean viewer but not by an outsider. Chile, of course, is a long strip of land sandwiched between the Andes and the Pacific, divided into twelve regions (the "first" being the furthest north). The scene does far more than just establish names and places: it sets out the geography of the dispute with Argentina and the various conscripts' relationships to it. The men come mostly from the central regions: Rojas, for instance, is from the capital Santiago, Mancilla from Talca (the director's birthplace) in the south-central (7th) region, Salazar from Talcahuano, near Concepción (8th region); Almonacid is a special case, not only as the fat boy: he is also an islander (from Chiloé). His rural background is something we return to subsequently, for instance when he is able correctly to predict rain. The zealous Orozco, the only professional soldier, is outside on guard duty, physically as well as psychologically removed from the group. The only southerner is sergeant Ferrer, from Coiaique in the 11th region: he sees all the conscripts as northerners. There is a clear reason for this perception: over 2,000 km separate Santiago from their base in the 12th region, while Chile in its entirety extends over twice that distance.

By the time we reach the lunch scene in the trenches (Chapter 3) there are discernible changes. Whereas the previous scene was shot with numerous cuts between those speaking, this very simple but effective scene is a single take: the camera pans constantly, hardly varying its pace.

Whereas before the soldiers are seen (and see themselves) in terms of differences, now they are considerably more united. The antagonist Orozco, who was on guard for the first scene, is still set apart in this by his exaggeratedly zealous conduct. Here, the camera takes in all the faces in the course of a conversation, involving all five men, about what it's like in Argentina. Ferrer says that it's "the same as here"; Almonacid (now with his geographically inspired nickname "Chilote") mentions people who cross the frontier to work, and Orozco comments that they are "traitors." Mancilla realizes the soldiers have been brought from the north because, unlike people from Chilean Patagonia, they have no family ties and will have no misgivings about fighting: he is told by Ferrer just to keep eating.

Linguistic Features

Chilean Spanish is the variation cited by other Latin Americans as the most difficult to understand. However, the dialogue in this film is relatively easy and, apart from a sprinkling of obscenities, less slang-laden than many others. Some slang is incidental, such as *china* (girl, in the dance scene), and *choro* (tough guy). In a key term the description of the soldiers as "*pelados conscriptos,*" "*pelado*" can mean "bald," or "stripped." In certain areas it refers to youth or to poverty — a combination of these is intended here.

For Discussion

1. What do you see as the advantages or disadvantages in this film being a coproduction?
2. Rojas talks at the beginning about mistrust, fear, and arrests in his town. To what is this attributable, and how is it transferred to the rest of the film?
3. The main theme music is more evocative of a Celtic setting than the South American *pampa*. Is there any reason for this? What other musical registers are there in the film?
4. To what effect does hand-held camera contrast with tripod and dolly use?
5. However tough the reality it portrays, *MME* depicts a far more benign treatment of recruits than that seen in *Iluminados*. Obviously the Chilean film has a comic element, but can it be put down entirely to this?
6. Apart from his girth and his place of origin, in what other ways is Almonacid set apart from the others?
7. What is brought to the film by the intercutting of shots of wildlife with the soldiers?
8. What is the dramatic function of the deserted farm?
9. Does the Chilean-Argentine encounter need to pan out in the way it does?
10. What do Rojas' two encounters with Gloria at the beginning and end tell us about the place of the ordinary conscript in this kind of situation?

23. *Hamaca paraguaya* (Paraguayan Hammock)

CREDITS: Paraguay/Argentina/France/Holland/Germany, 2006; *Produced by:* Lita Stantic, Marianne Slot, Ilse Hughan, in coproduction with José Maria Morales of Wanda Vision; *Director:* Paz Encina; *Script:* Paz Encina; *Sound:* Guido Berenblum, Víctor Tendler; *Director of Photography:* Willi Behnisch; *Art Direction:* Carlos Spatuzza; 35mm: 78 minutes.

CAST: Cándida (Georgina Genes), Ramón (Ramón del Río)

Synopsis

In 1935, an elderly peasant couple in rural Paraguay awaits the return of their son from the disastrous Chaco War with Bolivia. Ramón is initially convinced that Máximo will return, while Cándida is far more skeptical. These attitudes, though, will later fluctuate. Meanwhile they continue their everyday activities. They are comforted by their hammock, which offers respite from the intense heat as they also wait for the rains to come. They separately remember conversations with their son, and receive news from the front. Each is haunted by omens of various kinds.

About the Film

The first incarnation of *Hamaca paraguaya* was as an 8-minute short film in which constant rain impedes the son's arrival. As Encina told Ana Bianco in an online interview,[1] the idea of developing the short into a feature film was suggested by her former teacher, Jorge Laferia.

About the Film's Creators

Paz Encina studied at the Universidad del Cine in Buenos Aires, graduating in 2001. *Hamaca paraguaya* is her first feature: she had previously made short films including a brief version of the same theme.

Lita Stantic, one of Argentina's most eminent producers, was joined on this project by Ilse Hughan from France and Marianne Slot from the Netherlands who sought out funding for the film: ARTÉ, Fonds Sud, the World Cinema Fund and New Crowned Hope.

José María Morales of Wanda Vision in Madrid was the co-producer who provided financial help directly.

Willy Behnisch, Guido Berenblum, and Víctor Tendler are all technicians who usually work for the Argentine filmmaker Lucrecia Martel.

For Cultural Understanding

In the *Hamaca paraguaya* DVD's "making of," the actor Ramón del Río paraphrases the novelist Augusto Roa Bastos: if misfortune fell in love with Paraguay, then the country's leaders have facilitated this relationship as go-betweens.

The isolationist policies followed by José Gaspar Rodríguez de Francia (1766–1840) and Carlos Antonio López (1790–1862) led to another description of Paraguay by Roa Bastos as "an island surrounded by land." The ultra-nationalist Francia, who ruled the country from 1814 until his death, was the model for Roa Bastos's 1974 dictatorship novel *Yo el supremo* (*I, the Supreme* being one of the titles he assumed). López, another autocratic if charismatic leader, ran Paraguay from 1844 to 1862, during which the country entered the most calamitous episode in its history; the War of the Triple Alliance (1864–1870) saw this small, landlocked nation face the combined strength of Brazil, Uruguay and Argentina. Yet, however paradoxically, it is undeniable that both men oversaw social and institutional reforms and inspired genuine popular support.

The Chaco War (1932–1935), fought over possession of a region of hot brush land, proved ruinous for both participants. Bolivia invaded the Chaco region with ideas of obtaining a sea outlet (the country has been landlocked ever since defeat by Chile in the 1879 War of the Pacific). Two foreign oil companies were associated with the conflict; Standard on the Bolivian side and Royal Dutch Shell on the Paraguayan. The question of the scale of their involvement and precise role remains controversial. Paraguay, technically the victor, gained substantially in territory but forfeited over 40,000 lives. The Bolivians came off considerably worse in terms of casualties, economic costs and prestige.

Paz Encina conceived her film largely as a gesture to her country, one starved of filmic self-images. She offers a portrayal of the Paraguayan national character, which she sees as contrary to the effusive, extrovert Latin American stereotype. She describes her typical *compatriota* as "slow, silent and even distrustful, although not aggressively distrustful. He/she may not reply but stare at you for years, without answering."[2]

Film in Paraguay

Paraguay has long been an "invisible country" according to one of its filmmakers, Hugo Gamarra (2003, 156) one of the poorest in Latin America in terms of cinematic culture and history. As Paz Encina has said, "Cinema in Paraguay is scarce, inconstant, almost inexistent. I don't think that, even with *Paraguayan Hammock*, it can be said that cinema yet exists in Paraguay" (Russo 2008, 331). However, there has been a modest upturn in fortunes for audiovisual activity, partly resulting from the reduced cost of digital video. Productions such as *María Escobar* (Galia Giménez, 2002) and *Miramenometoquei* (Enrique Collar, 2003) have begun to address what Gamarra has termed "the inalienable right to one's own audiovisual expression" (2003, 162).[3]

The last entirely Paraguayan feature film before *Hamaca paraguaya* was *Cerro Corá* (Guillermo Vera, 1978), an epic made under the Stroessner dictatorship which glorifies a decisive battle in the War of the Triple Alliance. At the end of the ensuing slaughter the then Paraguayan president López led a pitiful band of 409 men, many of them old, very young, or even invalids; their apparent willingness to follow López reflects his considerable public support.

Hitherto the best-known film concerning the Chaco War is *Hijo de hombre* (*Son of Man*, Lucas Demare, Argentina, 1961) which adapts part of the famous 1960 novel by Paraguay's greatest writer, Augusto Roa Bastos. The only Paraguayan fiction film on the Chaco War besides *Hamaca paraguaya* is *Réquiem para un soldado* (*Requiem*, Galia Giménez, 2002).

La Guerra del Chaco (Agustín Carrón Quell, 1932) was a 20-minute documentary shot during the war itself. *El trueno entre las hojas* (*Thunder Among the Leaves*, Argentina/Paraguay, 1956) was based on short stories by Roa Bastos, dealing with a revolt among workers. Like many of the films made in or concerning Paraguay, co-productions with either Argentina or Brazil, this was made by the Argentine actor turned director and producer Armando Bo. *La sangre y la semilla* (*The Blood and the Seed*, Alberto Dubois, Argentina/Paraguay, 1959) was another co-production with Argentina, again using texts by Roa Bastos who co-wrote the script with Mario Halley Mora.

Influences on Paz Encina

Paz Encina has cited several filmmakers as influences,[4] at least three of whom are identifiable with her contemplative approach.

Encina's fascination with the Japanese master Yahujiro Ozu (1903–1963) is evident; she studied his work for her thesis when studying film in Buenos Aires. Stylistically, his influence on her work is visible in their shared preference for a stationary camera, with long takes from low angles and an interest in intimate, closely observed narratives. The poignancy of coming to terms with solitude in old age, inviting comparisons with *Hamaca paraguaya*, is a theme from both Ozu's last film, *An Autumn Afternoon* (1963) and his most famous, *Tokyo Story* (1953).

The Iranian director Abbas Kiarostami is famed for a poetic semi-documentary cinema which examines social issues through interaction between individuals, often from radically different backgrounds and viewpoints. Among the elements his cinema shares with *Hamaca paraguaya* is a preference for prolonged two-way dialogue, rural settings, and a fixed camera, one that is nonetheless far from passive.

The films of Argentine filmmaker Lisandro Alonso evince a fascination with stillness, observation of human behavior and the human figure in a natural landscape. Alonso is often misunderstood and even reviled for his uncompromising focus on the bare bones of existence and lone male protagonist. In *La libertad* (*Freedom*, 2001) the central character is a woodcutter and in *Los muertos* (*The Dead*, 2004) an ex-convict. The actor from *Los muertos* reappears as himself in *Fantasma* (2006). *Liverpool* (2008) shows a retired sailor's return to Patagonia. All these characters are in some way at odds with their filmed environment.

The case of Lucrecia Martel is somewhat different. One of the most renowned of contemporary Argentine directors, she has made three feature films to date. *La ciénaga* (*The Swamp*, 2001), *La niña santa* (*The Holy Girl*, 2004), and *La mujer sin cabeza* (*The Headless*

Woman, 2008) have in common the meticulous preparation of action and sound, latent violence, and moral and ethical transgressions.

Interview with Director Paz Encina

KR: Did you ever feel the temptation to use Spanish instead of Guaraní?
PE: Never. Before the full-length feature *Paraguayan Hammock*, I had already made a video-art short film with the same title, and that short was already in Guaraní. The thing is, Guaraní is built into Paraguayans, far more than people imagine; there have been many efforts to suppress it but that's impossible. Eighty percent of the population of Paraguay is Guaraní-speaking and it forms a part of everyday life.

You have spoken of cinematic influences (Ozu, Alonso, Martel, Kiarostami). Could you explain in which ways they influence you?
Really, what I have liked most about all those directors is that one can see in them the stamp of an auteur; I think that is something very difficult to have, and they have it. I always think, too, that they have been able to portray something that gave me the sensation that they really saw what they were filming... They do not do so from the outside... That happened to me in particular with Ozu, who found his own language in order to show to his people, his country, its way of life. That was something that always moved me about his films, from the beginning.

Staying with the theme of influences, would it be right to think there is something of the aesthetic of the absurd (Godot, for instance) in this vain waiting? Perhaps García Márquez's El coronel

Paz Encina explains a scene to Ramón del Río. Photograph by Cristián Núñez.

no tiene quien le escriba (Nobody Writes to the Colonel) *and some of Juan Rulfo's stories like* Nos han dado la tierra (They Have Given Us the Land)*?*

Of all those you mention, Rulfo is my main point of reference, but the story I like best, the one I could read over and over again, is *¿No oyes ladrar a los perros?* (*Don't You Hear the Dogs Bark?*) With respect to *Godot*, it has become the main reference for any wait there may be in history, and I think that for a long time, if not forever, anyone who waits will bear that name.

Do you see minimalism as a response to the epic (I haven't seen the film Cerro Corá *but I take it to be a kind of celebration of military "heroism").*

There's one thing about this subject, and it's that I never saw minimalism as anything that represents me. Perhaps what I do is look at the minimal, because it's true that I have the sensation that we are us. I think it's a word with which we coexist, and with which we have had to make do many times. And with regard to *Cerro Corá* I have mixed feelings, because cinematically speaking it's not something I could ever make, but it's the great Paraguayan film from my childhood, and because the character who plays the guitar in one of the camps was my teacher, and I loved that.

Analysis: Silence as an Element in Music and Dialogue

At the beginning of an article on the ideas behind this film (Russo 2008, 332), Paz Encina talks of the importance of silence both as a conditioning element of the Paraguayan psyche—a "great symptom of our history"—and as a challenge: "how to portray silence?" (Russo 2008, 332). For Encina, whose declared aim is partly to portray her country in film, silence is more than simply an absence of sound or speech. It raises a question: what does the Paraguayan variety consist of? "I felt I had to search with the utmost delicacy for the elements with which to convey *our* silence." Silence here is a sensation, a convergence of the loneliness and sadness experienced during what is an interminable wait.

Georgina Genes as Cándida. Photograph by Cristina Faire.

This feeling naturally conditions the way language, both verbal and filmic, is used in this film. The script contains numerous references to the weather, a commonplace in Paraguayan speech that suggests being locked into a scheme of repetition, where moments are linked chronologically but are infinitely divided by pauses that invite reflection (ibid., 333). Encina (2008, 336) talks of the importance of having learned to read music. Indeed, the musical element and the importance of silence are elements clearly present in any scene from this film, but in chapters 11–12 they have a particular relationship: Cándida is sitting, fanning herself by the oven when she is addressed (at least audibly; her interlocutor seems imaginary) by what proves to be the postman, one of only two voices from outside the family.

Like the veterinary surgeon heard in the previous scene in "conversation" with Ramón, the postman provides a verbal exchange that is imagined, or potential; this is presumably the news that Cándida dreads and is already prepared to deny. She has reasons for refusing the possibility of her son's death, quibbling over his identity and the whereabouts of his heart. The repetition of the young man's name, and of certain words like *izquierda*, are elements that add to the musicality in the sense of providing a kind of refrain. The uncomfortably long pauses remove the dialogue from any sense of reality: given the subject under discussion, these are highly unlikely. The same is true of the postman's not knowing where he is, and Cándida's refusal to acknowledge either the idea of "left" or the identity of her son.

Paz Encina adds, in the DVD extras, that her conception of sound seeks to convey the pervading sense that in Paraguay one always lives, simultaneously, in both past and present. For this reason the sound occupies one space and the image another; they coincide once in a while, for instance when Cándida's voice utters "*tira*" as she throws something into the oven. This brings the spectator into an almost voyeuristic intimacy with the character's innermost thoughts, largely explaining the use of dubbing: it would have been unthinkable to attempt the same effect with the actress "thinking out loud."[5] Two cuts, each time bringing the viewer closer to Cándida, intensify this powerful sense of intrusion.

Linguistic Features

Cándida and Ramón use both Guaraní and Spanish in *Hamaca paraguaya*, reflecting one fascinating aspect of their national reality: Paraguay is unique among Latin American countries in that an indigenous language is spoken by most of its people. Proficiency in the Guaraní language is practically a national badge of honor: the two languages are habitually used without a noticeable hierarchical relationship between them. The two are often interspersed in speech, a highly complex practice known as Jopara which, according to some linguists, is practically Paraguay's third language or even the true national tongue. Strict linguistic taxonomy, though, would class it as a combination of two languages in which both sets of grammar and syntax are kept intact and separate, yet are complementary. However, linguistic practice in Paraguay is by no means a perfectly smooth and idyllic blend; there are those who wish to curb the use of both Guaraní and Jopara, establishing Spanish as the sole official language.

For Discussion

1. Paz Encina has spoken of her decision to use dubbed sound as based on the desire to reflect the conjunction of past and present. What other effects are obtained by dubbing?

2. Is the absence of movement in this film, in both camera and actors, simply an affectation? Are there other reasons for this opposite extreme from the Hollywood norm?

3. What is the dramatic effect of setting the film in one day, beginning and ending in darkness?

4. The French filmmaker Robert Bresson has argued that sound film was what made the creative use of silence possible. Is this borne out in Paz Encina's film?

24. Writers as Characters

Cinema's brief history has been conditioned by its sometimes fraught and turbulent relationship with literature. The younger art form continues to seek ways of becoming independent, but there are still very few cinematic forms that do not involve writing in their preparation. Quite apart from the issue of cinema's independence from literature, in Latin America there is also the political dimension: the Western writing system, introduced with the European invasion, has long been associated with the preservation of colonial and elite power. At the same time, the region's writers have often been known for their liberationist position in both aesthetic and discursive terms. Film biographies of writers often celebrate the political activity of the individual as well as, or even instead of, the literary oeuvre.

While film's reliance upon and alliance with the written and spoken word continues to be challenged, in Latin America there is also the question of choice of language. Spanish and Portuguese are practically hegemonic, but not universal: their use can alienate, or make films inaccessible to, some indigenous audiences. With the recent growth of the indigenous video movement, far more films are made in aboriginal languages (see chapter on indigenous image in film).

The Mexican filmmaker Paul Leduc eschews the spoken word almost entirely in films like *Frida, naturaleza viva* (*Frida*, 1986) and *Dollar mambo* (1993) which audaciously use music, dance, body language and other aural and visual elements for narrative and expressive capacity, and demonstrate the redundancy of expository dialogue. If these films were extremist, Leduc has since restored dialogue (in, for instance, *Cobrador: In God We Trust*, 2006). The Argentine filmmaker Lisandro Alonso also keeps dialogue to a minimum, most recently in *Liverpool* (2008). The most radical treatment of silence comes in Esteban Sapir's remarkable *La antena* (*The Aerial*, Argentina, 2007). Sapir cites some of the greatest silent films, particularly German Expressionist classics, adopting their radical social and aesthetic positions to lend authority to his political fable. *La antena* also adapts inherent qualities of silent film, using muteness as an eloquent leitmotif and exploiting the visual possibilities of captions.

Such productions might serve as models in countries with little cinematic heritage, where films are often stifled by excessive use of verbal language and inadequate attention to cinematic syntax. Distrust of the non-verbal shows an unwarranted reverence for the word — spoken, but above all written. Ángel Rama's concept of the *La ciudad letrada* (*Lettered City*) (1984), arguing that colonial and republican power has been concentrated and protected by the (Western) writing system, has been applied to the audiovisual by Freya Schiwy (2008) who sees it as "a continuity in the collusion of power, knowledge and technologies of representation from the colonial period to the present" (23). Following up the work of Jean Franco (2002), Schiwy sees the growth of indigenous video as a challenge to the hegemony of writing. Rama's work was groundbreaking, but a new focus is required in view of tech-

177

nological developments in the late twentieth century: Schiwy (2008, 233–234, n6) also cites the work of Julio Ramos (2001) who argues that Rama's stigmatization of writing does not fully acknowledge the role of many literary figures in speaking against state oppression and envisaging alternatives.

Robert Stam lists eight roots of prejudice against film in relation to literature. These include cinema's perceived betrayal of literary sources, due to its relative infancy and alleged parasitism. A deep-seated distrust and aversion to the image as source of information corresponds to a faith only in the written word, the notion that cinema is suspiciously "easy" to create and consume, and the idea that the audiovisual is inherently inferior, as an intellectual vehicle, to the literary (Stam 2005, 3–8). Here Stam is specifically discussing film adaptations of books, but his categories define a pervasive distrust of cinema among elites and interest groups, even (or especially) where the reading of literature is waning and consumption of audiovisual material on the increase. There is considerable speculation on the prospect of a post-literate society and of the cinema's place within it. Meanwhile, literature continues to influence the audiovisual, providing narrative material from both literary works and the lives and positions of writers.

It is worth looking at a few particular instances of relationships between writer and screen that are not straight adaptations. Tomás Gutiérrez Alea's *Memorias del subdesarrollo* (*Memories of Underdevelopment*, 1968), widely considered the best Latin American film of all time, is based on a 1962 novel by Edmundo Desnoes about a skeptical middle-class individual who remains in Cuba after the Revolution, caught between his contempt for the island's bourgeoisie and his fascination (albeit distanced and doubtful) for the revolutionary process. An English-language version, *Inconsolable Memories*, appeared in 1967 after Desnoes had worked on the film: a translation of the original novel, it also incorporated some of the changes that had arisen through adaptation. The difference between the two titles marks a transformation in the works themselves which, as Michael Chanan puts it, "changes the emphasis from the personal to the public, and shifts the sense from the subjective to the historical" (1990, 3).

The Colombian Gabriel García Márquez, still Latin America's best-known writer, has had a long, multi-faceted, and well-documented relationship with the cinema. There have been numerous and generally unsuccessful adaptations of his work, of which the most satisfying is Ruy Guerra's *Eréndira* (1983). Alain Philippon wrote at the time that Guerra had been able to find a kind of filmic equivalent of the picaresque: this is an essentially heterogeneous play of codes, which here move between the burlesque and opera, passing en route through the western and the cartoon."[1] María Lourdes Cortés (1999, 205–214), who has traced the author's long and often paradoxical association with film through all manner of writings and collaborations, notes that *One Hundred Years of Solitude* (1967) is García Márquez's "revenge" on cinema. The first novel he wrote while consciously distancing himself from film, it aims to show that literature has a range of expression all its own: for this reason, he has never allowed the novel's screen adaptation.

Héctor Babenco's *Kiss of the Spider Woman* (already discussed in this book's chapter on sexuality) also explores the narrator's function. In the Scheherazade figure of the gay prisoner Molina, who "tells" films, cinema narrative reverts to the oral, the earliest form of storytelling. Molina is thus not only escaping into a self-enclosed metatext (to use the term employed by Santiago Colás (1994, 80) but also emulating the *1001 Nights* character's strategy in delaying the authorities' interrogation of Valentín, the cell-mate of whom he becomes increasingly fond.

As noted above, adaptation is far from being the only relationship between literature and film. The importance of the writer as public figure in Latin America has given rise to several films in which literary figures appear in some dramatic, narrative capacity (as played by an actor) or representative of an aesthetic or other tendency. The writer may be included as a fictional entity or as an unseen guiding force in a film's poetic vision or narrative strategy.

One of the two such films examined in this book is Eliseo Subiela's *El lado oscuro del corazón* (*The Dark Side of the Heart*) which enacts the aesthetic dissidence of poets Oliverio Girondo, Mario Benedetti, and Juan Gelman. The other, Mela Márquez's *Caída al cielo*, uses a fictional framework to parallel the biography and oeuvre of the great Bolivian writer Jaime Saenz. But the presence of the writer is also notable in Sergio Cabrera's *Perder es cuestión de método*, in which a journalist is engaged in writing the dietary memoirs of the police chief for whom he also works in a detective police capacity. It is an absurdly servile role, one reminiscent of the colonial scribe who simply penned the ideas of more powerful individuals. In *Cabeza de Vaca*, based on the chronicles of Álvar Núñez himself, the protagonist is also author. But Nicolás Echeverría's film focuses not on the man as writer but rather as pioneer and adventurer in both cultural and discursive terms.

There are signs that the importance of the writer as public figure in Latin America is waning: it is now less common for a literary figure to become involved in high-level politics. Today, Mario Vargas Llosa's candidacy in the 1990 Peruvian presidential elections seems to belong to another age (his triumph as 2010 Nobel winner returns him fully to the literary fold). There is not sufficient space here to debate the issue fully, but the general leftward shift in the region's politics seems to be contributory, as does the shift in political influence towards the sphere of social (indigenous, popular) movements: the leftist writer's position as critical of right-wing politics is, at least for now, almost obsolete. Meanwhile, rightist authors such as Vargas Llosa and Mexican Enrique Krauze attempt to fill the political vacuum and snipe at current leaders such as Venezuela's Hugo Chávez. These developments imply both a diminishing of literature's perceived importance generally, and the movement towards political representation from less rarefied spheres. With the widespread distrust of the old guard in terms of political and other institutional figures, even left-leaning writers today keep a lower profile. These figures were often emblematic, due to their role in political life or representation of a particular group or social tendency: today a figure like Eduardo Galeano, a best-selling leftist writer as well as a sought-after commentator, is relatively rare. This applies to the readiness of writers both to take up social themes, or to assume public office. Writers are still major contributors to certain leftist opposition dailies in response to continued social inequality (for instance, Carlos Monsiváis and Elena Poniatowska in Mexico's *La jornada*; Juan Gelman, Tomás Eloy Martínez and Eduardo Galeano in the Buenos Aires daily *Página/12*). In a sense, this helps today's filmmakers in that there is less pressure on filmmakers from the left to be open about the political intentions of their work.

John Beverley's concept of "neo–Arielism" (1999, 18) identifies the will to "a reassertion of the authority of Latin American literature, literary criticism and literary intellectuals ... to serve as the bearers of Latin America's cultural memory against forms of thought and theoretical practice identified with the United States." Writers, in this view, resent the removal of their traditional position of political authority.

Films on writers are made for various reasons: sometimes they reinforce the foundational nature of the individual and his/her work, whether as a contribution to the national project, or as an important dissenting figure in some social or political debate. At times they exploit the colorful or flamboyant nature of the life in question. Of course, a film can be inspired by the sheer literary quality of the oeuvre, but the writer in Latin America invariably has a role to play that exceeds the strictly literary and is detached from formal political power. The Cuban writer Pedro Juan Gutiérrez is not alone in arguing that writers are more trusted than politicians in Latin America, but this contention applies to an era in which people's identification with the state was tenuous, and is no longer strictly applicable considering the recent spate of popularly elected governments with a social agenda such as those of Morales, Chávez, or Correa. Traditionally, reception of official discourse was skeptical at best, and writers who have run for, or accepted, public office risked compromising their popularity and credibility. The revolutionary Sandinista government in Nicaragua (1979–1990) owed some of the public faith and popularity it enjoyed to its being, famously, an administration of poets (Sergio Ramírez, Tomás Borge and others). On the other hand Vargas Llosa's doomed tilt at his country's presidency in 1990 was heartily distrusted, partly because of the nature of the writer's work but also because of his representing a party seen as a new front for a long-established but discredited political hierarchy.

Argentina's writers have been the subject of film portrayals that celebrate both their public and literary personae. Given the nature of the country's political life, the former often involves an anti-authoritarian stance. Tristán Bauer's elegant documentary on Julio Cortázar (*Cortázar*, Argentina, 1994) looks at the work of this much-loved and influential writer largely through the growth of his political awareness during the "boom" years of the 1960s and '70s. On the other hand, with *Los libros y la noche* (*The Books and the Night*, Argentina, 1999), Bauer pays homage to another great Argentine writer, José Luis Borges, with far greater emphasis on the writing. The famously right-wing Borges has always been considered far more radical in his searching, eternally skeptical literature than in his at times insular and uninformed public pronouncements. Two of Argentina's most prominent literary feminists have been personified in film: *Alfonsina* (1957) is a biographical portrait by Austrian-born Kurt Land of the influential poet, journalist and advocate of women's rights Alfonsina Storni. Óscar Barney Finn's *Cuatro caras para Victoria* (*Four Faces for Victoria*, Argentina, 1992) portrays the four dimensions attributed to Victoria Ocampo, one of the country's most important literary figures of the early twentieth century. Four different actresses represent facets of Ocampo, as cosmopolitan, autochthonous, the American in Europe and the European in America.

In *Yo, la peor de todas* (*I, the Worst of All*, Argentina, 1990) the renowned Argentine director María Luisa Bemberg offers a biography of the great Mexican poet Sor Juana Inés de la Cruz, arguing that she chose life as a nun primarily in order to write and study, rather than for religious convictions. The film traces developments in the relationship between Sor Juana and her powerful allies, the viceroy and his wife, who protect her from the Inquisition. The stylized sets, visually rendering the baroque aesthetic within which Sor Juana created her distinctive poetics, complement the use of words as practically the raw material of this film (based on Octavio Paz's 1988 biography of Sor Juana). Here, literature is politically crucial in the context of Mexican independence, as well as in Sor Juana's individual fate, as she debates with those who later silence her.

The sons of three of Latin America's most famous writers have become filmmakers, all of them seeking to establish themselves as artists without being overshadowed by their illustrious progenitors. However, they have all developed projects that involve their fathers' work. *Del olvido al no me acuerdo* (*Juan, I Forgot I Don't Remember*, Juan Carlos Rulfo, Mexico, 1999) evokes the world created by the filmmaker's father, the great novelist Juan Rulfo, without recourse to the usual procedures of documentary. Rulfo sees this as analogous to the famous novel *Pedro Páramo* which relates a young man's doomed search for his father. The very old people interviewed in pitiless desert landscapes under glowering Jalisco skies, call to mind a "Juan" recreated from their own mnemonic resources rather than any convincing recall. This is a far more successful evocation of Rulfo's notoriously film-resistant fictional world than any of the more orthodox adaptations. Carlos Velo's 1967 adaptation of *Pedro Páramo* relies unduly on the spoken word; its use of actors fails to reproduce the novel's ethereal characterization, which gives us little idea of flesh and blood appearance. As Gabriela Yanes Gómez points out, "Rulfo is careful not to make explicit physical descriptions, so that the characters are sustained purely by their dialogues and actions"[2] (1996, 14). Yanes Gómez sees other problems in the second version (José Bolaños, 1978) which paradoxically suffers from an excessively large budget, encouraging the use of lavish sets that bear no relation to Rulfo's desolate fictional universe (op. cit., 21).

Mario Sábato exploits his genealogical advantage in the documentary *Ernesto Sábato, mi padre* (Argentina, 2008), which privileges some of the more intimate aspects of the writer's personality over literary and public considerations.

Gabriel García Márquez's son, the celebrated director Rodrigo García Barcha, plans to film his father's script *Tiempo de morir* (*Time to Die*), already filmed twice (by Arturo Ripstein in 1966 and Jorge Ali Triana in 1985).

Camilo Luzuriaga's *Entre Marx y una mujer desnuda* (*Between Marx and a Naked Woman*, Ecuador, 1996) adapts the homonymous novel by Jorge Enrique Adoum (1973) and deftly transfers to celluloid its atmosphere of political turmoil and frustration in 1970s Quito along with the subtext of novelists in dialogue. The novel incorporates parallel musings on the rigor and self-discipline required both to write validly and to maintain political integrity. These ruminations take place between the two main characters: "the writer" (an obvious alter ego for Adoum himself) and "Galo Gálvez," a personification of the Guayaquil-born novelist and essayist Joaquín Gallegos Lara. The considerations of validity and integrity apply also to cinema: as Gabriela Alemán (2009) has indicated, this important film marks a shift in Ecuadorean cinema away from slavish imitation of literary sources towards an imposition of filmic directorial authority over what is a complex and fiercely demanding novelistic source.

Before Night Falls (Julian Schnabel, USA, 2000) profiles Reinaldo Arenas (1943–1990), a gay Cuban writer who dodged persecution on the island until the opportunity presented by the Mariel boatlift in 1980. Admirably played by Javier Bardem, Arenas is seen attempting to establish a literary voice during an infamously repressive period in which Cuban gays, many of them real or potential supporters of the revolution, were alienated. Another writer embodying sexual aberrance and social prophesy was Teresa Wilms Montt, profiled in *Teresa* (Tatiana Gaviola, Chile, 2009).

León Ichaso's *Piñero* (2001) is the story of the New York–based Puerto Rican poet and playwright, Miguel Piñero (1946–1988), played by Benjamin Bratt. It follows the writer's trajectory through petty crime, drug addiction and cult status among the Latino literary community. The film's visual style and soundtrack seek to parallel the tone and cultural identification of Piñero's writing, embodying much of the jazz and hip-hop aesthetic of which he was a famed exponent.

Ardiente paciencia (*Burning Patience*, Antonio Skármeta, Chile, 1983) is based on the famous novel by Skármeta himself about poet Pablo Neruda's days on the island of Chiloë during the last days of the Allende government. The novel was later adapted for a second time in a highly successful international co-production as *Il postino* (*The Postman*, Michael Radford, Belgium/France/Italy, 1994). Nonetheless, despite its budgetary limitations and use of little-known actors, *Ardiente Paciencia* (also known as *El cartero de Neruda* or *Neruda's Postman*) conveys far more freshness and authenticity than the blockbuster re-make. Skármeta's film was shot in Portugal — another example of the Chilean "cinema in exile" during the dictatorship of Augusto Pinochet. *Ardiente paciencia* also incorporates a writer as filmmaker, actor and director. Skármeta himself (who also plays a cameo role in the film) is far better known as one of Chile's most prominent writers and here adapts his own book for the screen. Another Chilean poet's biography, also carrying a strong political charge, is *Teresa* (Tatiana Gaviola, Chile, 2009) telling of social repression of an audaciously unconventional woman, the poet Teresa Wilms Montt.

Júlio Bressane's curious *Dias de Nietzsche em Turim* (*Days of Nietzsche in Turin*, Brazil, 2001) combines subjective camerawork, seemingly designed to convey the philosopher's mental confusion, with objective shots that emphasize Nietzsche's isolation and alienation. The film, written and researched by Rosa Dias, was shot in both Turin and Rio de Janeiro. It not only makes use of the Brazilian city's architecture for interiors but also, in a deliberate viewer disorientation ploy, "tropicalizes" the setting with the use as locations of some of Rio's parklands. The soundtrack understandably includes Wagner and Bizet, composers both mentioned in Nietzsche's diaries, but also features the conscious anachronism and geographical inaccuracy in the use of samba, which appears to signal the filmmakers' origin as well as hinting at the philosopher's universal stature. The universality is also diachronic: there are shots of modern Turin including cars and other twentieth-century properties. Dialogues are oddly silent, enacted with voiceover readings of the diaries. There is also an intertextual use of soundtracks from other "literary" films that Ismail Xavier (2006, 9) has compared with Jean-Luc Godard's appropriation of, and dialogue with, literary and other precedents.

El dirigible (*The Airship*, Pablo Dotta, Uruguay, 1994) uses the figure of Juan Carlos Onetti (1909–1994), one of Uruguay's most renowned and recalcitrant novelists, who had only recently died when the film appeared. Onetti, who integrated withering criticism of his country into his literature, had chosen to remain in exile in Madrid for almost the last twenty years of his life after being imprisoned on flimsy grounds by the then military dictatorship. The film uses Onetti's contemptuous remarks about a land "without caste, devoid of history and lineage": the writer's opinions are, nonetheless, sought after and his personal legacy coveted. *El dirigible*, however, is not a biography of the writer or homage to him. The premise is slight: a French woman journalist arrives in Montevideo bringing tapes that purportedly contain Onetti's voice. The recordings, bogus or otherwise, become the object of intense interest and criminal activity. Dotta is concerned above all with the repression of images (in this case, those of a particular political assassination) as a failure to address what he sees as Uruguay's incapacity and unwillingness to face itself. *El Dirigible* was, unsurprisingly perhaps, not well received in Uruguay: nonetheless, it is a film that employs a literary figure in an inventive and revealing way (see Richards 2005, 149–152, for a fuller discussion of this film).

Three 1990s Brazilian biographies of national poets look at their political significance, particularly concerning the issue of race. Tom Job Azulay's *O judeo* (*The Jew*, Brazil, 1996) presents Antônio José da Silva (1705–1739), a Jewish Brazilian living in Lisbon whose work satirized Portuguese society. This aspect of his writing exacerbates his difficulties at a time when Jews were persecuted by the Inquisition. Radical Brazilian filmmaker Silvio Tendler's

Castro Alves: Retrato falado do poeta (1999) is a docufiction biography of the "slaves' poet" Antônio Frederico de Castro Alves (1847–1871), who played a foundational role in Brazilian history both as a campaigner for independence as well as an instrumental figure in the abolition of slavery. *Cruz e Souza: O poeta do desterro* (*The Banished Poet*, Sylvio Back, Brazil, 1999) is a controversial portrait of the Black Symbolist poet João da Cruz e Souza (1861–1898) who died at only 37, having endured the era's unbridled racism. Back's film is accused of excessive metaphorization of the poet's hardships, yet this transformation of spiritual and mental torment into metaphysics is arguably what Cruz e Souza sought to achieve in his work.

Future study of cinema and literature in Latin America must take into account the changing role of both media, and their respective relationships to the state and political power in general. It needs to ask whether the individual artist as institutional figure is on the wane, and whether the writer is still as important a social commentator or Socratic figure as the filmmaker. What does a hypothetical post-literate society have in store for cinema, or what storytelling possibilities are offered by less theoretical prospects such as 3D and other technological advances?

25. *El lado oscuro del corazón* (Dark Side of the Heart)

CREDITS: Argentina, 1992; *Production:* An Argentine-Canadian coproduction involving Roger Frappier (Canada) and associate producers Transeuropa S.A. Cinematografía and Fernando Sokolowicz, Suzanne Dessault, with support from INCAA (Argentina) and Téléfilm Canada; *Director:* Eliseo Subiela; *Script:* Eliseo Subiela; *Poetry:* Juan Gelman, Mario Benedetti, Oliverio Girondo; Dylan Thomas (epigraph); *Original Music:* Osvaldo Montes; *Director of Photography:* Hugo Colace; 35mm: 127 minutes (rated R)

CAST: Oliverio (Darío Grandinetti), Ana (Sandra Ballesteros), La Muerte (Nacha Guevara), Erik (André Mélançon), Gustavo (Jean-Pierre Reguerraz)

Synopsis

Poet Oliverio is never short of female company, but finds emotional satisfaction impossible. His exacting nature is epitomized by the trapdoor in his bed (called the Piranha Pit) through which "used" sexual partners are discarded. He searches for an ideal woman (one, in Girondo's words, who "knows how to fly"). This quest appears to have ended when he meets the prostitute Ana in a Montevideo cabaret; will true love triumph or will Death take Oliverio first?

About the Film

El lado oscuro is Eliseo Subiela's fourth feature film and the most concerned with literature as creative stimulation, thematic material, and social and philosophical reflection. A collection of essays edited by Nancy Membrez (2007) investigates the filmmaker's multiple approaches to both love and literature, and evinces the range of critical responses elicited by *El lado oscuro*. Membrez herself (213–230) finds numerous parallels to the Don Juan legend, though she sees Subiela's as a twentieth-century version that reflects social changes, particularly the far greater freedom enjoyed by women.

Geoffrey Kantaris (Membrez 2007, 151–168) argues that in both *El lado oscuro* and Subiela's *Últimas imagenes del naufragio* (*Last Images of the Shipwreck*, 1988), literature occupies a "*parergonal*" space, neither inside nor outside the film — asserting that "manifest in a proliferation of literary citations, proxy auteurs, and genre games, the space of literary representation in these films establishes a complex interplay of frame and reference, boundary

184

and signification" (152). As Kantaris indicates, *El lado oscuro* does not limit itself to adaptation, biography or simple reference but seeks a more fertile interaction between cinema and literature.

Olga Juzyn (Membrez 2007, 187–204) examines the relationship between Subiela and Girondo in the light of the poet's credo that poetry should be part of life praxis and not a mere commentary, or addenda, to it. Juzyn argues that this is reflected in the utilitarian dimension given to writing, which is regularly bartered for food, while Oliverio hangs his poetry out to dry, and Ana's books are secreted in household containers.

About the Film's Creators

Director **Eliseo Subiela** was born in Buenos Aires in 1944. He has achieved both fame and controversy with a unique style developed through features such as *Hombre mirando al sudeste* (*Man Facing Southeast*, 1986), *Últimas imagenes del naufragio* (*Last Images of the Shipwreck*, 1989), *No te mueras sin decirme adónde vas* (*Don't Die without Telling Me Where You're Going*, 1995), *Las aventuras de Dios* (*The Adventures of God*, 2000) and, most recently, *No mires para abajo* (*Don't Look Down*, 2008). He has also worked on television drama series and in advertising.

Subiela has had success with the viewing public in Argentina, but critical acceptance has been far from unanimous. His work's characteristics have been summed up as the "Subiela style" by Paraná Sendrós (1993, 50):

> Distance from the usual naturalism or realism, texts with literary weight, inclusion of so-called high culture, in particular Argentine writers, classical music and two painters, Edward Hopper and René Magritte, both of which are used from *Man Facing Southeast* onwards. A tendency also to work from the subconscious, an emotion alien to the conventions of standard melodrama. Sins of extension, excessive orality and reiteration, counterbalanced by the impact of ingenious images and phrases. Protagonists with sound cultural formation and painful existential dissatisfaction, confront others of lower status or greater strength whose women are generally more mature. If these are ex wives, then maternal comprehension is added; if they are abandoned wives, an understandable hatred.[1]

Octavio Getino (1998, 119–120) was writing of *Últimas imagenes del naufragio* but could have been referring to Subiela's work as a whole when he said it was "closer to artifice than conceptual solidity, but able to connect poetically with broad swathes of the public, including the younger sectors."[2]

These critics fail to mention surrealism, an undoubted influence on Subiela's visual and storytelling strategy. In *El lado oscuro* it is visible in cited images by the Belgian surrealist painter René Magritte (such as the burning key during the sexual encounter in C10) or in Oliverio's graphically giving Ana his heart. Subiela delights in visualizing hyperboles — here evoking the phrase "*llevar el corazón en la mano*" (wearing one's heart on one's sleeve).

Gustavo Noriega accuses Subiela of creating characters that are "incarnations of ... puerile ideas, lacking any secrets, enunciators of poetry and high-sounding phrases"[3] but it is nonetheless undeniable that this filmmaker has transferred aesthetic visions from "high" culture to films that are popularly accessible. An eclectic approach to the supposedly highbrow is also visible in his commercials. Whatever the criticisms of Subiela from the intelligentsia, he has certainly been a democratizing influence in placing "elite" artistic visions within reach of a general public.[4]

Subiela himself has described his notion of film as follows: "Cinema is magic, it's trick-ery. The tricks shouldn't be noticeable, but cheating is at the essence of cinema, and I'm prepared to set all the traps necessary to convince, to move the audience"[5] (Padrón Nodarse, 1991, 21).

Subiela's 13th feature, *Rehén de ilusiones* (*Hostage to Illusion*) was released in 2010.

For Cultural Understanding: Three Poets, Two Cities

The three poets whose work appears in *Dark Side of the Heart* are all representative of an avant-garde at odds with the prevailing social atmosphere of their time: Girondo's rebel-lion is his linguistic deviation and rejection of social and sexual mores. Gelman's and Benedetti's are notable more in their political opposition to the status quo (voiced particularly openly, if ingeniously, by the former).

Oliverio Girondo (Buenos Aires, 1891–1967), the most commonly cited poet in the film, was the most aesthetically subversive of the three yet the least politically active. Accord-ing to a note in the final credits, Girondo is not the basis for the protagonist; Subiela instead sees him as the film's "inspirer," adding that writers always present the "alter ego" in his work. There are similarities as well as differences between Subiela's Oliverio and the poet Girondo, who was from a wealthy family, thus able to travel unhindered as a means of exploring his literary interests (an essential part of vanguard literary experience) without distraction. Oliverio is usually penniless, though typically bourgeois in his bohemianism. He works in creative advertising—his occupation and upbringing echoing those of Subiela himself. Girondo was nevertheless no mere dilettante; he wrote in numerous journals and composed a manifesto for the Martín Fierro group which contributed to revolutionizing the country's cultural life. His poetry, in its various phases, reflects aesthetic interactions with Europe; the irreverent rejection of poetic solemnity; a surreal and at times aggressive taste for transgression; a tendency towards inner searches which eventually gives way to a political sensibility.

Juan Gelman (Buenos Aires, 1930) gave up university studies to follow his true inter-ests: journalism, politics and poetry. His poetry is constantly associated with an eloquent rage against injustice that nonetheless avoids the didactic. But not all his work has been angry and politically motivated: his love poetry displays moments of tenderness, and a playful tendency is seen, for instance, in his "translation" into Spanish of poems by an imag-inary English writer. However, his work as a whole has become increasingly identifiable with his politics, which since the early 1970s have become more discordant with those in power in a polarized Argentina. Gelman won the coveted Cervantes Prize in 2007. His work can be read in English in the volume *Unthinkable Tenderness* (1997).

Mario Benedetti (1920–2009) was one of Uruguay's best-loved writers. A member of the Generation of '45, he published over 80 books, including novels, short stories, essays and drama. He is best known, though, for his poetry—particularly his writings on love and the construction of relationships, which reflect a broader social panorama. Benedetti's political activism made him a target for the extreme right in the Uruguayan military, and after the 1973 coup he was forced into a ten-year period in Peru, Cuba and Spain that intro-duced the theme of exile to his work. He received numerous international prizes for services to literature and humanity, as well as receiving belated recognition in his own country.

Subiela's fictional poet contains identifiable aspects of all three men, mostly seen in the poems themselves. Oliverio represents Girondo's at times savage rejection of linguistic and perceptual normality. He also conveys something of Gelman's humanity, an eye for the topical and for political vehemence, as well as Benedetti's expression of the social through the amorous.

The Cities

Buenos Aires and Montevideo, which almost face each other across the River Plate, have a relationship rare among capital cities. The Argentine capital is far bigger, with a higher international profile and a population known for a self-confidence at times considered abrasive. Its Uruguayan counterpart is more modest and remoter from the rest of the world, but has produced a remarkable literature.

Despite Subiela's dismissal of my question about the use of architecture, it seems clear that his protagonists and other individuals interact with their urban environments in particularly expressive and revealing ways. A case in point is *El lado oscuro*'s scene of the phallic sculpture being pushed along Buenos Aires's main thoroughfare, the Avenida Corrientes, at one point partly obscuring Argentina's national monument, the distant obelisk. This visualizes sculptor Gustavo's assertion that our problems are due to sexual inadequacy among the powerful. A number of the Montevideo scenes are shot using as background another

Oliverio and Gustavo transport the phallic sculpture in the vicinity of a national symbol — the Buenos Aires obelisk. Photograph by Cristina Faire.

phallic landmark—the beacon or ventilation duct standing on the old city's southern shore. Neither monumental nor sculptural, this is a utilitarian yet somewhat outlandish erection, like a chimney without a factory, used tellingly when, for instance, Oliverio leaves it behind after the spat with Ana. Some of the architecture evokes the modernist era in which Girondo, in particular, was active. Often the unkempt good looks of the cityscapes frame similar qualities in Oliverio, while Ana is momentarily unglamorous in the humble Montevideo greengrocer's.

Interview with Director Eliseo Subiela

KR: According to a note placed at the end of Dark Side of the Heart, *the film is not based on the life of Oliverio Girondo. Given the use of Girondo's poetry, and of his name for the protagonist, how would you define his role in the film?*
     ES: He's the "inspirer." The film sets out to be a cinematographic "translation" of his poetry. And a declaration of love for his work.

Many of your films are peopled with writers or abound in literary references. I'm surprised there is no appearance (at least explicitly) from Juan Carlos Onetti, despite his provocative ideas about sexual and national identity. His Santa María, besides, had elements of both River Plate capitals. Is that something you would consider for the future?
     I love Onetti so I don't dismiss the possibility of filming something of his work one day.

Architecture plays a very important role in your films. There seems to be at times a dialogue between different forms of architectural language besides the dialogue between Buenos Aires and Montevideo. How consciously do you use these elements in your films?
     Not very "consciously."

Would you say the writer in your films acts as an accomplice in your intentions as a filmmaker?
     The writer in my films is my "alter ego," until the day when I decide to make a film about a filmmaker.

Your films incorporate a range of arts—music of all kinds, painting, sculpture, as well as the literature and architecture already mentioned. And at times you cite your previous films. However, the references to other filmmakers are less overt: is this due to the creation of a personal, unique style?
     In some of my films there is a more or less explicit "homage" to certain *cineastes* who have marked my career, like Godard, Buñuel or Tarkovsky. I agree with Bernardo Bertolucci who once said that all filmmakers are inspired by other filmmakers. Although we may search for, or have, a "personal" style.

Analysis: Poetry as Film Structure

     The use of literary references and quotes dominates the aesthetic structure of *Dark Side of the Heart*, but these are used in such a variety of ways that a pattern only emerges through an overview of their interactions.
     As Geoffrey Kantaris points out, "The space of literary representation ... establishes a

complex interplay of frame and reference, boundary and signification" that outstrips the "standard paradigms" of adaptation or influence (Membrez 2007, 152). The poet-protagonist, clearly an amalgam of three liberally quoted writers, is a character largely built out of a confluence in their aesthetic approaches and sentiments. The fourth "poet" is Subiela himself; as Nancy Membrez pointed out (personal communication, November 2009), he was working creatively in advertising while dreaming of making feature films for 20 years. It's no coincidence that his Oliverio makes a living doing the same kind of work — and hating it: as Ana tells him (C7): "You're a whore just like me!"[6]

Arguably, literary reference replaces narrative: according to Jesús Vega (1992, 12), "Unlike its predecessors, underpinned by strong, complex stories, this film is only sustained by a flimsy narrative whose dramatic events unfold around the characters' feelings, above all around poetry, thus taking flight towards other linguistic latitudes where thought, conflicts, and attitudes are centered on a universe in which the word and its resonances are the beginning and end."[7]

Poetry has somehow remained exempt from most prohibitions regarding the "contamination" of film by other artistic processes. Early filmmakers (Dziga Vertov, among others) and theorists such as Rudolf Arnheim, argued that film should maintain its distance from verbal and printed language, yet for some, poetry's abstraction makes it an ally of film. Roberto Forns-Broggi (Membrez 2007, 169–186) has argued that *Lado oscuro* is a "film-poem" in which the lyrics of popular *bolero* love songs complement the more rarefied imagery of Girondo, Gelman and Benedetti. But Forns-Broggi neglects to define "film-poem," an elusive and controversial concept which has been subject to many aesthetic visions.[8] Given the resistance among film purists to the written and spoken word, it is surprising that radical filmmakers like Maya Deren adopted the term "film-poem" and its variants; less so in the case of Subiela, for whom convention counts for little. The set of rules established by British director Ian Cottage[9] on the making of what he terms "poem-films" would certainly not be acceptable to Subiela's intuitive and anarchic approach.

Cottage's stipulations, such as "the poem film must be shot on film," or "no rushes can be shown to the poet. Sketches or storyboards are prohibited," would be anathema to Subiela, whose vehement opposition to Danish filmmaker Lars Von Trier's "Dogma 95" credo led him to declare himself "dogmatically anti-dogmatic."[10]

A look at some of the settings and treatment of the poems confirms that Subiela is, indeed, never prepared to be governed by a single aesthetic. For example, Girondo's "*Llorar a lágrima viva*" (C11: 1 hour 20 minutes into the film) reflects the emotional state of Oliverio and Ana after their breakup.

Accompanied by the romantic backdrop of the film's theme music, it consists of ten shots, in eight locations, of either Ana or Oliverio alone. Their solitude is evident, but the tears are left for the poetry to express. Subiela wisely never seeks to emulate poetic images through visual counterparts. Another Girondo work, *Comunión plenaria* (C4), is uttered as a direct challenge to Death's persistence in the utilitarian; when she gets up to leave, outraged by the chaotic effusion of imagery, Oliverio raises his voice to drown Death's protests, then follows her into the street. Here the poem has a directly diegetic, dramatic role.

Benedetti's "Rostro de vos" (C13, 1h 43m) has the two lovers separately waiting for service; Oliverio in a bank, Ana buying vegetables in her usual shop.

The various shots take in firstly the bank scene as he recites the poem to a teller who is at first surprised, then apparently intrigued (at least, she makes no attempt to stop him).

The poem is then continued in VO as it accompanies him into the street, and concludes as the two are seen on opposite banks of the river.

Juan Gelman's "Costumbres"[11] (Habits, C8) is one of the poems that Oliverio exchanges for a meal with the *parrillero* (grill chef) who reads laboriously (atrociously, as a non-poet). Meanwhile the camera travels left to right, as if perusing the wares about to be swapped for the poetry. The chef comments that it doesn't seem to be a love poem. The streetwise Gustavo, keen to eat, insists otherwise: "It's a special poem for women."[12]

The text would seem to support the chef's opinion, but he is impressed enough by previous results to accept the poem nonetheless; the price is a mixed grill for three. This is an example of what Olga Juzyn (Membrez 2007, 189–190) terms "the desire to transgress the threshold between art and life" that also includes Oliverio's recital of poetry for handouts in the Buenos Aires traffic.

Forns-Broggi (2007, 172) rightly states that some of the poems are transformed into dialogues by cross-cutting. Ana, for example, finishes the recital of Benedetti's "Táctica y estrategia"[13] (C3) that Oliverio begins. Benedetti's "Rostro de vos"[14] is rendered by Oliverio from the Buenos Aires side whilst standing in a bank — not the place most traditionally receptive to poetry. Ana listens from Montevideo, before they begin their dialogue from either side of the River Plate. On the other hand, the versions of "Me importa un pito"[15] differ in terms of audience: in the film's opening it is delivered almost as a monologue — an absent-minded ramble observed by Oliverio's puzzled bedfellow. Girondo's prose originally appears to confide in the reader: Oliverio recites the conclusion to the passage after he and Ana take to the sky: the experience has not finally sated him.

Subiela's approach is occasionally mimetic, incorporating the poetry into a diegetic role. But it should be borne in mind that his approach to choosing the poetry was completely instinctive: he simply kept the relevant books at hand while writing the screenplay, thumbing through them to find a poem that conveyed whatever feeling he wanted.[16] The heterogenic use of this material defies any established set of rules and is eminently individualistic.

Linguistic Features

The famous Uruguayan poet Mario Benedetti (1920–2009) surprised viewers by appearing in this film to recite one of his poems, "Corazón coraza," in German. There is no particular mystery here: as Benedetti has pointed out in interviews, he attended a German school as a child, doing homework and even writing his first poem in German. The choice of language suits the cosmopolitan air of a capital port-city, as well as Subiela's predilection for the offbeat — seen in this "foreign" personification of a writer who commanded great respect and affection in Uruguay.

For Discussion

1. Is there any feeling of anachronism in Subiela's transposition of poems from the 1920s onwards into a modern setting?

2. In explaining his work, the sculptor Gustavo opines that social problems are due to the sexual dissatisfaction and inadequacies of those in power (here, Subiela cites

Wilhelm Reich's radical ideas on sexual deprivation as a cardinal sin that leads to personality disorders). Is this borne out by the rest of the film?

3. How can the choice and use of the rest of the poetry in *El lado oscuro* be explained?
4. What are all the implications of "flying"? How does falling in love feel and how is it expressed visually in Subiela's film?
5. Is Oliverio sexist? Why or why not?

26. *Caída al cielo*
(Loud Whispers)

CREDITS: Bolivia, as yet unreleased; *Produced by:* Amarcord Producciones; *Director:* Mela Márquez; *Script:* Mela Márquez; *Literary Texts:* Jaime Saenz; *Music:* Cergio Prudencio; *Director of Photography:* Guillermo Medrano; *Art Direction:* Jorge Javier Altamirano

CAST: Sabine (Maria Teresa Dal Pero), Jaime Saenz, Hermenegildo Fernández, Feliciano Sirpa, the younger Huascárdenas (David Mondacca), Older Huascárdenas (Jorge Ortiz), Tía Esther (Sonia De Lazo)

Synopsis

Sabine, the only daughter of the writer Jaime Saenz, was taken from La Paz to Germany by her mother at the age of one, when her parents separated. After her father's death she defies her mother and travels to La Paz, drawn by a need to feel closer to a father she never saw again, despite corresponding with him from the age of twenty. Now, Sabine is legal heir to her father's intellectual rights. But she is also fascinated with his life and work, and begins a journey through the places, characters, and books her father created, in order to get to know the man everybody says was a genius, a madman, an accursed poet.

Guided by the enigmatic Huascárdenas, Sabine comes into contact with strange and intriguing people and situations in the labyrinthine alleys and backstreets of La Paz once frequented by the poet, as the film steers a passage between dreams, reality and the imaginary elements of Saenz's world.

About the Film

Caída al cielo is partly inspired by a one-man stage portrayal, by the actor David Mondacca, of the legendary La Paz poet and narrator Jaime Saenz. The work enjoyed considerable success in Bolivia and at festivals across Latin America, and includes a gallery of characters from both Saenz's life and the literary universe he created. However, the film expands upon and diverges from Mondacca's work; Mela Márquez's aesthetically ambitious film places Saenz, one of Bolivia's greatest writers, in his biographical and cultural context. Without reverting to the traditional "biopic" format, it weaves a fictional narrative based upon the poet's relationship with his daughter. This film, in which I have been to some extent personally involved, has had an extremely tough passage in terms of its financing and release, due to internal politics within Bolivia's reduced but conflictive film community. Despite the quality of the production and its portrayal of a central figure in the nation's cultural life, it still had not reached public exhibition at the time of this book's publication.

My own small role in this film is a cameo appearance in two scenes as Arturo Borda (1883–1953), an extraordinary writer and painter whose only published book, the novel *El loco*, runs to three large volumes. Borda's visionary canvases are mostly in private collections in Bolivia and elsewhere. I was chosen for the role having fortuitously been in the film's offices during casting to translate a letter for my friend, the director Mela Márquez.

Caída al cielo serves as an example of independent cinema in Latin America, driven by an individual vision intent upon telling a story whatever the cost. The film is inspired by a legendary figure central to the cultural history of La Paz, one that itself tells a story of sacrifice to art.

About the Film's Creators

Mela Márquez (La Paz, 1963) studied film at the renowned Centro Sperimentale in Rome, which produced some of the immortals of Italian cinema: Federico Fellini and Sergio Leone were among her mentors. The Centro was also a place of formation for many of the leading figures in the radical Latin American film movements of the 1960s and '70s; Fernando Birri, Fernando Solanas and Tomás Gutiérrez Alea all studied there, enthused by the possibilities of adapting the Italian Neo-Realist aesthetic to their own national realities.

Márquez has previously made one 75-minute film, *Sayariy* (1995; the title means "arise"

Above and top of following page: Sabine (Teresa Dal Pero) in a scene from *Caída al cielo*. Photographs by Rocío Rojas.

in the Quechua language). This semi-documentary also uses the poetry of Blanca Wietüchter to accompany its portrayal of the *tinku*, a ritual warfare enacted by inhabitants of some of Bolivia's most remote Andean communities. The *tinku*, which can result in fatal injury, "pays" the earth mother Pachamama for previous good harvests and guarantees future well-being. *Sayariy* has a dual meaning: "arise" evoking recovery after being knocked down, as well as the assertion of social standing and political rights. Much of Márquez's other film work has been in montage: influenced by the teaching of film editor Roberto Perpignani from her days in Rome, she has worked for directors of the stature of Sergio Cabrera and Antonio Eguino.

Guillermo Medrano, who graduated in 1990 from the famous EICTV[1] film school at San Antonio de los Baños, Cuba, is one of Bolivia's most sought-after directors of photography. Medrano emphasizes that art is born from art, rather than from a void: hence his use of images by the Bolivian painter Ricardo Pérez Alcalá (b. Potosí, 1939), who captures the crumbling facades and ravages of time in old La Paz. Moreover, as Medrano told me in June 2009, one of his main interests as a photographer lies in the transfer of texture from painting.

David Mondacca is among the country's most experienced and highly regarded actors. He has appeared in many of the most important Bolivian films as well as countless stage productions, among which are his many productions of Saenz plays and adaptations of fictional works.

Mondacca was among the students on Jaime Saenz's creative writing course in the mid–1980s at the Universidad Mayor de San Andrés in La Paz. He explains his fascination with the writer as largely due to the fact that "his life and work were one and the same, nobody like him could reveal the mystery that unites life and death. His solitude, his marginality, his search for the meaning of existence and of art, his interest in the occult. His perception of the Andean world... His sense of humor, at times merciless, is a constant in his life and work... He uncovered the city of La Paz for us ... revealed to us the character and temperament of the inhabitant of these highlands" (personal communication, August 2008).

David Mondacca as Jaime Saenz. Photograph by Rocío Rojas.

The La Paz–born composer and conductor **Cergio Prudencio** also researches and teaches music. He founded and directs an experimental orchestra for native instruments, as well as writing and interpreting in both classical and popular idioms. He has worked on music for numerous film projects.

For Cultural Understanding: Film Biography as Literary Appreciation

Jaime Saenz (1921–1986) was born and died in La Paz. He was a beacon for a generation of writers — particularly in the Bolivian capital[2] whose soul is captured in his work. He ran a workshop to tutor young writers; one acolyte, the novelist Homero Carvalho (1993, 70) has testified in the short story "*El viejo comealmas*" ("The Old Soul-Eater," 1985) to Saenz's utter dedication to his craft and the almost messianic figure he cut among aspiring writers: "The old man was a poet twenty-four hours of the day and night, conceiving the minutes as laden with symbols and visions to be deciphered and interpreted on paper."[3] Saenz's poetics incorporated La Paz's unique cultural heritage; the coexistence and sometimes fusion of indigenous Aymara, white and *mestizo* visions of the world, death and time. He conceived death not in the biological sense, but as a state to be attained within life, a detached poetic perspective, as Leonardo García Pabón (1998, 214) confirms:

> Death is present in each and every one of his texts as a constitutive element of the author's subjectivity.... But Saenz does not see death as simply a being's biological and/or spiritual end, but rather as a poetic-spiritual-imaginary state, which he calls "being dead," through which it is possible to accede to a better understanding of what living and dying mean. In this sense, his work is a radical affirmation that one can only write, think and love from this state of being dead, understood as a vital, corporeal process that is incarnate in the image and the materiality of the cadaver. For Saenz the topos of the cadaver becomes an essential symbol, since it represents both the materiality of the body and the dematerialization brought by death.[4]

Saenz's early life was dissolute: he was a voracious drinker who for years only left his house at night. In the 1960s he realized he had to make a choice between alcohol and poetry, he gave up drinking entirely for several years, only relapsing shortly before his death in 1986.

The young Saenz was one of a group of schoolboys invited as a study group by the German government in 1938. The experience left him with a fascination for Nazi paraphernalia and iconography, though whether this entails true belief in Hitlerian ideology is doubtful, given his union activity and participation in the National Revolution of 1952.

Caída al cielo is informed by various Saenz works. The atmosphere of La Paz comes from his *Imágenes paceñas* (*Images of La Paz*, 1979). The blind pianist in the bar appears in the collection of prose/poetry work *Piedra imán* (*Lodestone*, 1989).[5] Huascárdenas, Hermenegildo Fernández, Feliciano Sirpa and Arturo Borda are all taken from the collection of prose portraits of La Paz eccentrics entitled *Vidas y muertes* (*Lives and Deaths*, 1983). However, Aunt Esther was a flesh-and-blood relative, whose importance is underlined by Elías Blanco (1998, 11): "without Aunt Esther things would not have turned out the way they did, because she fulfilled the roles of mother, wife, friend and confidante."[6]

In the introduction to their excellent bilingual anthology of Saenz's poetry, Kent Johnson and Forrest Gander explain this writer's unique if somewhat unenviable position in Latin American letters during what for others were the boom years of the 1960s and 1970s:

> Saenz, stubbornly mystical and baroque, was on his own. His work was certainly innovative, absorbing the fantastic, the psychological, and the symbolic. But it wasn't formally radical enough to situate him among the international avant-garde; it wasn't politically specific enough to find favor with the ascendant literary left, and it was too weird to ride into popularity on the coattails of writers like Cortázar and Vargas Llosa during the Latin America boom of the 1970s. The artists and writers of his generation recognized him as a major force, but until Blanca Wietüchter [1975] wrote a tide-turning book-length study of his poetry, late in his career, Saenz's work was published to a general critical silence. Today, he is widely regarded as Bolivia's most original and visionary poet [Kent and Gander 2002, xii].

As Elizabeth Monasterios (2001, 126) has argued, this concern for the other side has always been central to Saenz's poetics and the fascination he provokes as a pioneer and a *poète maudit*.

Looking at what is different involves the unknown and has always been subversive since it implies dealing with what we do not see or do not wish to see, and, in Saenz's case, is manifested in a leap into dark areas of consciousness and reality, where we lose the consolation afforded to us by rational logic and are detached from the commonplace. Hence it is the spatial metaphor of the other side of things that best translates this epistemological will to transgress speculative knowledge and the immediate reality provided by the senses."[7]

Interview with Director Mela Márquez

KR: What gave you the courage to take on a cultural icon, for both La Paz and the nation, of the scale of Jaime Saenz?

MM: What motivated me to make a film about this famous and illustrious Bolivian poet stems from a very traumatic and painful family experience, and it was at this time that I began to reflect most seriously upon the meaning of our being here at this ephemeral instant. Why must we carry around this body that hurts, that wears out and that in the end turns to dust...? This marks the beginning of a long and tortuous love story with Jaime Saenz's imaginary and his poetic-existential quest.

With this film I hope partly to respond to many personal preoccupations linked to unraveling the enigma of death. It's in the poetry of Saenz where I discover this dramatic moment, this "demonstrated" idea of contemporary philosophy: that language testifies to the knowledge of our being through death. Because death is the fact of life, its true fact — not something that concludes it or is tacked on at the end. If death is the essential fact of life, at the same time it is the fact of our language, something that concerns us intimately and essentially. In Saenz this element is declined in terms of space and certainly also demarcates a touch of originality from the point of view of thought — beyond the terms in which he expresses it and in which, poetically, the problem resides. It was precisely this poetic idea that I wanted to transpose into cinematographic terms.

In this sense *Loud Whispers* sets out to capture the atmosphere of the literature of Saenz, the duality Life/Death; Light/Shade; Pain/Pleasure.

Through this film I wished to honor a debt to my ancestors, my roots, my land and especially my city, La Paz.[8]

You have spoken of uniting three elements in your film: literature, reality and dream. What does this imply with regard to your approaches to the script and the film's conception?

The film moves on three temporal/narrative levels. Each one receives a different photographic treatment.

1. The Present/Reality = The Body: Strong, vivid, highly contrasting colors
2. The Oniric/Imaginary = Literary: Black and white
3. The Past/Memory = Predominance of grays

On a visual and stylistic level I have tried to reproduce the atmosphere of the literature of Saenz: dichotomies of Life/Death. Light/Darkness, Pain/Happiness.

Each of the film's characters represents one of these narrative moments.

Sabine is the narrative thread running though the whole plot, as if weaving between present, past and imaginary where the characters move freely between those worlds.

Sabine is, besides, the very essence of the "foreign" being; an outsider, in relation to the world of the author, faced with an ethnically and culturally mixed, telluric city like La Paz. And above all in an existential sense: being a foreigner in the world.

Saenz: night, magic, memory and time.

Aunt Esther represents "the real," which is a level of narrative but at the same time the author's past, infancy, the enigma of time. This woman, who guards an indecipherable secret, is the bridge between present and past.

Huascárdenas is the marginal city, the *mestizo*, a bridge between the literary world of the author and the subterranean soul of La Paz. The relation between the onirical and real worlds, as well as the physical reality of the body, as fundamental reality of the human condition, the space where life and death, search and encounter, take place.

You've also declared that you seek a return to the "the essence of cinema" represented by Méliès. What do you mean by this?

I meant that having filmed in celluloid, which I consider a luxury today, I wanted to use celluloid in all its expressive possibilities. The effects were all achieved inside the camera, whether overprints or double exposures, and it is in this sense that I refer to Méliès — to the production of the image in the camera and not in post-production, which is the current tendency.

I've also used the black-and-white negative to explore shadows and light and a whole gamut of grays which gives me the film's range and which doesn't occur to the same extent with digital video, which, even if it's capable of very high resolution, doesn't have the same texture. In this film it comes down to exploring many textures, since it is also in some way a pictorial film, closer to an art film, through the textured use of color and black and white and the passage between the two, just like the film's art direction which is close to surrealism, but which I'd dare to call a La Paz surrealism.

You've fought admirably to get this film made against all manner of obstacles — logistic, financial and others. In view of this, how do you see the future of cinema in Bolivia?

Saenz used to say "where there's no pain there's no work of art": I believe this was, and remains, the challenge and the driving force of this film, which I am making come hell or high water, confronting obstacles produced by the moral smallness which, at the same time, provoked huge financial difficulties.

But in spite of everything, this film taught me one of the most important lessons of my life, namely that death is definitively the essential fact of life, the only one that brings sense and which in the final analysis is the leveler of vanities and fortunes. A film is not only the work in itself, but the entire life experience that it brings with it; artists confront their phantasms through their works, their deepest fears. For me the cinema is not a career but a reason for living. In this sense, despite the film being still unfinished, many fruits have already been gathered on this accident-strewn route.

One of the miracles of this film's gestation was a kind of "reencounter" for Yourlaine, Jaime Saenz's daughter, of whom nothing had been heard since before her father's death. It was she who contacted me when she found out from a webpage about the existence of this film. Now I maintain a very fluid correspondence with her and I hope, once the film is completed, that Yourlaine might be able to come to La Paz for the premiere, making a dream come true for both of us. This film was also a school for several young people who love this occupation; that's one of the collateral benefits of which I'm very proud.

As regards the future of Bolivian cinema, I'm reminded of Luis Espinal, who said that the future of Bolivian cinema lies not in prophecies but in action.

But I think that Bolivia, a space of encounter and contradiction, offers us a common battleground between cultures of fear and cultures of freedom, between what others deny us and those who deny us to ourselves. This "common frame," common space, or common battleground, is historic. It comes from the past, is nourished by the present and is projected as a need towards the future.

This "imaginary" stubbornly survives, although frequently wounded and shattered by attempts to negate our past and our perplexing identity, made up of love stories and violence, of native, white and *mestizo* peoples. I hope this "imaginary," which unites contradictions, may be told with intellectual honesty and rigor, in experimental or traditional ways, by young people or by yesterday's youth, whether with pencil and paper, watercolors, digitally or on celluloid.

Do you consider yourself in some way as an heir to Birri, Solanas, Alea and other radical film-makers of the '60s and '70s through your formation in the Centro Sperimentale di Cinematografia in Rome?

It was a great privilege and honor to have been trained at the Centro Sperimentale, together with great Italian and international masters, and I am very grateful to that country which brought so much to my formation, not only as a professional but also as a person.

Pieces of my life remain there, my best memories, and I firmly believe that the school, apart from its huge didactic and technological contribution, gifted me a unique experience shared with companions with whom I grew in a shared dream.

But I should also say that, as a person and as a filmmaker, I have known many influences. I gestated in that warm, aesthetic, spectacular, happily provincial womb that is Italian culture, protected by Latin America's creative generosity and magical ferocity.

The poet's daughter, the plastic artist **Yourlaine Saenz**, is a German citizen who lives near Heidelberg. She told me (personal communication, August 15, 2009) that the film had made her think seriously about following the footsteps of the fictional Sabine and of "visiting my home, La Paz, to find the traces of my father and the roots of my life. Mela expressed these ideas and this hope of mine without knowing me — there is great solidarity between us. I hope with all my heart that Mela will have the chance to bring this film to premiere."

Analysis: Painting as Visual Source

In the Andean countries, evidence of the process of conquest and colonization are eminently visible — in architecture, dress, speech and various other cultural manifestations, tangible or otherwise. Yet there is also a sense of a hidden dimension, product of the imperfect cohesion between indigenous and foreign influences. In Saenz's poetry there is also a metaphysical and ontological quest that may be seen as independent of these cultural and political questions. The matter of whether such elements can be captured in cinema is one of Mela Márquez's preoccupations. Her film opens with the following quote from Saenz's *Piedra Imán* (Magnet Stone), which establishes his essential aesthetic credo. It also illustrates ideas expounded in the above quote from Monasterios.

Moreover, there are unmistakable glimpses of Pérez Alcalá in Saenz, and vice versa. The film's first image derives from the watercolor *Cargando mis cosas* (*Carrying My Things*, 1990). But there are a number of differences: the animal bones seen in the original are human in the film: a *chullpa*,[9] suggesting the remains of Saenz's ancestors, or even his own. In the painting the sky is opaque, with an almost extinguished sun. The film, contrastingly, situates this figure against a limpid Andean sky: in fact, Mela Márquez had intended to film the scene at sunset, but logistical difficulties prevented this. Márquez also decided to turn the figure and show the face, not seen in the original painting. The painting's interpretation is also open to debate: Blanca

Ricardo Pérez Alcalá: *Cargando mis cosas* (*Carrying My Things*, 1990). Courtesy the artist.

Wietüchter (1997, 70) interprets it as an expression of Bolivia's colonized reality, "an act of solidarity with humble people and a world that presents itself to them, devastated without explanation."[10] However, for the cinematographer Guillermo Medrano, this image renders a mental or spiritual state rather than making a political statement. It also brings in another Saenzian preoccupation: death. Why is the figure walking away from the camera, across the empty *Altiplano*, despite Saenz being seen as an urban poet?

Jorge Javier Altamirano, who is credited as art director, stresses that this aspect of the film's art direction was very much a collective effort. Guillermo Medrano's decision to use elements from Pérez Alcalá took this artist's depiction of La Paz as a correspondence, in plastic terms, to Saenz's poetics. Contributions from the director Mela Márquez and actor David Mondacca were also crucial in giving the film a depth of visual language that would have been difficult with a single authorship.

Saenz's "looking at a look" could also be applied to the film's synesthetic aspect: i.e., the various dialogues it sets up between various arts. The subject's gaze takes himself in as well as external objects and stimuli, a process comparable to the interaction between film and poetry, film, painting, and acting. All these may be seen not simply as contributing elements to the film, but as integral parts. They illustrate the ability of cinema — practically its obligation — to incorporate and assimilate these other forms of expression.

Linguistic Features

La Paz slang is heavily influenced by Aymara, the main indigenous language in northern Bolivia and (Oruro and La Paz) and southern Peru (Puno and Juliaca) as well as some areas of northern Chile. The syntax of La Paz Spanish is greatly affected, as is the use of temporal adverbs and adverbial phrases. The verb often comes only at the end of even the longest sentence, and object often precedes verb. The scene in which Huascárdenas meets Feliciano Sirpa is particularly difficult for those unfamiliar with La Paz speech, because it uses thieves' cant: Sirpa's explanation that he has been in "*Canadá*" thinly disguises the slang term for jail, "*cana.*" The lady who runs the *picantería* (an eating establishment specializing in spicy food) berates Huascárdenas as "*q'encha*" (a jinx) for speaking of the dead.

For Discussion

1. Does the very strangeness of Saenz's universe make him incomprehensible to a non–Bolivian audience, or does *Caída al cielo* help it become a universal vision?
2. Is Saenz's literary world as clearly differentiated from "reality" as it should be?
3. Saenz speaks of how "*Only half of things appear to me.*" Is the "other half" represented in Márquez's film?

Chapter Notes

Introduction

1. "Todo ha cambiado afortunadamente, creo que hay una evolución, me parece que estos momentos están pasando cosas importantes, me parece que nos estamos librando de una especie de carga ideológica que nos limitaba bastante, yo siempre sentí que nos faltaba libertad, que al cine latinoamericano le faltaba el vuelo que tiene la literatura latinoamericana, me parece que lo está teniendo, me parece que están pasando cosas importantes aquí en Chile, en Argentina y no hemos dejado de soñar ni de creer en utopías, pero creo que ha pasado el tiempo y hemos aprendido, si no fuera así sería terrible, tenemos que hablar de mercado, tenemos que hablar de industria, en eso creo que hay un adelanto."

2. "La gente va al cine a que le cuenten una historia, no a que le den una lección." Dennis West. 1998. "Una conversación con Sergio Cabrera." In *Cine-Lit III: Essays on Hispanic Film and Fiction*, ed. George Cabello-Castelet, Jaume Martí-Olivella, and Guy H. Wood. 184–199. Portland: Oregon State University.

3. There is one exception: Mela Márquez's *Caida al cielo* has yet to be released.

4. "El nacimiento del cine marcó una nueva posibilidad a la expresión del hombre. Es en sí mismo un camino y recibe todos los aluviones que puedan enriquecerle sin quedar supeditado a ninguno. El cine ejemplifica la búsqueda eterna de la unidad por parte del hombre." José Lezama Lima, interviewed in "Entrevistas con directores de largometraje," *Cine Cubano* 23-24-25 (Dec 2009): 97–99 [http://cine-cubano-la-pupila-insomne.nireblog.com/post/2008/06/18/lezama-origenes-y-el-cine].

Chapter 1

1. Further examples of foreign enthusiasm in Latin American foundational cinema are the first versions of Alencar's novel — by the prolific Italian Vittorio Capellaro (who even remade his Iracema in 1919 after the 1918 version was destroyed through a laboratory accident), then two other Italians, Vittorio Cardineli and Gino Talamo (*Iracema* 1949). Jorge Bodanzky and Orlando Senna's eco-political allegory *Iracema — Uma transa Amazônica* (1917) — was followed in 1979 by Carlos Caoimbra's soft-porn *Iracema, a virgem dos lábios de mel* (*Iracema, the Virgin with Honey Lips*).

2. Ricardo Pacheco Colin. (2007, Jan. 9). Cineasta mexicano acusa a Mel Gibson de plagio por Apocalypto; robó ideas de Regreso a Aztlán, afirma Juan Mora Catlett, *La crónica de hoy* [http://www.cronica.com.mx/nota.php?id_nota=279751].

3. See chapter 3, "To be or not to be a cannibal" of Nagib's *Brazil on screen: Cinema novo, new cinema, Utopia.* 61–80. London, I.B. Tauris.

4. Su fuerza como una eficaz narrativa histórica nacional y nacionalista radica en su vinculación de dos tiempos: el tiempo pasado y mítico de Juan Diego — un indio cuya fe en la Virgen que se le aparece en el cerro del Tepeyac permite la incorporación de su raza (supuestamente bárbara) a la civilización criolla — y el tiempo presente que vuelve relevante la historia para un público del México contemporáneo.

5. See Ayala Blanco's chapter "Los indígenas." 1968. In *La aventura del cine mexicano*. 193–208. Mexico City: Era. Also Charles Ramírez Berg. 1992. *Cinema of solitude: A critical study of Mexican film*. Chapter 8: "The Indian Question." 137–156. Austin: University of Texas Press.

6. "Construyó un enemigo mítico, el indio que había que exterminar, que va sembrando la destrucción, hasta que aparece en el final del film combatiendo en el malón y arrasando vidas y fortines. El odio al indio no era metafórico.... La rememoración de la lucha contra el indio ahondaba una fractura entre la historia oficial de esa lucha y la memoria del exterminio de la población indígena, borrada del film."

7. "Tal vez Gerónima sea uno de los personajes más frágiles de la historia del cine.... Curiosamente, hoy la historia de Gerónima se nos revela actual, aunque ahora multiplicada en millones."

8. "El melodrama familiar y social ha dado lugar a un drama moral en el cual el abuso del poder y la discriminación racial se erigen como temas centrales."

9. "Utilizaba el romance como fachada para transmitir en el fondo un ideal de rebeldía y de lucha de clases."

10. "La cultura de quienes detentan el poder se impone a la de quienes llegaron como Isico portadores de valores culturales indios.... Rechazar no sólo una situación sin perspectiva y de opresión sino también el rechazar a los padres, al idioma, a las costumbres, a la cultura que le da identidad. Johnny es Isico devorado por la ciudad...."

11. The protagonists of *Hamaca paraguaya* are Guaraní speakers, but not indigenous.

Chapter 2

1. "Es probable que Ruiz se haya figurado a Eréndira como la imagen en negativa de doña Marina; aquélla, dueña de sí, patriota, con ideas propias, casta y nulípara, en frontal contraste con la Malinche, a quien la historiografía liberal decimonónica marcaba como traidora y puta."

2. Ana Cristina Ramírez Barreto. *Eréndira a caballo: Acoplamiento de cuerpos e historias en un relato de conquista y resistencia* [http://hemi.nyu.edu/journal/2_2/pdf/ramirez.pdf].

3. Goyas (Premios Goya): Film awards instituted in 1987 by the Spanish Academy of Film Arts and Sciences. The awards are presented annually in late January in Madrid.

4. Translation of script: ERENDIRA se borra con la mano la pintura facial y embarra con ella el rostro y pecho de NANUMA. HIRIPAN se escandaliza. En seguida ERENDIRA se da vuelta e intenta alejarse del enorme NANUMA, quien la sigue encolerizado. La coge por el pelo, zarandeándola y la tira al piso. Al caer, su mano se topa con una piedra e instintivamente se la arroja a NANUMA, golpeándolo en la frente. El cae sentado. HIRIPAN mira fascinado. Todos se quedan en suspenso. Cuando NANUMA se repone, se incorpora tambaleándose y se dispone a golpear a ERENDIRA, pero su TIA y las MUJERES DE TANGAXOAN la rodean para protegerla, blandiendo sus cañas. NANUMA recula y mira a las MUJERES. HIRIPAN intenta proteger a su hermano. Algunos NOBLES se ríen de la escena. NANUMA se da cuenta y se siente avergonzado.

5. "Mi trabajo es traducir sus ideas e intenciones en la plástica facial y corporal, como parte integral del mundo diegético.... Es una interpretación metafórica de lo que quizá fue la vida del pueblo purépecha. El referente para todo el trabajo de arte, fue el códice *La relación de Michoacan*, además de otras fuentes orales y bibliográficas. Estos sirvieron de inspiración, a partir de ellos diseñé el maquillaje."

Chapter 3

1. "El hechicero le sopla al escarabajo y Álvar siente un golpe de viento. El hechicero ata un hilito alrededor del cuerpo del bicho y Álvar se siente ahogado por una fuerza que no comprende, pero sigue corriendo en trechos. El hechicero ata el extremo del hilo a la estaca y pone al escarabajo en el suelo. El escarabajo comienza a girar y Álvar busca hacia dónde seguir su carrera. Los cantos del hechicero aumentan en intensidad mientras el escarabajo comienza a enredarse en la estaca. La imagen sincronizará los giros del bicho con el derrotero de Álvar. Cuando al fin el escarabajo se acerca a la estaca, Álvar decide un último cambio de dirección y lo toma, veloz. El hechicero calla. De pronto se abre la maleza cercana y Álvar aparece, jadeando, nuevamente en el campamento. Se da cuenta de que corrió en redondo y cae de bruces junto a sus compañeros, sofocado de fatiga y hartazgo. En ese momento vemos al escarabajo pegado a la estaca. Malacosa desata el escarabajo y se lo guarda."

2. "El destino cierra sus círculos: cuando tratamos de escapar de él, morimos poco a poco; lo que nos impulsa a vivir, a insistir en la liberación, es la ilusión de cambiar, o de resucitar en el intento y en el instante."

3. "1Dios! ¿Qué hago yo aquí en esta tierra? 1En este mundo, Dios! ... Siendo esclavo de un hijo de puta indio, brujo además. [Return to original shot Álvar Núñez.] Esto es el monstruoso. Maldigo el día que te conocí, Mala Cosa. 1Ríete, ríete ríete ríete! 1Endriago, en mi tierra te hubieran empalado!"

4. "Y hablo y hablo y hablo ... porque soy más humano que vosotros ... porque tengo un mundo, aunque estoy perdido, aunque soy un náufrago. Tengo un mundo, y un Dios. Creador del mundo. Creador del cielo y de la tierra. Y a vosotros también os ha creado Dios. Me llamo Álvar Núñez Cabeza de Vaca, tesorero de su Majestad Carlos I de España, y V de Alemania. Señor de estas Indias ... y estas son las Indias y yo soy de Sevilla ... y esto es el suelo ... y aquello el cielo ... Indias ... y esto es una mata ... ¿Y qué más? ¿Y qué más? ¿Y qué más? Y esta es arena ... arena. Y más allá el horizonte y el mar ... la mar ... en algún sitio la mar ... la mar. [Song.] Estaba la mar...."

5.

estaba la mar en calma	the sea was calm,
la luna estaba crecida	the moon was full,
moro que en tal signo nace	a Moor born under that sign
no debe decir mentira	should never lie.
siendo yo niño y muchacho	When I was still just a boy,
mi madre me lo decía	my mother would tell me
que mentira no dijese	that I should never tell lies
que era grande villanía	for it was a great villainy.
por tanto pregunta el rey,	Therefore ask me, king,
que la verdad te diría	and I will tell you the truth
yo te la diré señor	I'll tell you, sir,
aunque me cueste la vida	even though it cost me my life.
si tú quisieses, Granada,	If you wished, Granada,
contigo me casaría	I would marry you
dárete en alma y dote	and give you, as arms and dowry,
a Córdoba y a Sevilla	Cordoba and Seville.
Casada soy, Rey don Juan	I am married, King John,
casada, que no viuda	married and not widowed.
el moro que a mí me tiene	The Moor who I belong to
muy grande bien me tenía.	loved me deeply and well.

6. "Más al oportunismo quintocentenarista que a un intento serio de investigación histórica y filológica."

7. "Dexo aquí de contar esto más largo, porque cada uno puede pensar lo que passaría en tierra tan estraña y tan mala...."

8. "Aunque en ella se lean cosas muy nuevas y para

algunos muy difíciles de creer, pueden sin dubda creerlas...."

Chapter 4

1. See the overview given in the introduction to Bliss and French 2007, 1–30.

2. "El sueño de Bolívar, lo vamos a realizar nosotros. La unificación de América."

3. "Los pobres y los putos siempre coincidimos.... Ser puto, ser pobre, y ser Eva Perón, en este país despiadado, es la misma cosa."

4. *The Late Show*, BBC2 (UK), 1996.

5. "Porque el despertar sexual, y la marca de identidad que viene con el despertar sexual es el tema más universal del mundo. Es la impronta de la sexualidad en la identidad, más allá de la homosexualidad o la heterosexualidad.... La película elige hablar de un intersexual, pero también está hablando del momento en que dejamos de ser niños y elegimos nuestra identidad."

6. "También es metáfora de la Manuela, de quien quiere borrar los limites de un cuerpo-espacio de transgresiones" (Ripstein). "Invita a leer este 'lugar sin límites' como el infierno cotidiano colocando el cuerpo-infierno de Manuela como eje del texto fílmico."

Chapter 5

1. Production notes for Chijona's third feature *Perfecto amor equivocado* (2004).

2. "Películas musicales de folklore cubano, hechas con muy escasos medios, a base de mambos, congas, cha-cha-chas, etc., de asegurado éxito comercial debido a fórmulas probadas."

3. Oscar Quirós. 1996. "Critical mass of Cuban cinema: Art as the vanguard of society." *Screen* 37, 279–294.

4. Tomás Gutiérrez Alea's *Strawberry and Chocolate* (1992).

5. See *El Abuelo* (*The Grandfather*) by Cuban poet Nicolás Guillén, which reminds a young blonde woman of her partial African ancestry.

6. Michael Chanan recalls the skewed interpretation from some critics of Gutiérrez Alea's *Memorias del subdesarrollo*—"Andrew Sarris, for example, described him as a dissident, a kind of Cuban Solzhenitsin," whereas Gutiérrez Alea was a crucial figure in the cultural life of the Revolution and co-founder of the island's film institute, ICAIC. Michael Chanan. 1997, May. Remembering Titón. *Jump Cut* 41, 126–129 [http://www.ejumpcut.org/archive/onlinessays/JC41folder/TitonMemory.html]

7. "Por supuesto, que es uno de los tantos homenajes al buen cine de género que siempre hago en mis películas, como la escena de la alcantarilla es, como dices, un homenaje a Hitchcock" (personal communication, August 2007).

8. "Esta frase no es mía, sino de Luis Agüero, que era un experto en santería. Sobrevivió a todas las versiones del guión y sé que no quiere decir absolutamente nada, que fue un puro invento de Luis, que siempre estaba bromeando con la santería."

9. "Es el mundo de la prostitución institucional, la que viene desde arriba y no llega hasta las más bajas y desposeídas esferas de la sociedad sino después de haber arrasado con todos los buenos modales y preceptos sociales."

Chapter 6

1. "El cine, al igual que TODA aplicación del ARTE, es, por naturaleza y principio, experimental: en el sentido *en que no se conocen los resultados (la META), sólo los elementos y estructura, las causas pero no el efecto, puesto que depende de la humana experiencia, individual, única, intangible e incontrolable*— y, por lo tanto, constituye una búsqueda política, técnica, formal, estética, emocional y personal."

2. "El primer intento de reflexión en el cine boliviano sobre el sexo, sobre cómo se desarrollan las relaciones a partir de él, sobre cómo influye en nuestras vidas cotidianas y socioculturales ... plantea reflexiones más universales, más humanas ... es la primera cinta que retrata otra cara del sexo, de lo erótico, la menos idílica, la que duele, la que angustia...."

3. The main ethnic division in Bolivia, which carries political overtones, is between *cambas* (inhabitants of the eastern lowlands) and *collas* (Andean "Indians" or mestizos).

4. In Bolivia, *gringo* is a term generally used for a person from the United States, rather than (but not excluding) white or Caucasian.

5. The torture and murder of Matthew Shepard in 1998 was one of the most infamous cases of anti-gay hate crime in the U.S.

6. *Cumbia* is an extremely popular dance rhythm in Latin America.

Chapter 7

1. Karim Aïnouz. 2003. *Macabéa com raiva (Macabéa with Anger)*. *Cinémas d'Amérique Latine* 11, 10–20.

2. Maeve Mascarenhas de Cerqueira. A cultura cinematográfica brasileira: Uma leitura do filme Madame Satã [http://www.seara.uneb.br/sumario/professores/martaemaeve.pdf].

3. Rogério Durst. 1985. *Madame Satã: Com o diabo no corpo*. São Paulo: Editora Brasilense.

4. I use my own translations of Rodrigues's nomenclature.

Chapter 8

1. "¿Cómo poder revivir una actitud, una mirada, un gesto? Sólo con la imagen podemos reanimar o conservar esos signos del pasado tan añorados e imprecisos."

2. "Los pasajeros reaccionan ante el espectáculo de diversas maneras: algunos comentan, otros se muestran indiferentes, unos tiran monedas, otros restos de comida y de dulces, otros golosinas, mientras unos se muestran apenados o molestos, otros se burlan haciéndolos correr varios metros para darles o no, al final, una moneda."

3. "*Los rubios* trata de la furia y la pena de una hija cuyos padres, sus vivencias y sus cuerpos, le han sido arrebatados para siempre."

Chapter 9

1. R. Fandiño. 2000. *Revista Hispano Cubana* [http://www.hispanocubana.org/revistahc/pdf/REVISTA_HC_8.pdf].

2. "El hecho de ser una franja de tierra en la que diversos intereses geopolíticos han intervenido, produjo, en vez de integración entre los países, fragmentación, ausencia de comunicación y una tendencia a mirar hacia fuera, hacia lo extraño y extranjero. Ha sido una región no solo invadida por 'marines,' sino también por seductoras imágenes 'hollywoodenses.' El audiovisual centroamericano ha tenido que surgir entre los escombros de las guerras y los desastres naturales, ha debido sortear dictaduras e invasiones y, sobre todo, ha tenido que competir con pantallas copadas por las imágenes siempre impecables del cine dominante."

3. "La necesidad de los centroamericanos de construir su propio espejo, de reflejar sus múltiples identidades y de reconocerse en las pantallas propias."

4. *Ladino*, in this Central American context, applies to people of mixed descent who use Spanish; it distinguishes them from Indians. It is not to be confused with the Ladino language spoken by Sephardic Jews and discussed in the chapter on *Novia que te vea*.

Chapter 10

1. "La desesperanza derrotada a través de la música" (press release for *Maroa*, 2006).

2. Jonathan Jakubowicz's *Secuestro Express* (2005) has since improved upon this.

3. "Esa mezcla de inocencia, sensualidad, violencia y genio musical que debía ser MAROA" (press release for *Maroa*, 2006).

4. "¿Qué voy a hacer contigo? Muy fácil: Yo te limpio, te lavo, te cocino, y tú me coges."

5. "La selección del cuadro cinematográfico no se parece a la selección operada por nuestra mirada en la vida real. La selección de nuestra mirada no tiene unos *contornos definidos* ni un *límite* preciso" (author's emphasis).

Chapter 11

1. All the films mentioned here are Peruvian productions unless otherwise stated.

2. La forzada migración a Lima que emprendía un joven campesino desplazado, echado, desarraigado de su tierra como consecuencia de la guerra desatada por el movimiento subversivo Sendero Luminoso en los Andes peruanos.

3. "En el extranjero jodieron mucho. En cada proyección se levantaban y argumentaban que yo los había retratado muy esquemáticos y caricaturescos, pero en Lima me dijeron que yo lo había hecho muy bien y que así eran. También me dijeron a la salida de un cine en el centro de Lima que lo que salvaba la película es que al profesor Montes lo mataban de afuera."

4. "La facilidad increíble con la que ambos protagonistas sortean los obstáculos."

5. "No creo que haya cine en el mundo que deje de ser subjetivo y político."

Chapter 12

1. See Kimberley Theidon. 2009. *La teta asustada: Una teoría sobre la violencia de la memoria*. Praxis: Un Instituto para la Justicia Social [http://praxisweb.org/Documents/La%20teta%20asustada%20Theidon.pdf].

2. For English-speaking audiences, the title is simply given as *Iracema*; "transa" in Portuguese can translate as "affair" or "business," but also can refer to the sexual act.

3. See also discussion of the documentary *Evita, la tumba sin paz* (*Evita, the Unquiet Grave*, 1997) in this book's interview with the director, Tristán Bauer.

Chapter 13

1. "La imagen que ganó la primera posición en la cultura brasileña desde mediados del siglo XIX, fue el paisaje imaginario del Sertão, una región del interior considerada 'vacía' de civilización y entendida como antinomia de las templadas costas oceánicas" *Tal* (2005): 87–88.

2. See also Robert Stam. "The Favela: From Rio 40 Graus to Black Orpheus, 1954–1959." In *Tropical Multiculturalism: A Comparative History of Race in Brazilian Cinema and Culture*. 157–178. Durham, NC: Duke University Press.

3. *Minha vida nossa luta* (*My Life, Our Struggle*, 1979).

4. For a full discussion of the male narrator's role see the chapter How Does One Desire Wealth or Poverty in Hélène Cixous's *Reading with Clarice Lispector*, translated by Verena Andermatt Conley. University of Minnesota Press, 1990, pp. 143–163.

5. "Uma moça numa cidade toda feita contra ela," to quote Lispector's words: "a girl in a city all built against her" (my translation).

6. Earl E Fitz. 1991. Solitude: The evolution of an American literary motif." In *Rediscovering the New World*. 205–210. Iowa City: University of Iowa Press.

7. "O delicado equilíbrio entre a perspectiva social e o tom intimista ao delinear Macabéa, a nordestina."

Chapter 14

1. "La protagonista por ejemplo se da cuenta de que está cayendo en una trampa. Yo tampoco tengo a priori objeciones morales contra la prostitución, es una prostitución legal en mi país, y cada uno hace lo que quiere, ¿verdad? Se hace una explotación que trae mucho grotesco, tiene que ver con el humor, y la película está todo el tiempo en un filo entre el humor y lo trágico, lo realista y lo surrealista, lo exagerado y lo no exagerado, y para mantener un equilibrio permite que el espectador vaya sintiendo las emociones y la historia y al mismo tiempo reírse o llorar de momentos."

2. "El cine es muy eficaz para transmitir mensajes, pues construye realidades a través de la escenografía y las actuaciones de los protagonistas, que exageran o simplifican nuestros instintos, intuiciones y facultades para el manejo de conflictos."

3. "El recurrir a escenas con gran sentido del humor ayuda a bajar las resistencias al cambio y a divertirse."

Chapter 15

1. "El proyecto de incorporación de la perspectiva de las mujeres a una historia y cultura nacionales, que por tradición ha ignorado y borrado este punto de vista, se acompaña del uso y reevaluación de modos narrativos catalogados despectivamente como 'femeninos.'"

2. The titles would translate as "The Night's Not Only For Sleeping" and "The Journeys of My Body."

3. "Ha ayudado a la comprension de un México más diverso y multicultural, abordando temas como el de la inmigracvion, la adptacion social, la similacion y el apego a las tradiciones."

4. Sergio Wolf (53–54) has discussed the early critical opposition to dialogue, when full exploitation of what were considered film's inherent qualities was seen as practically obligatory.

5. "Intercambiables y fijos, tan fijos como las amarillentas fotos ancestrales."

Chapter 16

1. "La combinación del carácter documental del primer cine mexicano, de los elementos melodramáticos del cine italiano, y de los hallazgos técnicos del cine norteamericano."

2. See the website of Teatro de Ciertos Habitantes: http://www.ciertoshabitantes.com/index2.php?idioma=espanol&ira=obra_desc&menu_datos_obra=1&id=12.

3. "En el exiguo espacio de la carcel, la dinámica de cada uno es más clara: la clase media intelectual, el militar, el obrero, el joven, el viejo, la mujer, el hombre del nordeste y del sur del Brasil."

4. *Taratura y naturaleza muerta con cachimba* (1989).

5. "Efectivamente *El atraco* hace referencia al cine noir, del cual soy fanático. Hay varios aspectos de mi película que utilizan los clichés del cine noir: la rubia fatal (cantante de cabaret) que se enamora del policia bueno, aún estando involucrada con los malos. El policía corrupto; el policía honesto (aunque no totalmente integro). El uso de una música de inspiración jazz, aún siendo el jazz no propiamente un género muy común en el cine boliviano. La iluminación y el uso de una fotografía un poco 'sucia' en el burdel y el cabaret" (Paolo Agazzi, personal communication, 9 October 2009).

Chapter 17

1. The "Manhunt" project was abandoned in 2006.

2. "A diferencia de las otras artes figurativas o representativas, en el cine el encuadre puede ser móvil. No sólo porque los elementos del campo visual tienen la capacidad de desplazarse — en cuyo caso percibimos un movimiento interno en el encuadre incluso cuando la cámara se mantiene estática — sino porque la cámara es un aparato que, colocado sobre un soporte, puede variar su posición física respecto a los objetos filmados produciendo en el espectador la impresión de que los límites de la pantalla no son fijos y que las perspectivas visuales cambian con extraordinaria fluidez."

3. "La escena es casi un *sketch*, un guiño carnavalesco al espectador; una levedad que se irá perdiendo a medida que Ángel se convierte en el personaje central de *Ratas, ratones y rateros*. En la medida en que la jerarquía de la rata se impone sobre la de los ratones. Pero hasta este punto de la cinta los pequeños crímenes de los jóvenes parecen más bien un ensayo utópico de subversión de poderes, presente en el propio lenguaje."

4. "Aquí el mundo delictivo es mirado con realismo. No hay la más mínima oportunidad para simbolismos o discursos aleccionadores; todo es registrado de manera que la derrota y la autodestrucción compitan con la replana y el detalle pintoresco." *La gran ilusión* 13 (2003): 40–41.

Chapter 18

1. *Esperpento* is a hyperbolic grotesque aesthetic used to heighten and accentuate the absurd or unreal. It was originally developed by the Spanish writer Ramón María del Valle-Inclán (1866–1936).

2. "Rechazar la conformidad, la indolencia, la pasividad y el fatalismo a que nos hemos acostumbrado." [http://www.comohacercine.com/articulo.php?id_art=1201&id_cat=3].

3. Colombia's extraordinary 5–0 victory over Argentina in 1993 was greeted with such exultation that there were numerous accidental deaths.

4. McOndo is a literary tendency among younger writers intent upon a renewal of Latin American literature, freeing the thematic spectrum available to them in a move away from such perceived limitations as Magic Realism, representation of the nation, and politics.

5. "Ustedes han tenido la mala suerte de nacer y en el país más loco del planeta. No le sigan la corriente, no se dejen arrastrar por su locura...."

6. My thanks are due to Elizabeth Scott Blacud, the Bolivian journalist resident in Madrid who conducted this interview on my behalf, November 2008.

7. *Maquiladoras*: factories for making goods for transnational companies, situated in countries with low labor costs.

8. "Estaba retratado el viscoso y repugnante mundo de los especuladores y los corruptos, de las mafias que se organizan al abrigo de los pequeños espacios que el Estado les deja libres para enriquecerse a su antojo. Fue en ese momento cuando en la novela vi una película, una película de las que me gusta ver y de las que me gusta rodar" [http://www.comohacercine.com/articulo.php?id_art=1201&id_cat=3].

9. "El problema de la fidelidad es un falso problema. ¿Cómo se puede ser fiel en un traslado de códigos, de materias, de disciplinas que manejan, además, diferentes modos de producción y de recepción? Además, ¿cómo ser fiel a un texto cuando la única manera de aproximarnos a él es a través de la lectura y toda lectura es interpretación y, por lo tanto, toma de partido?"

Chapter 19

1. "Al crear un personaje para un guión de ficción, se está creando necesariamente aquellas acciones que permitirán definirlo como ser humano — imaginario pero verosímil — inmerso en la historia imaginada."

2. "La película trabaja el interior de los códigos de la tradición realista, pero se deshace del efecto de reconocimiento, del mimetismo y la verosimilitud convencionales. Allí están los detalles y signos de la cultura urbana, incluso los más estridentes, pero disueltos en una mecánica de obsesiones, reiteraciones, ideas fijas, diversos tratamientos audiovisuales, transfiguraciones que fuerzan la lógica de la percepción normal."

3. "Se desarrolla en una tensión permanente entre fuerzas contradictorias de destrucción y de integración, de irracionalidad y de caos."

4. "El progreso del personaje hacia un nuevo estado de conciencia es una de las formas en la que la trama suscita expectativa e intriga."

Chapter 20

1. Adolfo Colombres. *La encrucijada civilizatoria de Nuestra América*. Seminar organized jointly by the Universidad Mayor San Andrés and the Instituto de Estudios Bolivianos, La Paz, October 2007. See also Colombres's *América como civilización emergente* (in bibliography).

2. "Fueron filmadas en Cuba dudosas y breves tomas de emboscadas, escaramuzas, la famosa Toma de la Loma de San Juan, un panorama del Castillo del Morro de La Habana, y un combate naval en Santiago de Cuba ... que fue realmente filmado con maquetas en New York."

3. The term *mambí* refers to Cuban fighters against the Spanish.

4. Two other noteworthy documentaries on this theme are by Chileans: Gloria Camiruaga's *La venda* (*The Blindfold*, 1999) presents testimonies from a group of women tortured under military rule. The ironic title of *Fernando ha vuelto* (*Fernando Is Back*, Silvio Caiozzi, 1998) refers to the skeleton of a "disappeared" youth, which nonetheless proves eloquent under forensic examination.

5. "Una guerra fratricida cuyas causas están hoy dilucidadas: la instigación de los intereses de las ponderosas compañías, cifrados en los yacimientos del oro negro en las entrañas del inmenso territorio del Chaco Boreal."

6. *En el infierno del Chaco* and *El último malón* are among the Argentine silent films included in the collection Mosaico Criollo. Buenos Aires: Museo del Cine.

7. "Cuando nos ponemos a pensar en las películas que mediante confiscación y otros medios llegó a tener en su poder el ejército, soñamos con la cinemateca que hubiera podida establecerse del cine boliviano. Pero lo más seguro es que la ignorancia haya hecho desaparecer ya los originales de todas esas películas. Las latas habrían sido utilizadas como ceniceros en alguna cantina de cuartel."

8. Zuzana Pick. 2010. *Constructing the Image of the Mexican Revolution: Cinema and the Archive*. Austin: University of Texas Press.

Chapter 21

1. *Diario del Festival El Cine* 5.5 (7 Aug 2006): 6. (The journal of the annual Latin American film festival of the Catholic University of Lima, Peru.)

2. "Patriotism is the last refuge of a scoundrel."

3. Bauer told me his documentary embraces the human perspective and look at a little-known side of Guevara; the writer, theorist, and thinker. Aleida March was sufficiently impressed to allow them access to her personal archive of tapes, photographs, and intimate stories. This collection permitted much more closeness to their subject, not so much politically but fundamentally from a human perspective.

4. Raúl Alfonsín, first elected president of Argentina after the dictatorship, who ruled from 1983 to 1989.

5. "Las **formas de paso** entre secuencia y secuencia son otro de los componentes de la temporalidad del cine (30). Son formas de paso, por ejemplo, el fundido, el corte, el barrido, el iris.... Las formas de paso como los **signos de puntuación** (coma, punto...) en la escritura. Pero tienen un claro sentido temporal.

"Por ejemplo el **fundido encadenado** (funde una imagen mientras emerge otra sobre la pantalla) es una manera de decirnos que se suprime un trozo de tiempo. En cambio, el **fundido a negro** pone punto final a una escena y tiene el valor de un cambio de capítulo; por lo tanto denota un salto temporal. Por otra parte, el **barrido** acentúa la continuidad temporal dentro de un cambio espacial.

"Estas formas de paso pueden tener también un sentido de **causalidad**. Por ejemplo, un largo fundido encadenado, o una figura que emerge del desenfoque, puede ser el paso de la realidad al ensueño."

6. "El **sonoro** se ha convertido en uno de los componentes más importantes de la temporalidad cinematográfica. Este elemento no-plástico acentúa el tiempo que pasa. Pensemos, sobre todo, en el **ruido** como valor temporal: una sirena, el ruido monótono y repetido de una maquina.... El sonoro puede crear una temporalidad polifacética y múltiple, no solamente por el contenido de una conversación, sino por el **asincronismo**, al yuxtaponer una imagen con un sonoro que no corresponde con aquella imagen."

Chapter 22

1. This extraordinary story is ghost-written by Gabriel García Márquez and appears in English as *Clandestine in Chile: The Adventures of Miguel Littín.* New York: Henry Holt, 1988.

Chapter 23

1. Ana Bianco. n.d. En el Paraguay nos guían los mitos. *Latino America online: Musica e spetacolo* [http://www.latinoamerica-online.it/temi5/musica1-06.html#paraguay].

2. "Lento, callado y hasta desconfiado, aunque con su desconfianza no te agreda. Puede no contestarte y mirarte fijamente durante años, sin contestar." *La Nación* (Buenos Aires) 30 Oct 2006.

3. El derecho inalienable de una expresión audiovisual propia.

4. *La Nación* (Buenos Aires) 19 Sept 2006.

5. A contrast might be made here with the theatrical, stylized monologue in part 4 of *Dependencia sexual.*

Chapter 24

1. Alain Philippon. La poésie en contrabande. *Cahiers du Cinéma* 354 (December 1983).

2. "Rulfo se cuida de no hacer descripciones físicas explícitas, de tal manera que los personajes se sostienen únicamente por sus diálogos y acciones."

Chapter 25

1. "Distanciamiento del naturalismo y del realismo habituales, textos de peso literario, inclusión de la llamada cultura superior, particularmente escritores nacionales, clásicos musicales, y dos pintores, Hopper y Magritte, ambos a partir de *Hombre*.... También, trabajo desde el subconsciente, emoción ajena a las convenciones del melodrama standard, pecados de extensión, demasiada oralidad, y reiteración, compensados por imágenes impactantes y frases ingeniosas. Personajes protagónicos de buena formación cultural y dolida insatisfacción existencial, confrontados con otros de menor estrato u mayor fuerza, y con mujeres generalmente más maduras. Si se trata de ex esposas, se agrega comprensión maternal; si de esposas abandonadas, un comprensible odio."

2. "Más cercano a la artificiosidad que a la solidez conceptual, pero capaz de conectarse poéticamente con amplias franjas del público, incluidos los sectores más jóvenes."

3. "Encarnaciones de ... ideas pueriles, desprovistos de todo secreto, enunciadores de poesía y de frases altisonantes...."

4. A fuller discussion of the popular versus elite perceptions of Subiela's work can be found (Richards 2007) in the context of another of his films, *No te mueras sin decirme adónde vas* (*Don't Die without Telling Me Where You're Going*, 1995).

5. "El cine es magia, es truco, es engaño, es trampa. Los trucos no deben notarse, pero la trampa está en la esencia del cine, y yo estoy dispuesto a hacer todas las trampas necesarias para convencer, conmover."

6. "1Ah, sos una puta como yo!"

7. "A diferencia de sus predecesoras, apuntaladas por historias fuertes y complicadas, esta película sólo se sustenta en una levísima historia y despliega su acontecer dramático en torno a los sentimientos de los personajes, y, sobre todo, en torno a la poesía, levantando así el vuelo hacia otras latitudes del lenguaje, donde el pensamiento, los conflictos, las actitudes gravitarán en un universo en el cual la palabra y sus resonancias son principio y fin."

8. See "Poetry-Film & The Film Poem: Some Clarifications." 2009. *British Artists' Film and Video Study Collection* [http://www.studycollection.co.uk/poetry.html].

9. *Ian Cottage: Cinema and Stories: Blog.* 2009 [http://iancottage.blogspot.com/2009/03/poem-film-manifesto.html].

10. *La Nacion Espectáculos.* 2009 [http://www.lanacion.com.ar/nota.asp?nota_id=133503].

11. *Poema Costumbres de Juan Gelman.* 2006 [http://www.poemasde.net/costumbres-juan-gelman/].

12. "Es un poema especial para las mujeres."

13. Táctica y estrategia. 2010 [http://www.tinet.cat/~elebro/poe/benedetti/benedet2.html]. 14. Mario Benedetti. 2010. *Rostro de vos* [http://www.poemas-del-alma.com/rostro-de-vos.htm].

15. For complete text see http://amediavoz.com/girondo.htm [accessed November 2010].

16. I am grateful to Nancy Membrez for this information (personal communication, July 2010).

Chapter 26

1. Escuela Internacional de Cine y Televisión (EICTV) was founded in 1986 to train Latin American filmmakers and technicians. Its founders were the Colombian novelist Gabriel García Márquez alongside two legendary filmmakers: the Argentine Fernando Birri and the Cuban Julio García Espinosa.

2. Bolivia has two capital cities: Sucre is the judicial capital, La Paz the political.

3. "El viejo era poeta las veinticuatro horas del día y de la noche, concebía los minutos cargados de símbolos y visiones para descifrar e interpretar en el papel."

4. "La muerte está presente en todos y cada uno de sus textos como elemento constitutivo de la subjetividad del autor.... Pero Saenz no ve la muerte como simple final biológico y/o espiritual de los seres, sino como un estado poético-espiritual-imaginario, al que él llama 'estar muerto,' por el cual se puede acceder a un mejor entendimiento de lo que significa vivir y morir. En este sentido, su obra es una afirmación radical de que sólo se puede escribir, pensar y amar desde el estar muerto, entendido como un proceso vital y corporal, y que encarna en su imagen y la materialidad del cadáver. Para Saenz el topos del cadáver deviene un símbolo esencial, pues representa tanto la materialidad del cuerpo como la desmaterialización que trae la muerte."

5. The poetry used in the film's first scene is also the opening text of Jaime Saenz's poetic narrative: Jaime Saenz. 1989. *Piedra imán* (La Paz: Huayna Potosí), 7.

6. "Sin la tía Esther los hechos no habrían sucedido como sucedieron, porque ella cumplió el papel de madre, esposa, amiga y confidente."

7. "Mirar lo diferente, que entraña lo desconocido, siempre ha sido subversivo, ya que implica el trato con lo que no vemos o no queremos ver y que, en el caso de Saenz, se manifiesta en el salto hacia zonas oscuras de la conciencia y de la realidad, allí donde perdemos el consuelo que otorga la lógica racional y nos desvinculamos de los lugares comunes. De aquí que sea la metáfora espacial del otro lado de las cosas la instancia que mejor traduce esta voluntad epistemológica de transgredir el conocimiento especulativo y la realidad inmediata proporcionada por los sentidos."

8. At this point Mela Márquez refers the reader to Jaime Saenz's poem *Recorrer esta Distancia*, available at http://www.boliviaweb.com/poetry/saenz.htm#Recorrer. An English translation by Kent Johnson and Forrest Gander (as *To Cross This Distance*) is on page 87 of their book *Immanent Visitor*. The original can be found on page 107 of the same volume (see bibliography).

9. *Chullpa* is an Aymara term referring to both mummies and funerary monuments.

10. "Como un acto de solidaridad con los seres humildes y un mundo que se les presenta devastado sin explicación."

Bibliography

Adorno, R. 1993. "The Negotiation of Fear in Cabeza de Vaca's *Naufragios*." In *New World Encounters*, ed. S. Greenblatt. 48–84. Los Angeles: University of California Press.

_____, and C. Pautz, eds. 2003. *The Narrative of Cabeza de Vaca*. Lincoln: University of Nebraska Press.

Agramonte, A. 1966. *Cronología del cine cubano*. Havana: Ediciones ICAIC.

Aïnouz, K. 2003. Macabéa com raiva (Macabéa with rage). *Cinémas d'Amérique Latine* 11: 10–20.

Alcalá, M. 1973. *Buñuel (cine e ideología)*. Madrid: Edicusa.

Alemán, G. 2001. *Escupir al cielo: Ratas, ratones y rateros*. Edufuturo, 13 December 2009 [http://www.edufuturo.com/imageBDE/EF/11295.ratas.pdf].

_____. 2009. *Espectros de Marx*. Edufuturo, 13 December 2009 [http://www.edufuturo.com/image BDE/EF/11291.marx.pdf].

Alfassa, S. 1999. *A Quick Explanation of Ladino (Judeo-Spanish)*, 12 December 2009 [http://www.sephardicstudies.org/quickladino.html].

Almendros, N. 1992. *Cinemanía: Ensayos sobre cine*. Barcelona: Seix Barral.

Argueta, L., ed. 2005. *El silencio de Neto. Guión y artículos afines*. Guatemala City: Editorial Universitaria, Universidad de San Carlos de Guatemala.

Avellar, J. C., and Geraldo Sarno. 2003. Karim Aïnouz: Um olhar poético e político (Karim Aïnouz: A Poetic and Political Gaze). *Revista Cinemais* 35, 19–47.

Ayala Blanco, J. 2001. *La fugacidad del cine mexicano*. México City: Océano.

Balderstone, D., and D. J. Guy. 1997. *Sex and Sexuality in Latin America: An Interdisciplinary Reader*. New York: New York University Press.

Barillas, E. 2005. El mundo de Neto en *El silencio de Neto*. In *El silencio de Neto. Guión y artículos afines*, ed. L. Argueta. 11–33. Guatemala City: Editorial Universitaria, Universidad de San Carlos de Guatemala.

Barrow, S. 2005. "Images of Peru: A National Cinema in Crisis." In *Latin American Cinema: Essays on Modernity, Gender and National Identity*, ed. Stephanie Dennison and Lisa Shaw, 39–58. Jefferson, NC: McFarland.

Beaver, F. 1994. *Dictionary of Film Terms: The Aesthetic Companion to Film Analysis*. New York: Twayne.

Bedoya, R. 1995. *100 años de cine en el Perú. Una historia crítica*. Lima, Peru: Universidad de Lima / Fondo de Desarrollo Editorial.

_____. 1997. *Entre fauces y colmillos. Las películas de Francisco Lombardi*. Huesca, Spain: Festival de Cine de Huesca.

_____. 2008. Perú: Películas para después de una guerra. In *Hacer cine: Producción audiovisual en América Latina*, comp. E. A. Russo. 151–168. Buenos Aires, Paidós.

_____, and I. León-Frías. 2003. *Ojos bien abiertos: El lenguaje de las imágenes en movimiento*. Lima, Peru: Universidad de Lima/Fondo de Desarrollo Editorial.

Bellott, R. 2007. Los que me Amen que suban al Tren. In *Encuentro de cineastas sub-40*, ed. Patricia Suárez. 69–78. La Paz: Fundación Simón I. Patiño / Revista Alejandría.

Bermúdez, N. 2008. "Rosa Nissán y Guita Schyfter: Memorias, melodrama y negociación en *Novia que te vea*." In *Sujetos transnacionales: La negociación en cine y literatura*, ed. N. Bermúdez. 33–107. Universidad Autónoma de Ciudad Juárez.

Beverley, J. 1999. *Subalternity and Representation: Arguments in Cultural Theory*. Durham, NC: Duke University Press.

Beverly, J. 2003. "Los últimos serán los primeros": Notas sobre el cine de Gaviria. *Objeto Visual* 9, 16–21. In *Imagen y subalternidad: El cine de Víctor Gaviria*.

Blanco Mamani, E. 1998. *Jaime Saenz, el ángel solitario y jubiloso de la noche*. La Paz: Gobierno Municipal.

Blanco Pazos, R., and R. Clemente. 2004. *De la fuga a la fuga: El policial en el cine argentino*. Buenos Aires: Corregidor.

Bliss, K. E., and William E. French. 2007. *Gender, Sexuality, and Power in Latin America Since Independence*. Lanham, MD: Rowman and Littlefield.

Brenner, F. 1993. *Adolfo Aristarain*. Buenos Aires: Centro Editor de América Latina.

Buñuel, L. 1982. *Mi último suspiro*. Barcelona: Plaza y Janés.

Burnett, R. 1995. *Cultures of Vision: Images, Media, and the Imaginary*. Bloomington: Indiana University Press.

Burucúa, Constanza. 2005. Generando la historia: La "guerra sucia" en el cine de y por mujeres. In *La imagen como vehículo de la identidad nacional*, ed. Jorge Carman. 88–113. Buenos Aires: INCAA.

Cabeza de Vaca, A. N. 1993. *Naufragios*, ed. Trinidad Barrera. Madrid: Alianza.

Canclini, A. 2000. *Malvinas: Su historia en historias*. Buenos Aires: Editorial Planeta.

Carvalho, Homero. 1993. El viejo comealmas. In *Territorios invadidos*, ed. Homero Carvalho. 67–72. Hanover, NH: Ediciones del Norte.

Chanan, M. 2004. *Cuban Cinema*. Minneapolis: University of Minnesota Press.

_____, ed. 1990. *Memories of Underdevelopment*. New Brunswick: Rutgers University Press.

Cinemark Caballito. 2009. *7º Festival Internacional de Cine Judío en Argentina*, 13 December 2009 [http://www.ficja.com.ar/].

Cineteca Nacional. 1981. *El automóvil gris*. Mexico City: Dirección General de Cinematografía.

Close, Glen S. 2008. "Open Up a Few Corpses: Autopsied Cadavers in the Post-boom." *Journal of Latin American Cultural Studies* 17: 121–137.

Coates, T., ed. 2001. *War in the Falklands 1982*. London: The Stationery Office.

Cohen, J., M. Goodman, and D. Sorkin, eds. 2005. *The Oxford Handbook of Jewish Studies*. Oxford: Oxford University Press.

Colás, S. 1994. "Latin American Modernity in Crisis: *El beso de la mujer araña* and the Argentine National Left." In *Postmodernity in Latin America: The Argentine paradigm*, ed. Santiago Colás. 76–99. Durham, NC: Duke University Press.

Colombres, A. 2007. *América como civilización emergente*. La Paz: Tercera Piel.

Contreras, O. 2003. Ratas, rateros, ratones (review). *La gran ilusión* 13: 40–41.

Cortes, M. L. 1999. *Amor y traición: Cine y literatura en América Latina*. San José: Universidad de Costa Rica.

_____. 2006. *La pantalla rota: Cien años de cine en Centroamérica*. Mexico City: Taurus.

_____. 2006. *Centroamérica en celuloide: Mirada a un cine oculto. Istmo*. Denison University, 13 December 2009 [http://collaborations.denison.edu/istmo/n13/articulos/celuloide.html].

Craig, L. 2011. "Latin American Cinema." In *Introduction to Film Studies*, 5th ed, ed. Jill Nelmes. London and New York: Routledge.

D'Lugo, Marvin. 1993. "'Transparent Women': Gender and Nation in Cuban Cinema." In *Mediating Two Worlds*, ed. John King, et al. 279–290. London: BFI.

Dávalos Orozco, F. 1996. *Albores del cine mexicano*. México City: Clio.

De Cárdenas, F. 1995. Demasiados desencuentros: "Anda, corre, vuela." *La gran ilusión* 5: 93–95.

De la Mora, S. 2006. *Cinemachismo: Masculinities and Sexuality in Mexican Film*. Austin: University of Texas.

De los Reyes, A. 1997. *Medio siglo de cine mexicano, 1896–1947*. México City: Trillas.

Debs, S. 2007. Negro Brasil. *Cinémas d'Amérique Latine* 15: 54–70.

Del Rio, E. 2008. *Deleuze and the Cinemas of Performance: Powers of Affection*. Edinburgh: Edinburgh University Press.

Dennison, Stephanie. 2006. "The New Brazilian Bombshell: Sônia Braga, Race and Cinema in the 1970s." In *Remapping World Cinema: Identity, Culture and Politics in Film*, ed. Stephanie Dennison and Song Hwee Lim. 135–143. London: Wallflower.

Díaz, L. M. 2004. *Más Chaplin y menos Platón; Manejo de conflictos desde la sabiduría del cine y las canciones*. Santiago de Chile: Cuatro Vientos.

Dieleke, E. 2009. "*O sertão nao virou mar*: Images of Violence and the Position of the Spectator in Contemporary Brazilian Cinema." In *Visual Synergies in Fiction and Documentary Film from Latin America*, ed. M. Haddu and J. Page. 67–86. New York: Palgrave Macmillan.

Donelan, C. 1993. *The Politics of Gender in the New Latin American Cinema*. Morgantown: Department of Foreign Languages, West Virginia University.

Encina, P. 2008. Arrastrando la tormenta. In *Hacer cine: Producción audiovisual en América Latina*, ed. E. A. Russo. 331–342. Buenos Aires: Paidós.

Espinal, L. 1976. *Narrativa cinematográfica*. La Paz: Don Bosco.

Espinal, Luis. 1982. Narrativa cinematográfica. *Cuaderno de Cine No. 9*. 2nd ed. La Paz: Don Bosco.

Espinoza, S., and A. Laguna. 2009. *El cine de la nación clandestina: Aproximación a la producción cinematográfica boliviana de los últimos 25 años (1983–2008)*. La Paz: Gente Común.

Esteban, E. 1993. *Malvinas: Diario del regreso*. Buenos Aires: Editorial Sudamericana.

Fandiño, R. 2002. Jineterismo cinematográfico: *Un paraíso bajo las estrellas* de Gerardo Chijona. *Revista Hispano Cubana* 8: 207–210.

Forns-Broggi, R. 2007. "Poetic and Musical Re-enactment and Masculine Displacement: *Dark Side of the Heart* as a Film-poem." *The Cinematic Art of Eliseo Subiela, Argentine Filmmaker*, ed. N. J. Membrez, 169–186. Lewiston, NY: Edwin Mellen Press.

Foster, D. W. 1999. *Gender and Society in Contemporary Brazilian Cinema*. Austin: University of Texas Press.

Franco, J. 2002. *The Decline and Fall of the Lettered City: Latin America in the Cold War*. Cambridge, MA: Harvard University Press.

Fraunhar, Alison. 2005. *Mulata cubana*: The Problems of National Allegory. In *Latin American Cinema: Essays on Modernity, Gender and National Identity*, ed. Stephanie Dennison and Lisa Shaw. 160–179. Jefferson, NC: McFarland.

Gamarra Etcheverry, H. 2003. ¿Existe el cine paraguayo? *Cinémas d'Amérique Latine* 11, 156–162.

Gamboa, S. 2001. *Perder es cuestión de método*. Santiago de Chile: Editorial Cuarto Propio.

García Pabón, L. 1998. *La patria íntima: Alegorías nacionales en la literatura y el cine de Bolivia*. La Paz: Plural/CESU.

García Riera, E. 1998. *Breve historia del cine mexicano: Primer siglo, 1897–1997*. Mexico City: CONACULTA/IMCINE.

García Tsao, L. 1992. The conquistador as shaman. [Interview with Nicolás Echeverría, translated from the French by K. J. Richards.] *Positif*, 87–89.

García, M. E. 2007. Documento de identidad. [Interview with Lucía Puenzo.] *Haciendo Cine* 12.71: 34–35.

Getino, O. 1998. *Cine argentino: Entre lo posible y lo deseable*. Buenos Aires: Ciccus.

_____. 2007. *Cine iberoamericano: Los desafíos del nuevo siglo*. Buenos Aires: Ciccus/INCAA.

Glantz, M. 1992. Shipwreck as nakedness. *Travesía* 1.2: 88–105.

Gómez, L. S. 2003. *La mosca atrapada en una telaraña: Buñuel y "Los olvidados" en el contexto latinoamericano*. Bogotá: Universidad Nacional de Colombia.

González Casanova, M. 1992. Crónica del cine silente en México. In *Cine latinoamericano (1896–1930)*, ed. Héctor García Mesa. 227–277. Caracas: Fundación del Nuevo Cine Latinoamericano-Consejo Nacional de la Cultura-Foncine-Fundacine UC.

Graham-Yool, A. 1988. *Pequeñas guerras británicas en América Latina: Malvinas, crónica personal*. Buenos Aires: Belgrano.

Grupo Rev(b)elando Imágenes, comp. 2008. *Santiago Álvarez: Reflexiones, testimonios, relámpagos en un instante de peligro*. Buenos Aires: Cuadernos de Cine Latinoamericano.

Gumucio Dagron, A. 1982. *Historia del cine en Bolivia*. La Paz: Los Amigos del Libro.

Halevi-Wise, Y. 1998. Puente entre naciones: Idioma e identidad: *Novia que te vea* e *Hisho que te nazca* de Rosa Nissan. *Hispania* 81.2: 269–277.

Hershfield, J. 1995. Assimilation and identification in Nicolás Echeverría's *Cabeza de Vaca*. *Wide Angle* 16:3, 6–24.

Herzovich, Guido. 2007. *La pesadilla del amor* [interview with Ana Katz]. *Haciendo Cine* 12.71: 36–37.

Iampolski, M. 2008. *The Memory of Tiresias: Intertextuality and Film*. Berkeley: University of California Press.

Isaacson, J. 2003. *Geografía lírica argentina: Cuatro siglos de poesía XVII–XVIII–XIX–XX*. Buenos Aires: Corregidor.

Islas Malvinas. 2009. *Bibliografía*, 13 December 2009 [http://www.malvinasonline.com.ar/biblio.php].

Johnson, K., and F. Gander, eds. 2002. *Immanent Visitor: Selected Poems of Jaime Saenz*. Berkeley: University of California Press.

Juzyn, O. 2007. "Eliseo Subiela and Oliverio Girondo: Praxis from the Margins." *The Cinematic Art of Eliseo Subiela, Argentine Filmmaker*, ed. N. J. Membrez. 187–204. Lewiston, NY: Edwin Mellen Press.

Kantaris, G. 2007. "The Desire for Literature: Proxy Authors in *Last Images of the Shipwreck* and *Dark Side of the Heart*." In *The Cinematic Art of Eliseo Subiela, Argentine Filmmaker*, ed. N. J. Membrez, 151–168. Lewiston, NY: Edwin Mellen Press.

Kenny, S. 2009. *Buscando el otro cine: Un viaje al cine indigenista boliviano*. Mendoza, Argentina: Universidad Nacional de Cuyo.

King, John. 1990. *Magical Reels: A History of Cinema in Latin America*. London: Verso.

_____. 2000. "María Luisa Bemberg and Argentine Culture." In *An Argentine Passion: María Luisa Bemberg and Her Films*, ed. John King, Sheila Whitaker, and Rosa Bosch. 1–32. London: Verso.

King, John, and Nissa Torrents. 1991. *The Garden of Forking Paths: Argentine Cinema*. London, BFI: 115–121.

King, John, Sheila Whitaker, Rosa Bosch, eds. 2000. *An Argentine Passion: Maria Luisa Bemberg and Her Films*. London: Verso.

Kuhn, Annette. 1994. *Women's Pictures*. London: Verso.

Laikin Elkin, J. 1998. *The Jews of Latin America*. New York: Holmes & Meier.

Lebeau, V. 2008. *Childhood and Cinema*. London: Reaktion Books.

Lerner, J. 2009. *Dante Cerano—Día dos: Sexo, parentesco y video*, 12 December 2009 [http://theamericanegypt.blogspot.com/2009/05/dante-cerano-dia-dos-sexo-parentesco-y.html].

Lispector, C. 1987. *Hour of the Star* (translated from the Portuguese by Giovanni Pontiero). New York: Carcanet Press.

López, Ana M. "Are All Latins from Manhattan?" In *Mediating Two Worlds*, ed. John King, et al. 67–80. City: Publisher.

_____. 1993. "Tears and Desire: Women and Melodrama in the "Old" Mexican Cinema." In *Mediating Two Worlds: Cinematic Encounters in the Americas*, ed. John King, Ana M. López, and Manuel Alvarado. 147–165. London: BFI.

Lusnich, A. L. 2009. La condensación de estilos y de registros en el cine argentino silente. In *Mosaico Criollo: Primera antología del cine mudo argentino*, ed. Buenos Aires: INCAA/Museo del Cine/Gobierno de Buenos Aires.

Márquez, Carlos F. 2006. Eréndira Ikikunari *expone la leyenda desde el punto de vista indígena*. La Jornada, Michoacán [http://www.lajornadamichoacan.com.mx/2006/10/17/13n1cul.html].

Membrez, N. J. 2007. The Argentine Don Juan: The Case of *Dark Side of the Heart*. In *The Cinematic Art of Eliseo Subiela, Argentine Filmmaker*, ed. N. J. Membrez. 213–230. Lewiston, NY: Edwin Mellen Press.

_____, ed. 2007. *The Cinematic Art of Eliseo Subiela, Argentine Filmmaker*. Lewiston, NY: Edwin Mellen Press.

Mesa, C. 1985. *La aventura del cine boliviano 1952–1985*. La Paz: Gisbert.

Millán Agudo, F. J. 2004. *Las huellas de Buñuel: Influencias en el cine latinoamericano*. Teruel, Spain: Instituto de Estudios Turolenses.

Monasterios Pérez, E. 2002. La metáfora del otro lado de las cosas: Estudio de una estética y una poesía espaciales. In *Dilemas de la poesía de fin de siglo: José Emilio Pacheco y Jaime Saenz*, ed. Pérez Monasterios. 123–157. La Paz: Plural.

Monsiváis, C. 1995. Mythologies. In *Mexican Cinema*, ed. P. A. Paranagua. 117–127. London: BFI/IMCINE.

Mraz, J., 1993. "Absolved by History: On the Aesthetics and Ideology of History in the Cuban Film Institute." *Film-Historia* 3.3: 385–410 [http://www.publicacions.ub.es/bibliotecaDigital/cinema/filmhistoria/Art.%20Mraz.pdf].

Mulvey, Laura. 1999. "Visual Pleasure and Narrative Cinema." In *Film Theory and Criticism: Introductory Readings* (5th ed.), ed. Leo Braudy and Marshall Cohen. 833–844. Oxford University Press.

Nagib, Lúcia. 2007. "To Be or Not to Be a Cannibal." In *Brazil on Screen: Cinema Novo, New Cinema, Utopia*, ed. Lúcia Nagib. 61–80. London I. B. Tauris.

_____. 2007. The Urban Dystopia. In *Brazil on Screen: Cinema Novo, New Cinema, Utopia*, ed. Lúcia Nagib. 115–132. London: I. B. Tauris.

_____, ed. 2003. *The New Brazilian Cinema*. London and New York: I. B. Tauris.

Ni paraíso ni estrellas. 2003. Cubanet, 12 December 2009 [http://www.cubanet.org/CNews/y03/dec03/19a10.htm].

Noble, Andrea. 2005. *Mexican National Cinema*. Abingdon & New York: Routledge.

Noriega, G. 2003. Review of *Los rubios*. *El Amante Cine* 12.133: 26.

Ortiz, F. 1940. *Del fenómeno social de la "transculturación" y de su importancia en Cuba*. Caracas: Biblioteca Ayacucho, 1978.

Padrón Nodarse, F. 1991. Hombre mirando al naufragio (Review). *Cine cubano* 134: 21–25.

Paz, O. 1988. *Sor Juana, or, the Traps of Faith*. Cambridge, MA: Harvard University Press.

Peña-Ardid, C. 1996. *Literatura y cine*. Madrid: Cátedra.

Pick, Zuzana. 1993. *The New Latin América Cinema: A Continental Project*. Austin: University of Texas Press.

Pupo-Walker, E. 1993. *Castaways: The Narrative of Álvar Núñez Cabeza de Vaca*. Berkeley and Los Angeles: California University Press.

Quiroga, J. 2000. *Tropics of Desire: Interventions from Queer Latino America*. New York: New York University Press.

Rama, A. 1984. *La ciudad letrada*. Montevideo: Arca.

Ramírez Barreto, A. C. *Eréndira a caballo: Acoplamiento de cuerpos e historias en un relato de conquista y resistencia* [http://hemi.nyu.edu/journal/2_2/pdf/ramirez.pdf].

Ramírez Berg, C. 1992. *Cinema of Solitude: A Critical Study of Mexican Film, 1967–1983*. Austin: University of Texas Press.

Ramos González, A. 2006. De Sefarad a Yerushalayim: Escritoras de dos orillas. In *Desde Andalucía: Mujeres del Mediterráneo*, ed. M. Arriaga, J. Baca, C. Castaño, and M. Montoya. 400–408. Sevilla: ArCiBel.

Ramos, F., ed. 1987. *História do cinema brasileiro*. São Paulo: Art Editora.

Ramos, J. 2001. *Divergent Modernities: Culture and Politics in Nineteenth-century Latin America*, trans. John D. Blanco. Durham, NC: Duke University Press.

Rangil, Viviana. 2005. *Otro punto de vista: Mujer y cine en Argentina*. Rosario, Argentina: Beatriz Viterbo Editora.

Rashkin, Elissa J. 2001. "Guita Schyfter: The Chicken and the Egg." In *Women Filmmakers in Mexico: The Country of Which We Dream*, ed. Elissa J. Rashkin. 141–166. Austin: University of Texas Press.

Richards, Keith J. 2006. "Born at Last? Cinema and Social Imaginary in 21st-Century Uruguay." In *Remapping World Cinema: Identity, Culture and Politics in Film*, ed. S. Dennison and S. H. Lim. 137–159. London: Wallflower.

_____. 2006. "Export Mythology: Primitivism and Paternalism in Pasolini, Hopper and Herzog." In *Remapping World Cinema: Identity, Culture and Politics in Film*, ed. S. Dennison and S. H. Lim. 55–64. London: Wallflower.

_____. 2007. Moving Images: Technology and the Affective in Subiela's *No te mueras sin decirme adónde vas: The Cinematic Art of Eliseo Subiela, Argentine Filmmaker*, ed. N. J. Membrez, 231–247. Lewiston, NY: Edwin Mellen Press.

_____. 2010. A Shamanic Transmodernity: Juan Mora Catlett's *Eréndira ikikunari*. In *Latin American Cinemas: Local Views and Transnational Connections*, ed. N. Bermúdez. 176–200. Calgary: University of Calgary Press.

Roa Bastos, A. 1993. *Mis reflexiones sobre el guión cinematográfico y el guión de* Hijo de hombre. Asunción: RP Ediciones.

Rodrigues, A. 2008. *O Rio no cinema*. Rio de Janeiro: Nova Fronteira.

Rodrigues, J. C. 2007. *Arquetipos y caricaturas do negro no cinema brasileiro [Black Archetypes and Caricatures in Brazilian Cinema]*. *Cinémas d'Amérique Latine* 15: 4–16.

Rowe, W., and Vivian Schelling. 1991. *Memory and Modernity: Popular Culture in Latin America*. London: Verso.

Rueda, M. H. 2003. El cine latinoamericano y su búsqueda de la infancia callejera: El giro de Víctor Gaviria. *Objeto Visual* 9: 54–61.

Ruggiero, K., ed. 2007. *The Jewish Diaspora in Latin America: Fragments of Memory*. Brighton: Sussex Academic Press.

Saenz, J. 1979. *Imágenes paceñas*. La Paz: Difusión.

_____. 1986. *Vidas y muertes*. La Paz: Editorial Huayna Potosí.

Salas, E. 1990. *Soldaderas in the Mexican Military: Myth and History*. Austin: University of Texas Press.

Sanjinés, J. 1979. *Teoría y práctica de un cine junto al pueblo*. Mexico City: Siglo XXI.

Satarain, M., ed. 2004. *Plano secuencia: 20 películas argentinas para reafirmar la democracia*. Buenos Aires: Crujía.

Schiwy, F. 2008. "Indigenous Media and the End of the Lettered City." *Journal of Latin American Cultural Studies* 17: 23–40.

_____. 2009. *Indianizing Film: Decolonization, the Andes, and the Question of Technology*. New York: Rutgers.

Schyfter, G. n.d. *Guita Schyfter, directora de cine* [http://www.guitaschyfter.com/].

Sellers, S. 1988. *Writing Differences: Readings from the Seminar of Hélène Cixous.* Ann Arbor: University of Michigan.

Sendrós, P. 1993. *Eliseo Subiela.* Buenos Aires: Centro Editor de América Latina / INCAA.

Shaw, D., 2003. *Contemporary Cinema of Latin America: Ten Key Films.* New York: Continuum Books.

———, ed. 2007. *Contemporary Latin American Cinema: Breaking into the Global Market.* Lanham and Plymouth: Rowman and Littlefield.

Shaw, L., and M. Conde. 2006. "Brazil Through Hollywood's Gaze: From the Silent Screen to the Good Neighbor Policy Era. In *Remapping World Cinema: Identity, Culture and Politics in Film*, ed. S. Dennison and S. H. Lim. 180–208. London: Wallflower.

Sheridan, G., and N. Echeverría. 1994. *Cabeza de Vaca* (original script). Mexico City: Ediciones El Milagro.

Smith, P. J. 1989. *The Body Hispanic: Gender and Sexuality in Spanish and Spanish-American Literature.* Oxford: Clarendon.

———. 1996. *Vision Machines: Cinema, Literature, and Sexuality in Spain and Cuba, 1983–93.* London: Verso.

Sofair, M. 2006. "*Sexual Dependency*: The Split Screen of Globalization." *Cine-Action* 69: 48–55 [http://www.thefreelibrary.com/Sexual+Dependency%3a+the+split+image+of+globalisation.-a0147339317].

Somerlate Barbosa, M. J. 1989. "*A hora da estrela*: A Reinforced Affirmative Reply." *Romance Notes* 29.3: 233–239.

Stam, R. 1997. *Tropical Multiculturalism. A Comparative History of Race in Brazilian Cinema and Culture.* Durham and London: Duke University Press.

———. 2006. "Cabral and the Indians: Filmic Representation of Brazil's 500 Years." In *The New Brazilian Cinema*, ed. Lúcia Nagib. 205–228. London: I. B. Tauris.

———, and A. Rengo. 2005. *Literature and Film: A Guide to the Theory and Practice of Film Adaptation.* Malden, MA: Blackwell.

Tal, T. 2005. *Pantallas y revolución: Una visión comparativa del Cine de Liberación y el Cinema Novo.* Tel Aviv: Universidad de Tel Aviv.

Tamayo, A. 1996. *Teoría y práctica del guión de ficción.* Lima: Universidad de Lima/Fondo de Desarrollo Editorial.

Toledo, T. 1990. *10 años del nuevo cine latinoamericano.* Madrid: Quinto Centenario.

Torrents, N. 1987. "Contemporary Argentine Cinema." In *The Garden of Forking Paths: Argentine Cinema*, ed. J. King and N. Torrents. 93–113. London: BFI.

———. 1993. "Mexican Cinema Comes Alive." In *Mediating Two Worlds: Cinematic Encounters in the Americas*, ed. J. King et al. 222–229. London: British Film Institute.

Tranchini, E. 2005. Cordilleras y exilios. In *La imagen como vehículo de la identidad nacional*, ed. J. Carman. 11–29. Buenos Aires: INCAA.

Urruzola, M. 2001. *El huevo de la serpiente.* Montevideo: Ediciones del Caballo.

Uzel, M. 2007. Profil/Perfil Lázaro Ramos. *Cinémas d'Amérique Latine* 15: 45–53.

Valdivia, J. A., ed. 1998. *Testigo de la realidad. Jorge Ruiz: Memorias del cine documental boliviano.* La Paz: CONACINE/Cinemateca boliviana.

Vandromme, P. 1960. *Los niños en la pantalla.* Madrid: RIALP.

Vega, J. 1992. Subiela: La poética de lo insólito. *Cine cubano* 137: 6–16.

Waldman, Stuart, and Tom McNeely. 2003. *We Asked for Nothing: The Remarkable Journey of Cabeza De Vaca.* New York: Mikaya Press.

Wietüchter, Blanca. 1975. Las estructuras de lo imaginario en la obra poética de Jaime Saenz. In *Jaime Saenz: Obra Poética*, ed. Blanca Wietuchter. 267–425. La Paz: Sesquicentenario de la República.

———. 1997. *Pérez Alcalá o los melancólicos senderos del tiempo.* La Paz: Plural.

Wolf, S. 2001. *Cine/literatura: Ritos de pasaje.* Buenos Aires: Paidós.

Wood, D. 2006. "Indigenismo and the Avant-garde: Jorge Sanjinés's Early Films and the National Project." *Bulletin of Latin American Research* 25.1: 63–82.

Xavier, I. 2006. Roteiro de Júlio Bressane: Apresentação de uma poética. *ALCEU* 6.12: 5–26.

Yanes Gómez, G. 1996. *Juan Rulfo y el cine.* Universidad de Guadalajara.

Index